EDITORIAL

WITH the publication of this REVIEW begins a completely new adventure in the history of mankind. Whatever knowledge may previously have been imputed to men, it has always been fenced in with conditions and restrictions. The time has come to speak plainly, and so far as may be in the language of the multitude.

Thus, the Brothers of the A∴ A∴ announce themselves without miracle or mystery. It is easy for every charlatan to perform wonders, to bewilder and even to deceive not only fools but all persons, however shrewd, untrained in observation; nor does the trained observed always succeed instantly in detecting the fraud. Again, what the A∴ A∴ propose to do is to enable such men as are capable of advancement to a higher interpretation of manhood to do so; and the proof of their ability lies in their success, and not in any other irrelevant phenomenon. *The argument from miracles is a* non sequitur.

Nor is there anything mysterious in the A∴ A∴; one must not confuse the mysterious with the unknown. Some of the contents of this REVIEW may be difficult or impossible to understand at first, but only in the sense that Homer is unintelligible to a person ignorant of Greek.

But the Brothers of the A∴ A∴ make no mystery; They give you not only the Text, but the Comment; not only the Comment, but the Dictionary, the Grammar, and the Alphabet. It is necessary to be thoroughly grounded in the language before you can appreciate its masterpieces; and if while totally ignorant of the former you despise the latter, you will forgive the more frivolous onlookers if their amusement matches your indignation.

The Brothers of the A∴ A∴ have set their faces against all charlatanism, whether of miracle-mongering or obscurantism; and all those persons who have sought reputation or wealth by such means may expect ruthless exposure, whether of their vanity or their dishonesty; for by no gentler means can they be taught.

The Brothers of the A∴ A∴ will advise simple experiments, and will describe them, by the pens of their chosen delegates, in the simplest available language. If you fail to obtain good results, blame either yourself or Their method, as you will; if you succeed, thank either yourself or Them, as you will.

In this first number are published three little books; the first an account of Their character and purpose, restored from the writings of von Eckartshausen; the second an ethical essay restored from the Cipher MSS. of the G∴ D∴ (of which MSS. a complete account will later be given); these two books chiefly for the benefit of those who will understand wrongly or not at all the motto "THE METHOD OF SCIENCE — THE AIM OF RELIGION," in which (if rightly interpreted) all is expressed; the third a series of scientific experiments, designed to instruct beginners in the groundwork of Scientific

EDITORIAL

Illuminism, and to prevent them from falling into the self-deception which pride always prepares for the unwary.

From time to time further knowledge will be published, as fast as the diligence of the persons employed to write it down will permit.

It is the intention of the Brothers of the A∴ A∴ to establish a laboratory in which students may be able to carry out such experiments as require too much time and toil to suit with their ordinary life; and Their further plans will be explained fully as opportunity permits.

Any person desirous of entering into the communication with the A∴ A∴ may do so by addressing a letter to the Chancellor of the Order, at the offices of this paper.

AN ACCOUNT OF A∴A∴

FIRST WRITTEN IN THE LANGUAGE
OF HIS PERIOD
BY
THE COUNCILLOR VON ECKARTSHAUSEN
AND
NOW REVISED AND REWRITTEN
IN THE UNIVERSAL CIPHER

A∴ A∴
Official Publication in Class C.
Issued by Order :
D.D.S. 7° = 4°
O.S.V. 6° = 5°
N.S.F. 5° = 6°

AN ACCOUNT OF A∴A∴

[The Revisers wish to acknowledge gratefully
the translation of Madame de Steiger, which
they have freely quoted.]

IT is necessary, my dear brothers, to give you a clear idea of the interior Order; of that illuminated community which is scattered throughout the world, but which is governed by one truth and united in one spirit.

This community possesses a School, in which all who thirst for knowledge are instructed by the Spirit of Wisdom itself; and all the mysteries of nature are preserved in this school for the children of light. Perfect knowledge of nature and of humanity is taught in this school. It is from her that all truths penetrate into the world; she is the school of all who search for wisdom, and it is in this community alone that truth and the explantation of all mystery are to be found. It is the most hidden of communities, yet it contains members from many circles; nor is there any Centre of Thought whose activity is not due to the presence of one of ourselves. From all time there has been an exterior school based on the interior one, of which it is but the outer expression. From all time, therefore, there has been a hidden assembly, a society of the

Elect, of those who sought for and had capacity for light, and this interior society was the Axle of the R.O.T.A. All that any external order possesses in symbol, ceremony, or rite is the letter expressive outwardly of that spirit of truth which dwelleth in the interior Sanctuary. Nor is the contradiction of the exterior any bar to the harmony of the interior.

Hence this Sanctuary, composed of members widely scattered indeed but united by the bonds of perfect love, has been occupied from the earliest ages in building the grand Temple (through the evolution of humanity) by which the reign of L.V.X. will be manifest. This society is in the communion of those who have most capacity for light; they are united in truth, and their Chief is the Light of the World himself, V.V.V.V.V., the One Anointed in Light, the single teacher for the human race, the Way, the Truth, and the Life.

The interior Order was formed immediately after the first perception of man's wider heritage had dawned upon the first of the adepts; it received from the Masters at first-hand the revelation of the means by which humanity could be raised to its rights and delivered from its misery. It received the primitive charge of all revelation and mystery; it received the key of true science, both divine and natural.

But as men multiplied, the frailty of man necessitated an exterior society which veiled the interior one, and concealed the spirit and the truth in the letter, because many people were not capable of comprehending great interior truth. Therefore, interior truths were wrapped in external and perceptible ceremonies, so that men, by the perception of the outer which is the symbol of the interior, might by degrees be enabled safely to approach the interior spiritual truths.

But the inner truth has always been confided to him who in his day had the most capacity for illumination, and he became the sole guardian of the original Trust, as High Priest of the Sanctuary.

When it became necessary that interior truths should be enfolded in exterior ceremony and symbol, on account of the real weakness of men who were not capable of hearing the Light of Light, then exterior worship began. It was, however, always the type or symbol of the interior, that is to say, the symbol of the true and Secret Sacrament.

The external worship would never have been separated from interior revel but for the weakness of man, which tends too easily to forget the spirit in the letter; but the Masters are vigilant to note in every nation those who are able to receive light, and such persons are employed as agents to spread the light according to man's capacity and to revivify the dead letter.

Through these instruments the interior truths of the Sanctuary were taken into every nation, and modified symbolically according to their customs, capacity for instruction, climate, and receptiveness. So that the external types of every religion, worship, ceremonies and Sacred Books in general have more or less clearly, as their object of instruction, the interior truths of the Sanctuary, by which man will be conducted to the universal knowledge of the one Absolute Truth.

The more the external worship of a people has remained united with the spirit of esoteric truth, the purer its religion; but the wider the difference between the symbolic letter and the invisible truth, the more imperfect has become the religion. Finally, it may be, the external form has entirely parted from its inner truth, so that ceremonial observances without soul or life have remained alone.

In the midst of all this, truth reposes inviolable in the inner Sanctuary.

Faithful to the spirit of truth, the members of the interior Order live in silence, but in real activity.

Yet, besides their secret holy work, they have from time to time decided upon political strategic action.

Thus, when the earth was night utterly corrupt by reason of the Great Sorcery, the Brethren sent Mohammed to bring freedom to mankind by the sword.

This being but partially a success, they raised up one Luther to teach freedom of thought. Yet this freedom soon turned into a heavier bondage than before.

Then the Brethren delivered unto man the knowledge of nature, and the keys thereof; yet this also was prevented by the Great Sorcery.

Now then finally in nameless ways, as one of our Brethren hath it now in mind to declare, have they raised up One to deliver unto men the keys of Spiritual Knowledge, and by His work shall He be judged.

This interior community of light is the reunion of all those capable of receiving light, and it is known as the Communion of Saints, the primitive receptacle for all strength and truth, confided to it from all time.

By it the agents of L.V.X. were formed in every age, passing from the interior to the exterior, and communicating spirit and life to the dead letter, as already said.

AN ACCOUNT OF A∴ A∴

This illuminated community is the true school of L.V.X.; it has its Chair, its Doctors; it possesses a rule for students; it has forms and objects for study.

It has also its degrees for successive development to greater altitudes.

This school of wisdom has been for ever most secretly hidden from the world, because it is invisible and submissive solely to illuminated government.

It has never been exposed to the accidents of time and to the weakness of man, because only the most capable were chosen for it, and those who selected made no error.

Through this school were developed the germs of all the sublime sciences, which were first received by external schools, then clothed in other forms, and hence degenerated.

According to time and circumstances, the society of sages communicated unto the exterior societies their symbolic hieroglyphs, in order to attract man to the great truths of their Sanctuary.

But all exterior societies subsist only by virtue of this interior one. As soon as external societies wish to transform a temple of wisdom into a political edifice, the interior society retires and leaves only the letter without the spirit. It is thus that secret external societies of wisdom were nothing but hieroglyphic screens, the truth remaining inviolable in the Sanctuary so that she might never be profaned.

In this interior society man finds wisdom and with her All—not the wisdom of this world, which is but scientific knowledge, which revolves round the outside but never touches the centre (in which is contained all strength), but true wisdom, understanding and knowledge, reflections of the supreme illumination.

All disputes, all controversies, all the things belonging to the false cares of this world, fruitless discussions, useless germs of opinions which spread the seeds of disunion, all error, schisms, and systems are banished. Neither calumny nor scandal is known. Every man is honoured. Love alone reigns.

We must not, however, imagine that this society resembles any secret society, meeting at certain times, choosing leaders and members, united by special objects. All societies, be what they may, can but come after this interior illuminated circle. This society knows none of the formalities which belong to the outer rings, the work of man. In this kingdom of power all outward forms cease.

L.V.X. is the Power always present. The greatest man of his times, the chief himself, does not always know all the members, but the moment when it is necessary that he should accomplish any object he finds them in the world with certainty ready to his hand.

This community has no outside barriers. He who may be chosen is as the first; he presents himself among the others without presumption, and he is received by the others without jealousy.

It if be necessary that real members should meet together, they find and recognize each other with perfect certainty.

No disguise can be used, neither hypocrisy nor dissimulation could hide the characteristic qualities which distinguish the members of this society. All illusion is gone, and things appear in their true form.

No one member can choose another; unanimous choice is required. Though not all men are called, many of the called are chosen, and that as soon as they become fit for entrance.

Any man can look for the entrance, and any man who is within can teach another to seek for it; but only he who is fit can arrive within.

Unprepared men occasion disorder in a community, and disorder is not compatible with the Sanctuary. Thus it is impossible to profane the Sanctuary, since admission is not formal but real.

Worldly intelligence seeks this Sanctuary in vain; fruitless also will be the efforts of malice to penetrate these great mysteries; all is indecipherable to him who is not ripe; he can see nothing, read nothing in the interior.

He who is fit is joined to the chain, perhaps often where he though least likely, and at a point of which he knew nothing himself.

To become fit should be the sole effort of him who seeks wisdom.

But there are methods by which fitness is attained, for in this holy communion is the primitive storehouse of the most ancient and original science of the human race, with the primitive mysteries also of all science. It is the unique and really illuminated community which is absolutely in possession of the key to all mystery, which knows the centre and source of all nature. It is a society which unites superior strength to its own, and counts its members from more than one world. It is the society whose members form the republic of Genius, the Regent Mother of the whole World.

LIBER LIBRÆ

SVB FIGVRÂ
XXX

A∴ A∴ Publication in Class B.
Issued by Order:

D.D.S. 7° = 4° Præmonstrator
O.S.V. 6° = 5° Imperator
N.S.F. 5° = 6° Cancellarius

LIBER LIBRÆ

SVB FIGURÂ
XXX

0. Learn first—Oh thou who aspirest unto our ancient Order!—that Equilibrium is the basis of the Work. If thou thyself hast not a sure foundation, whereon wilt thou stand to direct the forces of Nature?

1. Know then, that as man is born into this world amidst the Darkness of Matter, and the strife of contending forces; so must his first endeavour be to seek the Light through their reconciliation.

2. Thou then, who has trials and troubles, rejoice because of them, for in them is Strength, and by their means is a pathway opened unto that Light.

3. How should it be otherwise, O man, whose life is but a day in Eternity, a drop in the Ocean of time; how, were thy trials not many, couldst thou purge thy soul from the dross of earth?

Is it but now that the Higher Life is best with dangers and difficulties; hath it not ever been so with the Sages and Hierophants of the past? They have been persecuted and reviled, they have been tormented of men; yet through this also has their Glory increased.

4. Rejoice, therefore, O Initiate, for the greater thy trial

the greater thy Triumph. When men shall revile thee, and speak against thee falsely, hath not the Master said, "Blessed art thou!"?

5. Yet, oh aspirant, let thy victories bring thee not Vanity, for with increase of Knowledge should come increase of Wisdom. He who knoweth little, thinketh he knoweth much; but he who knoweth much hath learned his own ignorance. Seest thou a man wise in his own conceit? There is more hope of a fool, than of him.

6. Be not hasty to condemn others; how knowest thou that in their place, thou couldest have resisted the temptation? And even were it so, why shouldst thou despise one who is weaker than thyself?

7. Thou therefore who desirest Magical Gifts, be sure that thy soul is firm and steadfast; for it is by flattering thy weaknesses that the Weak Ones will gain power over thee. Humble thyself before thy Self, yet fear neither man not spirit. Fear is failure, and the forerunner of failure: and courage is the beginning of virtue.

8. Therefore fear not the Spirits, but be firm and courteous with them; for thou hast no right to despise or revile them; and this too may lead thee astray. Command and banish them, curse them by the Great Names if need be; but neither mock nor revile them, for so assuredly wilt thou be lead into error.

9. A man is what he maketh himself within the limits fixed by his inherited destiny; he is a part of mankind; his actions affect not only what he calleth himself, but also the whole universe.

10. Worship and neglect not, the physical body which is

thy temporary connection with the outer and material world. Therefore let thy mental Equilibrium be above disturbance by material events; strengthen and control the animal passions, discipline the emotions and the reason, nourish the Higher Aspirations.

11. Do good unto others for its own sake, not for reward, not for gratitude from them, not for sympathy. If thou art generous, thou wilt not long for thine ears to be tickled by expressions of gratitude.

12. Remember that unbalanced force is evil; that unbalanced severity is but cruelty and oppression; but that also unbalanced mercy is but weakness which would allow and abet Evil. Act passionately; think rationally; be Thyself.

13. True ritual is as much action as word; it is Will.

14. Remember that this earth is but an atom in the universe, and that thou thyself art but an atom thereon, and that even couldst thou become the God of this earth whereon thou crawlest and grovellest, that thou wouldest, even then, be but an atom, and one amongst many.

15. Nevertheless have the greatest self-respect, and to that end sin not against thyself. The sin which is unpardonable is knowingly and wilfully to reject truth, to fear knowledge lest that knowledge pander not to thy prejudices.

16. To obtain Magical Power, learn to control thought; admit only those ideas that are in harmony with the end desired, and not every stray and contradictory Idea that presents itself.

17. Fixed thought is a means to an end. Therefore pay attention to the power of silent thought and meditation. The

material act is but the outward expression of thy thought, and therefore hath it been said that "the thought of foolishness is sin." Thought is the commencement of action, and if a chance thought can produce much effect, what cannot fixed thought do?

18. Therefore, as hath already been said, Establish thyself firmly in the equilibrium of forces, in the centre of the Cross of the Elements, that Cross from whose centre the Creative Word issued in the birth of the Dawning Universe.

19. Be thou therefore prompt and active as the Sylphs, but avoid frivolity and caprice; be energetic and strong like the Salamanders, but avoid irritability and ferocity; be flexible and attentive to images like the Undines, but avoid idleness and changeability; be laborious and patient like the Gnomes, but avoid grossness and avarice.

20. So shalt thou gradually develop the powers of thy soul, and fit thyself to command the Spirits of the elements. For wert thou to summon the Gnomes to pander to thine avarice, thou wouldst no longer command them, but they would command thee. Wouldst thou abuse the pure beings of the woods and mountains to fill thy coffers and satisfy thy hunger of Gold? Wouldst thou debase the Spirits of Living Fire to serve thy wrath and hatred? Wouldst thou violate the purity of the Souls of the Waters to pander to thy lust of debauchery? Wouldst thou force the Spirits of the Evening Breeze to minister to thy folly and caprice? Know that with such desires thou canst but attract the Weak, not the Strong, and in that case the Weak will have power over thee.

21. In the true religion there is no sect, therefore take heed

LIBER LIBRÆ

that thou blaspheme not the name by which another knoweth his God; for if thou do this thing in Jupiter thou wilt blaspheme יהוה and in Osiris יהשוה. Ask and ye shall have! Seek, and ye shall find! Knock, and it shall be opened unto you!

LIBER
E. VEL EXERCITIORVM
SVB FIGVRÂ
IX

A∴ A∴ Publication in Class B.
Issued by Order:

D.D.S. 7° = 4° Præmonstrator
O.S.V. 6° = 5° Imperator
N.S.F. 5° = 6° Cancellarius

LIBER

E. VEL EXERCITIORVM
SVB FIGVRÂ
IX

I

1. It is absolutely necessary that all experiments should be recorded in detail during, or immediately after, their performance.
2. It is highly important to note the physical and mental condition of the experimenter or experimenters.
3. The time and place of all experiments must be noted; also the state of the weather, and generally all conditions which might conceivably have any result upon the experiment either as adjuvants to or causes of the result, or as inhibiting it, or as sources of error.
4. The A∴ A∴ will not take official notice of any experiments which are not thus properly recorded.
5. It is not necessary at this stage for us to declare fully the ultimate end of our researches; nor indeed would it be understood by those who have not become proficient in these elementary courses.
6. The experimenter is encouraged to use his own intelligence, and not to rely upon any other person or persons, however distinguished, even among ourselves.

7. The written record should be intelligibly prepared so that others may benefit from its study.

8. The book John St. John published in this first number of the "Equinox" is an example of this kind of record by a very advanced student. It is not as simply written as we could wish, but will shew the method.

9. The more scientific the record is, the better.

Yet the emotions should be noted, as being some of the conditions.

Let then the record be written with sincerity and care, and with practice it will be found more and more to approximate to the ideal.

II

Physical Clairvoyance

1. Take a pack of (78) Tarot playing cards. Shuffle; cut. Draw one card. Without looking at it, try and name it. Write down the card you name, and the actual card. Repeat, and tabulate results.

2. This experiment is probably easier with an old genuine pack of Tarot cards, preferably a pack used for divination by some one who really understood the matter.

3. Remember that one should expect to name the right card once in 78 times. Also be careful to exclude all possibilities of obtaining the knowledge through the ordinary senses of sight and touch, or even smell.

There was once a man whose finger-tips were so sensitive that he could feel the shape and position of the pips, and so judge the card correctly.

4. It is better to try first, the easier form of the experiment, by guessing only the suit.

5. Remember that in 78 experiments you should obtain 22 trumps and 14 of each other suit; so that, without any clairvoyance at all, you can guess right twice in 7 times (roughly) by calling trumps each time.

6. Note that some cards are harmonious.

Thus it would not be a bad error to call the five of Swords ("The Lord of Defeat") instead of the ten of Swords ("The Lord of Ruin"). But to call the Lord of Love (2 Cups) for the Lord of Strife (5 Wands) would show that you were getting nothing right.

Similarly, a card ruled by Mars would be harmonious with a 5, a card of Gemini with "The Lovers."

7. These harmonies must be thoroughly learnt, according to the numerous tables given in 777.

8. As you progress, you will find that you are able to distinguish the suit correctly three times in four, and that very few indeed inharmonious errors occur, while in 78 experiments you are able to name the card aright as many as 15 or 20 times.

9. When you have reached this stage, you may be admitted for examination; and in the event of your passing, you will be given more complex and difficult exercises.

III

Asana—Posture

1. You must learn to sit perfectly still with every muscle tense for long periods.

2. You must wear no garment that interferes with the posture in any of these experiments.

3. The first position: (The God). Sit in a chair; head up, back straight, knees together, hands on knees, eyes closed.

4. The second position: (The Dragon). Kneel; buttocks resting on the heels, toes turned back, back and head straight, hands on thighs.

5. The third position: (The Ibis). Stand; hold left ankle with right hand (and alternately practise right ankle in left hand, &c.) free forefinger on lips.

6. The fourth position: (The Thunderbolt). Sit: left heel pressing up anus, right foot poised on its toes, the heel covering the phallus; arms stretched out over the knees: head and back straight.

7. Various things will happen to you while you are practising these positions; they must be carefully analysed and described.

8. Note down the duration of the pracitce, the severity of the pain (if any) which accompanies it, the degree of rigidity attained, and any other pertinent matters.

9. When you have progressed up to the point that a saucer filled to the brim with water and poised upon the head does not spill one drop during a whole hour, and when you can no longer perceive the slightest tremor in any muscle; when, in short, you are perfectly steady and easy, you will be admitted for examination; and, should you pass, you will be instructed in more complex and difficult practices.

LIBER E

IV

Pranayama—Regularisation of the Breathing

1. At rest in one of your positions, close the right nostril with the thumb of the right hand and breath out slowly and completely through the left nostril, while your watch marks 20 seconds. Breathe in through the same nostril for 10 seconds. Changing hands, repeat with the other nostril. Let this be continuous for one hour.

2. When this is quite easy to you, increase the periods to 30 and 15 seconds.

3. When this is quite easy to you, but not before, breathe out for 15 seconds, in for 15 seconds, and hold the breath for 15 seconds.

4. When you can do this with perfect ease and comfort for a whole hour, practise breathing out for 40, in for 20 seconds.

5. This being attained, practise breathing out for 20, in for 10, holding the breath for 30 seconds.

When this has become perfectly easy to you, you may be admitted for examination, and should you pass, you will be instructed in more complex and difficult practices.

6. You will find that the presence of food in the stomach, even in small quantities, makes the practices very difficult.

7. Be very careful never to overstrain your powers; especially never get so short of breath that you are compelled to breathe out jerkily or rapidly.

8. Strive after depth, fulness, and regularity of breathing.

9. Various remarkable phenomena will very probably occur during these practices. They must be carefully analysed and recorded.

V

Dharana—Control of Thought

1. Constrain the mind to concentrate itself upon a single simple object imagined.

The five tatwas are useful for this purpose; they are: a black oval; a blue disk; a silver crescent; a yellow square; a red triangle.

2. Proceed to combinations of simple objects; *e.g.*, a black oval within a yellow square, and so on.

3. Proceed to simple moving objects, such as a pendulum swinging, a wheel revolving, &c. Avoid living objects.

4. Proceed to combinations of moving objects, *e.g.*, a piston rising and falling while a pendulum is swinging. The relation between the two movements should be varied in different experiments.

Or even a system of fly-wheels, eccentrics, and governor.

5. During these practices the mind must be absolutely confined to the object determined upon; no other thought must be allowed to intrude upon the consciousness. The moving systems must be regular and harmonious.

6. Note carefully the duration of the experiments, the number and nature of the intruding thoughts, the tendency of the object itself to depart from the course laid out for it, and any other phenomena which may present themselves. Avoid overstrain. This is very important.

7. Proceed to imagine living objects; as a man, preferably some man known to, and respected by, yourself.

8. In the intervals of these experiments you may try to

imagine the objects of the other senses, and to concentrate upon them.

For example, try to imagine the taste of chocolate the smell of roses, the feeling of velvet, the sound of a waterfall, or the ticking of a watch.

9. Endeavour finally to shut out all objects of any of the senses, and prevent all thoughts arising in your mind. When you feel that you have attained some success in these practices, apply for examination, and should you pass, more complex and difficult practices will be prescribed for you.

VI

Physical Limitations

1. It is desirable that you should discover for yourself your physical limiations.
2. To this end ascertain for how many hours you can subsist without food or drink before your working capacity is seriously interfered with.
3. Ascertain how much alcohol you can take, and what forms of drunkenness assail you.
4. Ascertain how far you can walk without once stopping; likewise with dancing, swimming, running, &c.
5. Ascertain for how many hours you can do without sleep.
6. Test your endurance with various gymnastic exercises, club-swinging and so on.
7. Ascertain for how long you can keep silence.
8. Investigate any other capacities and aptitudes which may occur to you.

9. Let all these things be carefully and conscientiously recorded; for according to your powers will it be demanded of you.

VII

A Course of Reading

1. The object of most of the foregoing practices will not at first be clear to you; but at least (who will deny it?) they will have trained you in determination, accuracy, introspection, and many other qualities which are valuable to all men in their ordinary avocations, so that in no case will your time have been wasted.

2. That you may gain some insight into the nature of the Great Work which lies beyond these elementary trifles, however, we should mention that an intelligent person may gather more than a hint of its nature from the following books, which are to be taken as serious and learned contributions to the study of nature, though not necessarily to be implicitly relied upon.

> "The Yi *K*ing" [S.B.E. Series, Oxford University Press].
> "The Tao Teh *K*ing" [S.B.E. Series].
> "Tannhäuser" by A. Crowley.
> "The Upanishads."
> "The Bhagavad-Gita."
> "The Voice of the Silence."
> "Raja Yoga" by Swami Viveklnanda.
> "The Shiva Sanhita."

LIBER E

"The Aphorisms of Patanjali."
"The Sword of Song."
"The Book of the Dead."
"Rituel et Dogme de la Haute Magie."
"The Book of the Sacred Magic of Abramelin the Mage."
"The Goetia."
"The Hathayoga Pradipika."
Erdmann's "History of Philosophy."
"The Spiritual Guide of Molinos."
"The Star in the West" (Captain Fuller).
"The Dhammapada" [S.B.E. Series, Oxford University Press].
"The Questions of King Milinda" [S.B.E. Series].
"777. vel Prolegomena, &c."
"Varieties of Religious Experience" (James).
"Kabbala Denudata."
"Konx Om Pax."

3. Careful study of these books will enable the pupil to speak in the language of his master and facilitate communication with him.

4. The pupil should endeavour to discover the fundamental harmony of these very varied works; for this purpose he will find it best to study the most extreme divergences side by side.

5. He may at any time that he wishes apply for examination in this course of reading.

6. During the whole of this elementary study and practice, he will do wisely to seek out, and attach himself to, a master, one competent to correct him and advise him. Nor

should he be discouraged by the difficulty of finding such a person.

7. Let him further remember that he must in no wise rely upon, or believe in, that master. He must rely entirely upon himself, and credit nothing whatever but that which lies within his own knowledge and experience.

8. As in the beginning, so at the end, we here insist upon the vital importance of the written record as the only possible check upon error derived from the various qualities of the experimenter.

9. Thus let the work be accomplished duly; yea, let it be accomplished duly.

[If any really important or remarkable results should occur, or if any great difficulty presents itself, the A∴ A∴ should be at once informed of the circumstances.]

THE WIZARD WAY

THE WIZARD WAY

VELVET soft the night-star glowed
Over the untrodden road,
Through the giant glades of yew
Where its ray fell light as dew
Lighting up the shimmering veil
Maiden pure and aery frail
That the spiders wove to hide
Blushes of the sylvan bride
Earth, that trembled with delight
At the male caress of Night.

Velvet soft the wizard trod
To the Sabbath of his God.
With his naked feet he made
Starry blossoms in the glade,
Softly, softly, as he went
To the sombre sacrament,
Stealthy stepping to the tryst
In his gown of amethyst.

Earlier yet his soul had come

THE EQUINOX

To the Hill of Martyrdom,
Where the charred and crookèd stake
Like a black envenomed snake
By the hangman's hands is thrust
Through the wet and writhing dust,
Never black and never dried
Heart's blood of a suicide.

He had plucked the hazel rod
From the rude and goatish god,
Even as the curved moon's waning ray
Stolen from the King of Day.
He had learnt the elvish sign;
Given the Token of the Nine:
Once to rave, and once to revel,
Once to bow before the devil,
Once to swing the thurible,
Once to kiss the goat of hell,
Once to dance the aspen spring,
Once to croak, and once to sing,
Once to oil the savoury thighs
Of the witch with sea-green eyes
With the unguents magical.
Oh the honey and the gall
Of that black enchanter's lips
As he croons to the eclipse
Mingling that most puissant spell
Of the giant gods of hell
With the four ingredients

THE WIZARD WAY

Of the evil elements;
Ambergris from golden spar,
Musk of ox from Mongol jar,
Civet from a box of jade,
Mixed with fat of many a maid
Slain by the inchauntments cold
Of the witches wild and old.

He had crucified a toad
In the basilisk abode,
Muttering the Runes averse
Mad with many a mocking curse.

He had traced the serpent sigil
In his ghastly virgin vigil.
Sursum cor! the elfin hill,
Where the wind blows deadly chill
From the world that wails beneath
Death's black throat and lipless teeth.
There he had stood—his bosom bare—
Tracing Life upon the Air
With the crook and with the flail
Lashing forward on the gale,
Till its blade that wavereth
Like the flickering of Death
Sank before his subtle fence
To the starless sea of sense.

Now at last the man is come

THE EQUINOX

Haply to his halidom.
Surely as he waves his rod.
In a circle on the sod
Springs the emerald chaste and clean
From the duller paler green.
Surely in the circle millions
Of immaculate pavilions
Flash upon the trembling turf
Like the sea-stars in the surf—
Millions of bejewelled tents
For the warrior sacraments.
Vaster, vaster, vaster, vaster,
Grows the stature of the master;
All the ringed encampment vies
With the infinite galaxies.
In the midst a cubic stone
With the Devil set thereon;
Hath a lamb's virginal throat;
Hath the body of a stoat;
Hath the buttocks of a goat;
Hath the sanguine face and rod
Of a goddess and a god!

Spell by spell and pace by pace!
Mystic flashes swing and trace
Velvet soft the sigils stepped
By the silver-starred adept.
Back and front, and to and fro,
Soul and body sway and flow
In vertiginous caresses

THE WIZARD WAY

To imponderable recesses,
Till at last the spell is woven,
And the faery veil is cloven
That was Sequence, Space, and Stress
Of the soul-sick consciousness.

"Give thy body to the beasts!
Give thy spirit to the priests!
Break in twain the hazel rod
On the virgin lips of God!
Tear the Rosy Cross asunder!
Shatter the black bolt of thunder!
Such the swart ensanguine kiss
Of the resolute abyss!"
Wonder-weft the wizard heard
This intolerable word.

Smote the blasting hazel rod
On the scarlet lips of God;
Trampled Cross and rosy core;
Brake the thunder-tool of Thor;
Meek and holy acolyte
Of the priestly hells of spite,
Sleek and shameless catamite
Of the beasts that prowl by night!

Like a star that streams from heaven
Through the virgin airs light-riven,
From the lift there shot and fell

THE EQUINOX

An admirable miracle.
Carved minute and clean, a key
Of purest lapis-lazuli
More blue than the blind sky that aches
(Wreathed with the stars, her torturing snakes),
For the dead god's kiss that never wakes;
Shot with golden specks of fire
Like a virgin with desire.
Look, the levers! fern-frail fronds
Of fantastic diamonds,
Glimmering with ethereal azure
In each exquisite embrasure.
On the shaft the letters laced,
As if dryads lunar-chaste
With the satyrs were embraced,
Spelled the secret of the key:
Sic pervenias. And he
Went his wizard way, inweaving
Dreams of things beyond believing.

When he will, the weary world
Of the senses closely curled
Like a serpent round his heart
Shakes herself and stands apart.
So the heart's blood flames, expanding,
Strenuous, urgent, and commanding;
And the key unlocks the door
Where his love lives evermore.

She is of the faery blood;

THE WIZARD WAY

All smaragdine flows its flood.
Glowing in the amber sky
To ensorcelled porphyry.
She hath eyes of glittering flake
Like a cold grey water-snake.
She hath naked breasts of amber
Jetting wine in her bed-chanber,
Whereof whoso stoops and drinks
Rees the riddle of the Sphinx.

She hath naked limbs of amber
Whereupon her children clamber.
She hath five navels rosy-red
From the five wounds of God that bled;
Each wound that mothered her still bleeding,
And on that blood her babes are feeding.
Oh! like a rose-winged pelican
She hath bred blessed babes to Pan!
Oh! like a lion-hued nightingale
She hath torn her breast on thorns to avail
The barren rose-tree to renew
Her life with that disastrous dew,
Building the rose o' the world alight
With music out of the pale moonlight!
O She is like the river of blood
That broke from the lips of the bastard god,
When he saw the sacred mother smile
On the ibis that flew up the foam of Nile

THE EQUINOX

Bearing the limbs unblessed, unborn,
That the lurking beast of Nile had torn!
So (for the world is weary) I
These dreadful souls of sense lay by.
I sacrifice these impure shoon
To the cold ray of the waning moon.
I take the forkèd hazel staff,
And the rose of no terrene graff,
And the lamp of no olive oil
With heart's blood that alone may boil.
With naked breast and feet unshod
I follow the wizard way to God.

Wherever he leads my foot shall follow;
Over the height, into the hollow,
Up to the caves of pure cold breath,
Down to the deeps of foul hot death,
Across the seas, through the fires,
Past the palace of desires;
Where he will, whether he will or no,
If I go, I care not whither I go.

For in me is the taint of the faery blood.
Fast, fast, its emerald flood
Leaps within me, violent rude
Like a bestial faun's beatitude.
In me the faery blood runs hard:
My sires were a druid, a devil, a bard,

THE WIZARD WAY

A beast, a wizard, a snake and a satyr;
For—as my mother said—what does it matter?
She was a fay, pure of the faery;
Queen Morgan's daughter by an aery
Demon that came to Orkney once
To pay the Beetle his orisons.

So, it is I that writhe with the twitch
Of the faery blood, and the wizard itch
To attain a matter one may not utter
Rather than sink in the greasy splutter
Of Britons munching their bread and butter;
Ailing boys and coarse-grained girls
Grown to sloppy women and brutal churls.
So, I am off with staff in hand
To the endless light of the nameless land.

Darkness spreads its sombre streams,
Blotting out the elfin dreams.
I might haply be afraid,
Were it not the Feather-maid
Leads me softly by the hand,
Whispers me to understand.
Now (when through the world of weeping
Light at last starrily creeping
Steals upon my babe-new sight,
Light—O light that is not light!)
On my mouth the lips of her
Like a stone on my sepulchre

THE EQUINOX

Seal my speech with ecstasy,
Till a babe is born of me
That is silent more than I;
For its inarticulate cry
Hushes as its mouth is pressed
To the pearl, her honey breast;
While its breath divinely ripples
The rose-petals of her nipples,
And the jetted milk he laps
From the soft delicious paps,
Sweeter than the bee-sweet showers
In the chalice of the flowers,
More intoxicating than
All the purple grapes of Pan.

Ah! my proper lips are stilled.
Only, all the world is filled
With the Echo, that dips over
Like the honey from the clover.
Passion, penitence, and pain
Seek their mother's womb again,
And are born the triple treasure,
Peace and purity and pleasure.

—Hush, my child, and come aloft
Where the stars are velvet soft!

ALEISTER CROWLEY.

THE MAGIC GLASSES

THE MAGIC GLASSES

ONE raw November morning, I left my rooms near the British Museum and turned down Regent street. It was cold and misty: the air like shredded cotton-wool. Before I reached the Quadrant, the mist thickened to fog, with the colour of muddied water, and walking became difficult. As I had no particular object in view, I got into talk with a policeman, and, by his advice, went into the Vine Street Police Court, to pass an hour or two before lunch. Inside the court, the atmosphere was comparatively clear, and I took my seat on one of the oak benches with a feeling of vague curiosity. There was a case going on as I entered: an old man, who pretended to be an optician, had been taken up by the police for obstructing the traffic by selling glasses. His green tray, with leathern shoulder-straps, was on the solicitor's table. The charge of obstruction could not be sustained, the old man had moved on as soon as the police told him to, and the inspector had substituted a charge of fraud, on the complaint of a workman and a shopkeeper. A constable had just finished his evidence when I came into the court. He left the box with a self-satisfied air and the muttered remark that the culprit was "a rare bad 'un."

I glanced about for the supposed criminal and found that he was seated near me on a cross-bench in the charge of a sturdy policeman. He did not look like a criminal: he was tall, thin and badly dressed in a suit of rusty black, which seemed to float about his meagre person; his complexion was tallowy-white, like the sprouts of potatoes which have been kept a long time in a dark cellar; he seemed about sixty years old. But he had none of the furtive glances of the criminal; none of the uneasiness: his eye rested on mine and passed aside with calm indifference, contemplative and not alarmed.

The workman who was produced by the police in support of the charge of fraud amused me. He was a young man, about middle height, and dressed in corduroys, with a rough jacket of dark tweed. He was a bad witness: he hesitated, stopped and corrected himself, as if he didn't know the meaning of any words except the commonest phrases of everyday use. But he was evidently honest: his brown eyes looked out on the world fairly enough. His faltering came from the fact that he was only half articulate. Disentangled from the mist of inappropriate words, his meaning was sufficiently clear.

He had been asked by the accused, whom he persisted in calling "the old gentleman," to buy a pair of spectacles: they would show him things truer-like than he could see 'em; and so he "went a bob on 'em." Questioned by the magistrate as to whether he could see things more plainly through the glasses, he shook his head:

"No; about the same."

Then came the question: had he been deceived? Apparently he didn't know the meaning of the word "deceived."

"Cheated," the magistrate substituted.

THE MAGIC GLASSES

"No"; he hadn't been cheated.

"Well, disappointed then?"

"No"; he couldn't say that.

"Would he spend another shilling on a similar pair of glasses?"

"No," he would not; "one bob was enough to lose."

When told he might go, he shuffled out of the witness-box, and on his way to the door attempted more than once to nod to the accused. Evidently there was no malice in him.

The second police witness had fluency and self-possession enough for a lawyer: a middle-aged man, tall, florid and inclined to be stout; he was over-dressed, like a spruce shopman, in black frock-coat, grey trousers and light-coloured tie. He talked volubly, with a hot indignation which seemed to match his full red cheeks. If the workman was an undecided and weak witness, Mr. Hallett, of High Holborn, was a most convinced and determined witness. He had been induced to buy the glasses, he declared, by the "old party," who told him that they would show him things exactly as they were—the truth of everything. You'd only have to look through 'em at a man to see whether he was trying to "do" you or not. That was why he bought them. He was not asked a shilling for them, but a sovereign and he gave it—twenty shillings. When he put the glasses on, he could see nothing with them, nothing at all; it was a "plant": and so he wanted the "old party" to take 'em back and return his sovereign; that might have caused the obstruction that the policeman had objected to. The "old man" refused to give him his money back; said he had not cheated him; had the impudence to pretend that he (Hallett) had no eyes for truth,

THE EQUINOX

and, therefore, could see nothing with the glasses. "A blamed lie," he called it, and a "do," and the "old man" ought to get six months for it.

Once or twice, the magistrate had to direct the stream of emphatic words. But the accusation was formal and precise. The question now was: How would the magistrate deal with the case? At first sight, Mr. Brown, the magistrate, made a good impression on me. He was getting on in life: the dark hair was growing thin on top and a little grey at the sides. The head was well-shaped; the forehead notably broad; the chin and jaw firm. The only unpleasant feature in the face was the hard line of mouth, with thin, unsympathetic lips. Mr. Brown was reputed to be a great scholar, and was just the type of man who would have made a pedant; a man of good intellect and thin blood, who would find books and words more interesting than men and deeds.

At first, Mr. Brown had seemed to be on the side of the accused: he tried to soften Mr. Hallett's anger. One or two of his questions, indeed, were pointed and sensible:

"You wouldn't take goods back after you had sold them, would you, Mr. Hallett?" he asked.

"Of course I would," replied Mr. Hallett, stoutly: "I'd take any of my stock back at a twenty per cent. reduction; my goods are honest goods: prices marked plain on 'em. But 'e would not give me fifteen shillings back out of my sovereign; not 'e; 'e meant sticking' to it all."

The magistrate looked into the body of the court and addressing the accused, said:

"Will you reserve your defence, Mr. Henry?"

"Penry, your worship: Matthew Penry," corrected the

THE MAGIC GLASSES

old man in a quiet, low-pitched voice, as he rose to his feet. "If I may say so: the charge of fraud is absurd. Mr. Hallett seems to be angry because I sold one pair of glasses for a shilling and another pair to him for a sovereign. But they were not the same glasses and, if they had been, I am surely allowed to ask for my wares what I please."

"That is true," interrupted the magistrate; "but he says that you told him he would see the truth through them. I suppose you meant that he would see more truly through them than with his own eyes?"

"Yes," replied Mr. Penry, with a certain hesitation.

"But he did not see more truly through them," continued the magistrate, "or he would not have wanted you to take them back."

"No," Mr. Penry acknowledged; "but that is this fault, not the fault of the glasses. They would show the truth, if he had any faculty for seeing it: glasses are no good to the blind."

"Come, come," said the magistrate; "now you are beginning to confuse me. You don't really pretend that your glasses will show the truth of things, the reality; you mean that they will improve one's sight, don't you?"

"Yes," replied Mr. Penry, "One's sight for truth, for reality."

"Well," retorted the magistrate smiling, "That seems rather metaphysical than practical, doesn't it? If your spectacles enabled one to discern the truth, I'd buy a pair myself: they might be useful in this court sometimes," and he looked about him with a smile, as if expecting applause.

With eager haste, the old man took him at his word,

threw open his case, selected a pair of glasses, and passed them to the clerk, who handed them up to Mr. Brown.

The magistrate put the glasses on; looked round the court for a minute or two, and then broke out:

"Dear me! Dear me! How extraordinary! These glasses alter every one in the court. It's really astonishing. They don't improve the looks of people; on the contrary, a more villainous set of countenances it would be difficult to imagine. If these glasses are to be trusted, men are more like wild animals than human beings, and the worst of all are the solicitors; really a terrible set of faces. But this may be the truth of things; these spectacles do show one more than one's ordinary eyes can perceive. Dear me! Dear me! It is most astonishing; but I feel inclined to accept Mr. Penry's statement about them," and he peered over the spectacles at the court.

"Would you like to look in a glass, your worship?" asked one of the solicitors drily, rising, however, to his feet with an attitude of respect at the same time; "perhaps that would be the best test."

Mr. Brown appeared to be a little surprised, but replied:

"If I had a glass I would willingly."

Before the words were out of his mouth, his clerk had tripped round the bench, gone into the magistrate's private room and returned with a small looking-glass, which he handed up to his worship.

As Mr. Brown looked in the glass, the smile of expectancy left his face. In a moment or two, he put down the glass gravely, took off the spectacles and handed them to the clerk,

THE MAGIC GLASSES

who returned them to Mr. Penry. After a pause, he said shortly:

"It is well, perhaps, to leave all these matters of fact to a jury. I will accept a small bail, Mr. Penry," he went on; "but I think you must be bound over to answer this charge at the sessions."

I caught the words, "£50 a-piece in two sureties and his own recognisances in £100," and then Mr. Penry was told by the policeman to go and wait in the body of the court till the required sureties were forthcoming. By chance, the old man came and sat beside me and I was able to examine him closely. His moustache and beard must have been auburn at one time, but now the reddish tinge seemed only to discolour the grey. The beard was thin and long and unkempt, and added to the forlorn untidiness of his appearance. He carried his head bent forward, as if the neck were too weak to support it. He seemed feeble and old and neglected. He caught me looking at him, and I noticed that his eyes were a clear blue, as if he were younger than I had thought. His gentle, scholarly manner and refined voice had won my sympathy; and, when our eyes met, I introduced myself and told him I should be glad to be one of his sureties, if that would save him time or trouble. He thanked me with a sort of detached courtesy: he would gladly accept my offer.

"You stated your case," I remarked, "so that you confused the magistrate. You almost said that you glasses were—magic glasses," I went on, smiling and hesitating, because I did not wish to offend him, and yet hardly knew how to convey the impression his words had left upon me.

"Magic glasses," he repeated gravely, as if weighing the words; "yes, you might call them magic glasses."

To say that I was astonished only gives a faint idea of my surprise and wonder:

"Surely, you don't mean that they show things as they are," I asked: "the truth of things?"

"That is what I mean," he replied quietly.

"Then they are not ordinary glasses?" I remarked inanely.

"No," he repeated gravely; "not ordinary glasses."

He had a curious trick, I noticed, of peering at one very intently with narrowed eyes and then blinking rapidly several times in succession as if the strain were too great to be borne.

He had made me extremely curious, and yet I did not like to ask outright to be allowed to try a pair of his glasses; so I went on with my questions:

"But, if they show truth, how was it that Mr. Hallett could see nothing through them?"

"Simply because he has no sense of reality; he has killed the innate faculty for truth. It was probably at not time very great," went on this strange merchant, smiling; "but his trader's habits have utterly destroyed it; he has so steeped himself in lies that he is now blind to the truth, incapable of perceiving it. The workman, you remember, could see fairly well through his spectacles."

"Yes," I replied laughing; "and the magistrate evidently saw a good deal more through his than he cared to acknowledge."

The old man laughed too, in an ingenuous, youthful way that I found charming.

At last I got to the Rubicon.

THE MAGIC GLASSES

"Would you let me buy a pair of your glasses?" I asked.

"I shall be delighted to give you a pair, if you will accept them," he replied, with eager courtesy; "my surety ought certainly to have a pair"; and then he peered at me in his curious, intent way. A moment later, he turned round, and opening his tray, picked out a pair of spectacles and handed them to me.

I put them on with trembling eagerness and stared about me. The magistrate had told the truth; they altered everything: the people were the same and yet not the same; this face was coarsened past all description; that face sharpened and made hideous with greed; and the other brutalized with lust. One recognized, so to speak, the dominant passion in each person. Something moved me to turn my glasses on the merchant; if I was astounded before, I was now lost in wonder: the glasses transfigured him. The grey beard was tinged with gold, the blue eyes luminous with intelligence; all the features ennobled; the countenance irradiated sincerity and kindliness. I pulled off the glasses hastily and the vision passed away. Mr. Penry was looking at me with a curious little pleased smile of anticipation: involuntarily, I put out my hand to him with a sort of reverence:

"Wonderful," I exclaimed; "your face is wonderful and all the others grotesque and hideous. What does it mean? Tell me! Won't you?"

"You must come with me to my room," he said, "where we can talk freely, and I think you will not regret having helped me. I should like to explain everything to you. There are so few men," he added, "who proffer help to another man in difficulty. I should like to show you that I am grateful."

"There is no cause for gratitude," I said hastily; "I have done nothing."

His voice now seemed to me to be curiously refined and impressive, and recalled to me the vision of his face, made beautiful by the strange glasses. . . .

I have been particular to put down how Mr. Penry first appeared to me, because after I had once seen him through his spectacles, I never saw him again as I had seen him at first. Remembering my earliest impressions of him, I used to wonder how I could have been so mistaken. His face had refinement and gentleness in every line; a certain courage, too, that was wholly spiritual. Already I was keenly interested in Mr. Penry; eager to know more about him; to help him, if that were possible, in any and every way.

Some time elapsed before the formalities for his bail were arranged, and then I persuaded him to come out with me to lunch. He got up quietly, put the leathern straps over his shoulders, tucked the big case under his arm and walked into the street with perfect self-possession; and I was not now in any way ashamed of his appearance, as I should have been an hour or two before: I was too excited even to feel pride; I was simply glad and curious.

And this favourable impression grew with everything Mr. Penry said and did, till at last nothing but service would content me; so, after lunch, I put him into a cab and drove him off to my own solicitor. I found Mr. Morris, of Messrs. Morris, Coote and Co., quite willing to take up his case at the sessions; willing, too, to believe that the charge was "trumped

THE MAGIC GLASSES

up" by the police and without serious foundation. But, when I drew Mr. Morris aside and tried to persuade him that his new client was a man of extraordinary powers, he smiled incredulously.

"You are enthusiastic, Mr. Winter," he said half reproachfully; "but we solicitors are compelled to see things in the cold light of reason. Why should you undertake to defend this Mr. Penry? Of course if you have made up your mind," he went on, passing over my interruption, "I shall do my best for him; but if I were you, I'd keep my eyes open and do nothing rashly."

In order to impress him, I put on a similar cold tone and declared that Mr. Penry was a friend of mine and that he must leave no stone unturned to vindicate his honesty. And with this I went back to Mr. Penry, and we left the office together.

Mr. Penry's lodging disappointed me; my expectations, I am afraid, were now tuned far above the ordinary. It was in Chelsea, high up, in a rickety old house overlooking a dingy road and barges drawn up on the slimy, fetid mud-banks. And yet, even here, romance was present for the romantic; the fog-wreaths curling over the river clothed the houses opposite in soft mystery, as if they had been draped in blue samite, and through the water-laden air the sun glowed round and red as a fiery wheel of Phaeton's chariot. The room was very bare; by the broad low window stood a large deal table crowded with instruments and glasses; strong electric lamps on the right and left testified to the prolonged labours of the optician. The roof of the garret ran up towards the centre, and by the wall there was a low truckle-bed, fenced off by a cheap Japanese paper-screen. The whole of the wall between the bed and the window was furnished with pine-shelves, filled with books; everything was neat, but the room seemed friendless and cold in the thick, damp air.

There we sat and talked together, till the sun slid out of sight and the fog thickened and night came on: there our acquaintance, so strangely begun, grew to friendship. Before we went to dinner, the old man had shown me the portraits of his two daughters and a little miniature of his wife, who had died fifteen years before.

It was the first of many talks in that room, the first of many confidences. Bit by bit, I heard the whole of Mr. Penry's history. It was told to me piecemeal and inconsequently, as a friend talks to a friend in growing intimacy; and, if I now let Mr. Penry tell his tale in regular sequence and at one stretch, it is mainly in order to spare the reader the tedium of interrupted narration and needless repetitions.

* * * * *

"My father was an optician," Mr. Penry began, "and a maker of spectacles in Chelsea. We lived over the shop in the King's Road, and my childhood was happy enough, but not in any way peculiar. Like other healthy children, I liked play much better than lessons; but my school-days were too uneventful, too empty of love to be happy. My mother died when I was too young to know or regret her, and my father was kind, in spite of his precise, puritanical ways. I was the only boy, which perhaps made him kinder to me, and very much younger than my two sisters, who were grown up when I was in short clothes and who married and left my father's house before I had got to know them, or to feel much affection for them.

THE MAGIC GLASSES

"When I was about sixteen, my father took me from school and began teaching me his own trade. He had been an admirable workman in his time, of the old English sort --- careful and capable, though somewhat slow. The desire was always present in him to grind and polish each glass as well as he could, and this practice had given him a certain repute with a circle of good customers. He taught me every part of his craft as he had learnt it; and, in the next five or six years, imbued me with his own wish to do each piece of work as perfectly as possible. But this period of imitation did not last long. Before I reached manhood, I began to draw apart from my father, to live my own life and to show a love of reading and thinking foreign to his habit. It was religion which separated us. At school I had learnt some French and German, and in both languages I came across sceptical opinions which slowly grew in my mind, and in time led me to discard and almost to dislike the religion of my father. I mention this simply because any little originality in me seemed to spring from this inquiry and from the mental struggle that convulsed three or four years of my youth. For months and months I read feverishly to conquer my doubts, and then I read almost as eagerly to confirm my scepticism.

"I still remember the glow of surprise and hope which came over me the first time I read that Spinoza, one of the heroes of my thought, had also made his living by polishing glasses. He was the best workman of his time, the book said, and I determined to become the best workman of my time; and, from that moment, I took to my trade seriously, strenuously.

"I learned everything I could about glass, and began to

make my own material, after the best recipes. I got books on optics, too, and studied them, and so, bit by bit, mastered the science of my craft.

"I was not more than nineteen or twenty when my father found out that I was a much better workman than his assistant Thompson. Some glasses had been sent to us from a great oculist in Harley Street, with a multitude of minute directions. They had been made by Thompson, and were brought back to us one afternoon by a very fidgety old gentleman who declared that they did not suit him at all. The letter which he showed from Sir William Creighton, the oculist, hinted that the glasses were not carefully made. My father was out, and in his absence I opened the letter. As soon as I had looked at the glasses, I saw that the complaint was justified, and I told the old gentleman so. He turned out to be the famous parliamentary speaker, Lord B. He said to me testily:

"All right, young man; you make my glasses correctly and I shall be satisfied; but not till then; you understand, not till then."

"I smiled at him and told him I would do the work myself, and he went out of the shop muttering, as if only half reassured by my promises. Then I determined to show what I could do. When my father returned, I told him what had happened, and asked him to leave the work to me. He consented, and I went off at once to the little workshop I had made in our back-yard and settled down to the task. I made my glass and polished it, and then ground the spectacles according to the directions. When I had finished, I sent them to Sir William Creighton with a note, and a few days afterwards we had another visit from Lord B., who told my

THE MAGIC GLASSES

father that he had never had such glasses and that I was a "perfect treasure." Like many very crochety people, he was hard to satisfy, but one satisfied he was as lavish in praise as in blame. Lord B. made my reputation as a maker of spectacles, and for years I was content with this little triumph. . . .

"I married when I was about two- or three-and-twenty, and seven or eight years afterwards my father died. The gap caused by his death, the void of loss and loneliness, was more than filled up by my young children. I had two little girls who, at this time, were a source of perpetual interest to me. How one grows to love the little creatures, with their laughter and tears, their hopes and questions and make-believe! And how one's love for them is intensified by all the trouble one takes to win their love and by all the plans one weaves for their future! But all this is common human experience and will only bore you. A man's happiness is not interesting to other people, and I don't know that much happiness is good for a man himself; at any rate, during the ten or fifteen years in which I was happiest, I did least; made least progress, I mean, as a workman and the least intellectual advantage as a man. But when my girls began to grow up and detach themselves from the home, my intellectual nature began to stir again. One must have some interests in life, and, if the heart is empty, the head becomes busier, I often think.

"One day I had a notable visit. A man came in to get a pair of spectacles made: a remarkable man. He was young, gay and enthusiastic, with an astonishing flow of words, an astonishing brightness of speech and manner. He seemed to light up the dingy old shop with his vivacity and happy frankness. He wanted spectacles to correct a slight dissimilarity between his right eye and his left, and he had been advised to come to me by Sir William Creighton, as the glasses would have to be particularly well made. I promised to work at them myself, and on that he burst out:

" 'I shall be very curious to see whether perfect eyes help or hurt my art. You know I am a painter,' he went on, throwing his hair back from his forehead, 'and each of us painters sees life in his own way, and beauty with certain peculiarities. It would be curious, wouldn't it? if talent came from a difference between one's eyes!'

"I smiled at his eagerness, and took down his name, then altogether unknown to me; but soon to become known and memorable above all other names: Dante Gabriel Rossetti. I made the glasses and he was enthusiastic about them, and brought me a little painting of himself by way of gratitude.

"There it is," said Penry, pointing to a little panel that hung by his bedside; "the likeness of an extraordinary man—a genius, if ever there was one. I don't know why he took to me, except that I admired him intensely; my shop, too, was near his house in Chelsea, and he used often to drop in and pass an hour in my back parlour and talk—such talk as I had never heard before and have never heard since. His words were food and drink to me, and more than that. Either his thoughts or the magic of his personality supplied my mind with the essence of growth and vigour which had hitherto been lacking to it; in a very real sense, Rossetti became my spiritual father. He taught me things about art that I had never imagined; opened to me a new heaven and a new earth and, above all, showed me that my craft, too, had artistic possibilities in it that I had never dreamed of before.

THE MAGIC GLASSES

"I shall never forget the moment when he first planted the seed in me that has grown and grown till it has filled my life. It was in my parlour behind the shop. He had been talking in his eager, vivid way, pouring out truths and thoughts, epigrams and poetry, as a great jeweller sometimes pours gems from hand to hand. I had sat listening open-mouthed, trying to remember as much as I could, to assimilate some small part of all that word-wealth. He suddenly stopped, and we smoked on for a few minutes in silence; then he broke out again:

" 'Do you know, my solemn friend,' he said abruptly, 'that I struck an idea the other day which might suit you. I was reading one of Walter Scott's novels: that romantic stuff of his amuses me, you know, though it isn't as deep as the sea. Well, I found out that, about a hundred years ago, a man like you made what they call Claude-glasses. I suppose they were merely rose-tinted,' he laughed, 'but at any rate, they were supposed to make everything beautiful in a Claude-like way. Now, why shouldn't you make such glasses? It would do Englishmen a lot of good to see things rose-tinted for a while. Then, too, you might make Rossetti-glasses,' he went on, laughingly, 'and, if these dull Saxons could only get a glimpse of the passion that possesses him, it would wake them up, I know. Why not go to work, my friend, at something worth doing? Do you know,' he continued seriously, 'there might be something in it. I don't believe, if I had had your glasses at the beginning, I should ever have been the artist I am. I mean,' he said, talking half to himself, 'if my eyes had been all right from the beginning, I might perhaps have been contented with what I saw. But as my eyes were imperfect I tried to see things as my soul saw them, and so invented looks and gestures that the real world would never have given me.'

"I scarcely understood what he meant," said Mr. Penry, "but his words dwelt with me: the ground had been prepared for them; he had prepared it; and at once they took root in me and began to grow. I could not get the idea of the Claude-glasses and the Rossetti-glasses out of my head, and at last I advertised for a pair of those old Claude-glasses, and in a month or so a pair turned up.

"You may imagine that while I was waiting, time hung heavy on my hands. I longed to be at work; I wanted to realize the idea that had come to me while Rossetti was talking. During my acquaintance with him, I had been to his studio a dozen times, and had got to know and admire that type of woman's beauty which is now connected with his name; the woman, I mean, with swanlike throat and languid air and heavy-lidded eyes, who conveys to all of us now something of Rossetti's insatiable passion. But, while I was studying his work and going about steeped in the emotion of it, I noticed one day half a dozen girls whom Rossetti could have taken as models. I had begun, in fact, to see the world as Rossetti saw it; and this talk of his about the Claude-glasses put the idea into my head that I might, indeed, be able to make a pair of spectacles which would enable people to see the world as Rossetti saw it and as I saw it when Rossetti's influence had entire possession of me. This would be a great deal easier to do, I said to myself, than to make a pair of Claude-glasses; for, after all, I did not know what Claude's eyes were really like and I did know the peculiarity of Rossetti's eyes. I accordingly began to study the disparate

THE MAGIC GLASSES

quality in Rossetti's eyes and, after making a pair of spectacles that made my eyes see unequally to the same degree, I found that the Rossettian vision of things was sharpened and intensified to me. From that moment on, my task was easy. I had only to study any given pair of eyes and then to alter them so that they possessed the disparity of Rossetti's eyes and the work was half done. I found, too, that I could increase this disparity a little and, in proportion as I increased it, I increased also the peculiarity of what I called the Rossettian view of things; but, if I made the disparity too great, everything became blurred again.

"My researches had reached this point, when the pair of old Claude-glasses came into my hands. I saw at a glance that the optician of the eighteenth century had no knowledge of my work. He had contented himself, as Rossetti had guessed, with colouring the glasses very delicately and in several tints; in fact, he had studied the colour-peculiarities of the eye as I had studied its form-peculiarities. With this hint, I completed my work. It took me only a few days to learn that Rossetti's view of colour was just as limited, or, I should say, just as peculiar, as his view of form; and, when I once understood the peculiarities of his colour-sight, I could reproduce them as easily as I could reproduce the peculiarities of his vision of form. I then set to work to get both these peculiarities into half a dozen different sets of glasses.

"The work took me some six or eight months; and, when I had done my best, I sent a little note round to Rossetti and awaited his coming with painful eagerness, hope and fear swaying me in turn. When he came, I gave him a pair of the spectacles; and, when he put them on and looked out into the street, I watched him. He was surprised—that I could see—and more than a little puzzled. While he sat thinking, I explained to him what the old Claude-glasses were like and how I had developed his suggestion into this present discovery.

" 'You are an artist, my friend,' he cried at last, 'and a new kind of artist. If you can make people see the world as Claude saw it and as I see it, you can go on to make them see it as Rembrandt saw it and Velasquez. You can make the dullards understand life as the greatest have understood it. But that is impossible,' he added, his face falling: 'that is only a dream. You have got my real eyes, therefore you can force others to see as I see; but you have not the real eyes of Rembrandt, or Velasquez, or Titian; you have not the physical key to the souls of the great masters of the past; and so your work can only apply to the present and to the future. But that is enough, and more than enough,' he added quickly. 'Go on: there are Millais' eyes to get too; and Corot's in France, and half a dozen others; and glad I shall be to put you on the scent. You will do wonderful things, my friend, wonderful things.'

"I was mightily uplifted by his praise and heart-glad, too, in my own way; but resolved at the same time not to give up the idea of making Velasquez-glasses and Rembrandt-glasses; for I had come to know and to admire these masters through Rossetti's talk. He was always referring to them, quoting them, so to say; and, for a long time past, I had accustomed myself to spend a couple of afternoons each week in our National Gallery, in order to get some knowledge of the men who were the companions of his spirit.

"For nearly a year after this, I spent every hour of my spare

THE MAGIC GLASSES

time studying in the National; and at last it seemed to me that I had got Titian's range of colour quite as exactly as the old glasses had got Claude's. But it was extraordinarily difficult to get his vision of form. However, I was determined to succeed; and, with infinite patience and after numberless attempts, success began slowly to come to me. To cut a long story short, I was able, in eight or ten years, to construct these four or five different sorts of glasses. Claude-glasses and Rossetti-glasses, of course; and also Titian-glasses, Velasquez-glasses and Rembrandt-glasses; and again my mind came to anchor in the work accomplished. Not that I stopped thinking altogether; but that for some time my thoughts took no new flight, but hovered round and about the known. As soon as I had made the first pair of Rossetti-glasses, I began to teach my assistant, Williams, how to make them too, in order to put them before the public. We soon got a large sale for them. Chelsea, you know—old Chelsea, I mean—is almost peopled with artists, and many of them came about me and began to make my shop a rendezvous, where they met and brought their friends and talked; for Rossetti had a certain following, even in his own lifetime. But my real success came with the Titian-glasses. The great Venetian's romantic view of life and beauty seemed to exercise an irresistible seduction upon every one, and the trade in his glasses soon became important.

"My home life at this time was not as happy as it had been. In those long years of endless experiment, my daughters had grown up and married, and my wife, I suppose, widowed of her children, wanted more of my time and attention, just when I was taken away by my new work and began to give her less. She used to complain at first; but, when she saw that complaints did not alter me, she retired into herself, as it were; and I saw less and less of her. And then, when my work was done and my new trade established, my shop, as I have told you, became the rendezvous for artists, and I grew interested in the frank, bright faces and the youthful, eager voice, and renewed my youth in the company of the young painters and writers who used to seek me out. Suddenly, I awoke to the fact that my wife was ill, very ill, and, almost before I had fully realised how weak she was, she died. The loss was greater than I would have believed possible. She was gentle and kind, and I missed her every day and every hour. I think that was the beginning of my dislike for the shop, the shop that had made me neglect her. The associations of it reminded me of my fault; the daily requirements of it grew irksome to me.

"About this time, too, I began to miss Rossetti and the vivifying influences of his mind and talk. He went into the country a great deal and for long periods I did not see him, and, when at length we met, I found that the virtue was going out of him: he had become moody and irritable, a neuropath. Of course, the intellectual richness in him could not be hidden altogether: now and then, he would break out and talk in the old magical way:

> And conjure wonder out of emptiness,
> Till mean things put on beauty like a dress
> And all the world was an enchanted place.

But, more often, he was gloomy and harassed, and it saddened and oppressed me to meet him. The young artists who came

THE MAGIC GLASSES

to my shop did not fill his place; they chattered gaily enough, but none of them was a magician as he had been, and I began to realise that genius such as his is one of the rarest gifts in the world.

"I am trying, with all brevity, to explain to you the causes of my melancholy and my dissatisfaction: but I don't think I have done it very convincingly; and yet, about this time, I had grown dissatisfied, ill at ease, restless. And once again my heart-emptiness drove me to work and think. The next step forward came inevitably from the last one I had taken.

"While studying the great painters, I had begun to notice that there was a certain quality common to all of them, a certain power they all possessed when working at highest pressure: the power of seeing things as they are—the vital and essential truth of things. I don't mean to say that all of them possessed this faculty to the same degree. Far from it. The truth of things to Titian is overlaid with romance: he is memorable mainly for his magic of colour and beauty; while Holbein is just as memorable for his grasp of reality. But compare Titian with Giorgione or Tintoretto, and you will see that his apprehension of the reality of things is much greater than theirs. It is that which distinguishes him from the other great colourists of Venice. And, as my own view of life grew sadder and clearer, it came to me gradually as a purpose that I should try to make glasses that would show the reality, the essential truth of things, as all the great masters had seen it; and so I set to work again on a new quest.

"About this time, I found out that, though I had many more customers in my shop, I had not made money out of my artistic enterprises. My old trade as a spectacle-maker was really the most profitable branch of my business. The sale of the Rossetti-glasses and the Titian-glasses, which at first had been very great, fell off quickly as the novelty passed away, and it was soon apparent that I had lost more than I had gained by my artistic inventions. But whether I made £1500 a year, or £1000 a year, was a matter of indifference to me. I had doubled that cape of forty which to me marks the end of youth in a man, and my desires were shrinking as my years increased. As long as I had enough to satisfy my wants, I was not greedy of money.

"This new-born desire of mine to make glasses which would show the vital truth of things soon began to possess me; and, gradually, I left the shop to take care of itself, left it in the hands of my assistant, Williams, and spent more and more time in the little workshop at the back, which had been the theatre of all my achievements. I could not tell you how long I worked at the problem; I only know that it cost me years and years, and that, as I gave more time and labour to it and more and more of the passion of my soul, so I came to love it more intensely and to think less of the ordinary business of life. At length, I began to live in a sort of dream, possessed by the one purpose. I used to get up at night and go on with the work and rest in the day. For months together, I scarcely ate anything, in the hope that hunger might sharpen my faculties; at another time, I lived almost wholly on coffee, hoping that this would have the same effect; and, at length, bit by bit, and slowly, I got nearer to the goal of my desire. But, when I reached it, when I had constructed glasses that would reveal the naked truth, show things as they were and men and

THE MAGIC GLASSES

women as they were, I found that circumstances about me had changed lamentably.

"In the midst of my work, I had known without realising it that Williams had left me and started a shop opposite, with the object of selling the artistic glasses, of which he declared himself the inventor; but I paid no attention to this at the time, and when, two or three years afterwards, I awoke again to the ordinary facts of life, I found that my business had almost deserted me. I am not sure, but I think it was a notice to pay some debts which I hadn't the money to pay, that first recalled me completely to the realities of everyday life. What irony there is in the world! Here was I, who had been labouring for years and years with the one object of making men see things as they are and men and women as they are, persecuted now and undone by the same reality which I was trying to reveal.

"My latest invention, too, was a commercial failure: the new glasses did not not sell at all. Nine people out of ten in England are truthblind, and could make nothing of the glasses; and the small minority, who have the sense of real things, kept complaining that the view of life which my glasses showed them, was not pleasant: as if that were any fault of mine. Williams, too, my assistant, did me a great deal of harm. He devoted himself merely to selling my spectacles; and the tradesman succeeded where the artist and thinker starved. As soon as he found out what my new glasses were, he began to treat me contemptuously; talked of me at times as a sort of half-madman, whose brain was turned by the importance given to his inventions; and at other times declared that I had never invented anything at all, for the idea of the artistic glasses had been suggested by Rossetti. The young painters who frequented his shop took pleasure in spreading this legend and attributing to Rossetti what Rossetti would have been the first to disclaim. I found myself abandoned, and hours used to pass without any one coming into my shop. The worst of it was that, when chance gave me a customer, I soon lost him: the new glasses pleased no one.

"At this point, I suppose, if I had been gifted with ordinary prudence, I should have begun to retrace my steps; but either we grow more obstinate as we grow older, or else the soul's passion grows by the sacrifices we make for it. Whatever the motives of my obstinacy may have been, the disappointment, the humiliation I went through seemed only to nerve me to a higher resolution. I knew I had done good work, and the disdain shown to me drove me in upon myself and my own thoughts."

* * * * *

So much I learned from Mr. Penry in the first few days of our acquaintance, and then for weeks and weeks he did not tell me any more. He seemed to regard the rest of his story as too fantastic and improbable for belief, and he was nervously apprehensive lest he should turn me against him by telling it. Again and again, however, he hinted at further knowledge, more difficult experiments, a more arduous seeking, till my curiosity was all aflame, and I pressed him, perhaps unduly, for the whole truth.

In those weeks of constant companionship, our friendship had grown with almost every meeting. It was impossible to escape the charm of Penry's personality! He was so absorbed in his work, so heedless of the ordinary vanities and greeds of

THE MAGIC GLASSES

men, so simple and kindly and sympathetic, that I grew to love him. He had his little faults, of course, his little peculiarities; surface irritabilities of temper; moments of undue depression, in which he depreciated himself and his work; moments of undue elation, in which he over-estimated the importance of what he had done. He would have struck most people as a little flighty and uncertain, I think; but his passionate devotion to his work lifted the soul, and his faults were, after all, insignificant in comparison with his noble and rare qualities. I had met no one in life who aroused the higher impulses in me as he did. It seemed probable that his latest experiments would be the most daring and the most instructive, and, accordingly, I pressed him to tell me about them with some insistence, and, after a time, he consented:

"I don't know how it came about," he began, "but the contempt of men for my researches exercised a certain influence on me, and at length I took myself seriously to task: was there any reason for their disdain and dislike? Did these glasses of mine really show things as they are, or was I offering but a new caricature of truth, which people were justified in rejecting as unpleasant? I took up again my books on optics and studied the whole subject anew from the beginning. Even as I worked, a fear grew upon me: I felt that there was another height before me to climb, and that the last bit of the road would probably be the steepest of all. . . . In the Gospels," he went on, in a low, reverent voice, "many things are symbolic and of universal application, and it alway seemed to me significant that the Hill of Calvary came at the end of the long journey. But I shrank from another prolonged effort; I said to myself that I couldn't face another task like the last.

But, all the while, I had a sort of uncomfortable prescience that the hardest part of my life's work lay before me.

"One day, a casual statement stirred me profoundly. The primary colours, you know, are red, yellow and blue. The colours shown in the rainbow vary from red to blue and violet; and the vibrations, or lengths, of the light-waves that give us violet grow shorter and shorter and, at length, give us red.

"These vibrations can be measured. One day, quite by chance, I came across the statement that there were innumerable light-waves longer than those which give violet. At once the question sprang: were these longer waves represented by colours which we don't see, colours for which we have no name, colours of which we can form no conception? And was the same thing true of the waves which, growing shorter and shorter, give us the sensation of red? There is room, of course, for myriads of colours beyond this other extremity of our vision. A little study convinced me that my guess was right; for all the colours which we see are represented to our sense of feeling in degrees of heat: that is, blue shows one reading on the thermometer and red a higher reading; and by means of this new standard, I discovered that man's range of vision is not even placed in the middle of the register of heat, but occupies a little space far up towards the warmer extremity of it. There are thousands of degrees of cold lower than blue and hundreds of degrees of heat above red. All these gradations are doubtless represented by colours which no human eye can perceive, no human mind can imagine. It is with sight as with sound. We know now that there are noises louder than thunder which we cannot hear, the roar that lies on the other side of silence. We men are

THE MAGIC GLASSES

poor restless prisoners, hemmed in by our senses as by the walls of a cell, hearing only a part of nature's orchestra and that part imperfectly; seeing only a thousandth part of the colour-marvels about us and seeing that infinitesimal part incorrectly and partially. Here was new knowledge with a vengeance! Knowledge that altered all my work! How was I to make glasses to show all this? Glasses that would reveal things as they are and must be to higher beings—the ultimate reality. At once, the new quest became the object of my life and, somehow or other I knew before I began the work that the little scraps of comfort or of happiness which I had preserved up to this time, I should now forfeit. I realised with shrinking and fear, that this new inquiry would still further remove me from the sympathy of my fellows.

"My prevision was justified. I had hardly got well to work—that is, I had only spent a couple of years in vain and torturing experiments—when I was one day arrested for debt. I had paid no attention to the writ; the day of trial came and went without my knowing anything about it; and there was a man in possession of my few belongings before I understood what was going on. Then I was taught by experience that to owe money is the one unforgivable sin in the nation of shopkeepers. My goods were sold up and I was brought to utter destitution"—the old man paused—"and then sent to prison because I could not pay."

"But," I asked, "did your daughters do nothing? Surely, they could have come to your help?"

"Oh! they were more than kind," he replied simply, "the eldest especially, perhaps because she was childless herself. I called her Gabrielle," he added, lingering over the name; "she was very good to me. As soon as she heard the news, she paid my debt and set me free. She bought things, too, and fitted out two nice rooms for me and arranged everything again quite comfortably; but you see," he went on with a timid, depreciating smile, "I tired out even her patience: I could not work at anything that brought in money and I was continually spending money for my researches. The nice furniture went first; the pretty tables and chairs and then the bed. I should have wearied an angel. Again and again, Gabrielle bought me furniture and made me tidy and comfortable, as she said, and again and again, like a spendthrift boy, I threw it all away. How could I think of tables and chairs, when I was giving my life to my work? Besides, I always felt that the more I was plagued and punished, the more certain I was to get out the best in me: solitude and want are the twin nurses of the soul."

"But didn't you wish to get any recognition, any praise?" I broke in.

"I knew by this time," he answered, "that, in proportion as my work was excellent, I should find fewer to understand it. How many had I seen come to praise and honour while Rossetti fell to nerve-disease and madness; and yet his work endures and will endure, while theirs is already forgotten. The tree that grows to a great height wins to solitude even in a forest: its highest outshoots find no companions save the winds and stars. I tried to console myself with such similes as this," he went on, with a deprecatory smile, "for the years passed and I seemed to come no nearer to success. At last, the way opened for me a little, and, after eight or ten years of incessant experiment, I found that partial success was all I

THE MAGIC GLASSES

should ever accomplish. Listen! There is not one pair of eyes in a million that could ever see what I had taught myself to see, for the passion of the soul brings with it its own reward. After caring for nothing but truth for twenty years, thinking of nothing but truth, and wearying after it, I could see it more clearly than other men: get closer to it than they could. So the best part of my labour—I mean the highest result of it—became personal, entirely personal, and this disappointed me. If I could do no good to others by it, what was my labour but a personal gratification? And what was that to me—at my age! I seemed to lose heart, to lose zest.... Perhaps it was that old age had come upon me, that the original sum of energy in me had been spent, that my bolt was shot. It may be so.

"The fact remains that I lost the desire to go on, and, when I had lost that, I woke up, of course, to the ordinary facts of life once again. I had no money: I was weak from semi-starvation and long vigils, prematurely old and decrepit. Once more, Gabrielle came to my assistance. She fitted up this room, and then I went out to sell my glass, as a pedlar. I bought the tray and made specimens of all the spectacles I had made, and hawked them about the streets. Why shouldn't I? No work is degrading to the spirit, none, and I could not be a burden to the one I loved, now I knew that my best efforts would not benefit others. I did not get along very well: the world seemed strange to me, and men a little rough and hard. Besides, the police seemed to hate me; I don't know why. Perhaps, because I was poor, and yet unlike the poor they knew. They persecuted me, and the magistrates before whom they brought me always believed them and never believed me. I have been punished times without number for obstruction, though I never annoyed any one. The police never pretended that I had cheated or stolen from any one before; but, after all, this latest charge of theirs brought me to know you and gave me your friendship; and so I feel that all the shame has been more than made up to me."

My heart burned within me as he spoke so gently of his unmerited sufferings. I told him I was proud of being able to help him. He put his hand on mine with a little smile of comprehension.

A day or two later curiosity awoke in me again, and I asked him to let me see a pair of the new glasses, those that show the ultimate truth of things.

"Perhaps, some day," he answered quietly. I suppose my face fell, for, after a while, he went on meditatively: "There are faults in them, you see, shortcomings and faults in you, too, my friend. Believe me, if I were sure that they would cheer or help you in life, I would let you use them quickly enough; but I am beginning to doubt their efficacy. Perhaps the truth of things is not for man."

*   *   *   *   *

When we entered the court on the day of Penry's trial, Morris and myself were of opinion that the case would not last long and that it would certainly be decided in our favour. The only person who seemed at all doubtful of the issue was Penry himself. He smiled at me, half pityingly, when I told him that in an hour we should be on our way home. The waiting seemed interminable, but at length the case was called. The counsel for the prosecution got up and talked perfunctorily for

THE MAGIC GLASSES

five minutes, with a sort of careless unconcern that seemed to me callous and unfeeling. Then he began to call his witnesses. The workman, I noticed, was not in the court. His evidence had been rather in favour of the accused, and the prosecution, on that account, left it out. But Mr. 'Allett, as he called himself, of 'Igh 'Olborn, was even more voluble and vindictive than he had been at the police-court. He had had time to strengthen his evidence, too, to make it more bitter and more telling, and he had used his leisure malignantly. It seemed to me that every one should have seen his spite and understood the vileness of his motives. But no; again and again, the judge emphasised those parts of his story which seemed to tell most against the accused. The judge was evidently determined that the jury should not miss any detail of the accusation, and his own bias appeared to me iniquitous. But there was a worse surprise in store for us. After Hallett, the prosecution called a canon of Westminster, a stout man, with heavy jowl and loose, suasive lips, Canon Bayton. He told us how he had grown interested in Penry and in his work, and how he had bought all his earlier glasses, the Rossetti-glasses, as he called them. The cannon declared that these artistic glasses threw a very valuable light on things, redeemed the coarseness and commonness of life and made reality beautiful and charming. He was not afraid to say that he regarded them as instruments for good; but the truth-revealing glasses seemed to excite his utmost hatred and indignation. He could not find a good word to say for them: they only showed, he said, what was terrible and brutal in life. When looking through them, all beauty vanished, the charming flesh-covering fell away and you saw the death's-head grinning at you. Instead of parental affection, you found personal vanity; instead of the tenderness of the husband for the wife, gross and common sensuality. All high motives withered, and, instead of the flowers of life, you were compelled to look at the wormlike roots and the clinging dirt. He concluded his evidence by assuring the jury that they would be doing a good thing if they put an end to the sale of such glasses. The commerce was worse than fraudulent, he declared; it was a blasphemy against God and an outrage on human nature. The unctuous canon seemed to me worse than all the rest; but the effect he had on the jury was unmistakable, and our barrister, Symonds, refused to cross-examine him. To do so, he said, would only strengthen the case for the prosecution, and I have no doubt that he was right, for Morris agreed with him.

But even the prosecuting witnesses did not hurt us more than the witnesses for the defence. Mr. Penry had been advised by Mr. Morris to call witnesses to his character, and he had called half a dozen of the most respectable tradesmen of his acquaintance. One and all did him harm rather than good; they all spoke of having known him twenty years before, when he was well-to-do and respectable. They laid stress upon what they called "his fall in life." They all seemed to think that he had neglected his business and come to ruin by his own fault. No one of them had the faintest understanding of the man, or of his work. It was manifest from the beginning that these witnesses damaged our case, and this was apparently the view of the prosecuting barrister, for he scarcely took the trouble to cross-examine them.

It was with a sigh of relief that I saw Mr. Penry go into the box to give evidence on his own behalf. Now, I thought, the

THE MAGIC GLASSES

truth will come to light. He stated everything with the utmost clearness and precision; but no one seemed to believe him. The wish to understand him was manifestly wanting in the jury, and from the beginning the judge took sides against him. From time to time, he interrupted him just to bring out what he regarded as the manifest falseness of his testimony.

"You say that these glasses show truth," he said. "Who wants to see truth?"

"Very few," was Penry's reply.

"Why, then, did you make the glasses," went on the judge, "if you knew that they would disappoint people?"

"I thought it my duty to," replied Penry.

"Your duty to disappoint and anger people?" retorted the judge, "a strange view to take of duty. And you got money for this unpleasant duty, didn't you?"

"A little," was Penry's reply.

"Yes; but still you got money," persisted the judge. "You persuaded people to buy your glasses, knowing that they would be disappointed in them, and you induced them to give you money for the disappointment. Have you anything else to urge in your defence?"

I was at my wit's end; I scarcely knew how to keep quiet in my seat. It seemed to me so easy to see the truth. But even Penry seemed indifferent to the result, indifferent to a degree that I could scarcely explain or excuse. This last question, however, of the judge aroused him. As the harsh, contemptuous words fell upon the ear, he leaned forward, and, selecting a pair of spectacles, put them on and peered round the court. I noticed that he was slightly flushed. In a moment or two, he took the glasses off and turned to the judge:

"My lord," he said, "you seem determined to condemn me, but, if you do condemn me, I want you to do it with some understanding of the facts. I have told you that there are very few persons in this country who have any faculty for truth, and that the few who have, usually have ruined their power before they reach manhood. You scoff and sneer at what I say, but still it remains the simple truth. I looked round the court just now to see if there was any one here young enough, ingenuous enough, pure enough, to give evidence on my behalf. I find that there is no one in the court to whom I can appeal with any hope of success. But, my lord, in the room behind this court there is a child sitting, a girl with fair hair, probably your lordship's daughter. Allow me to call her as a witness, allow her to test the glasses and say what she sees through them, and then you will find that these glasses do alter and change things in a surprising way to those who can use them."

"I don't know how you knew it," broke in the judge, "but my daughter is in my room waiting for me, and what you say seems to have some sense in it. But it is entirely unusual to call a child, and I don't know that I have any right to allow it. Still, I don't want you to feel that you have not had every opportunity of clearing yourself; so, if the jury consent, I am quite willing that they should hear what this new witness may have to say."

"We are willing to hear the witness," said the foreman, "but really, your lordship, our minds are made up about the case."

THE MAGIC GLASSES

The next moment, the child came into the court—a girl of thirteen or fourteen, with a bright, intelligent face, a sort of shy fear troubling the directness of her approach.

"I want you to look through a pair of spectacles, my child," said Penry to her, "and tell us just what you see through them," and, as he spoke, he peered at her in his strange way, as if judging her eyes.

He then selected a pair of glasses and handed them to her. The child put them on and looked round the court, and then cried out suddenly:

"Oh, what strange people; and how ugly they all are. All ugly, except you who gave me the glasses; you are beautiful." Turning hastily round, she looked at her father and added, "Oh, papa, you are—Oh!" and she took off the glasses quickly while a burning flush spread over her face.

"I don't like these glasses," she said indignantly, laying them down. "They are horrid! My father doesn't look like that."

"My child," said Penry, very gently, "will you look through another pair of glasses? You see so much that perhaps you can see what is to be, as well as what is. Perhaps you can catch some glimpse even of the future."

He selected another pair and handed them to the child. There was a hush of expectancy in the court; people who had scoffed at Penry before and smiled contempt, now leaned forward to hear, as if something extraordinary were about to happen. All eyes were riveted on the little girl's face; every ear strained to hear what she would say. Round and round the court she looked through the strange glasses and then began to speak in a sort of frightened monotone:

"I see nothing," she said. "I mean there is no court and no people, only great white blocks, a sort of bluey-white. Is it ice? There are no trees, no animals; all is cold and white. It is ice. There is no living creature, no grass, no flowers, nothing moves. It is all cold, all dead." In a frightened voice she added: "Is that the future?"

Penry leaned towards her eagerly:

"Look at the light, child," he said; "follow the light up and tell us what you see."

Again a strange hush; I heard my heart thumping while the child looked about her. Then, pulling off the glasses, she said peevishly:

"I can't see anything more: it hurts my eyes."

*   *   *   *   *

DEATH IN PRISON.

"Matthew Penry, whose trial for fraud and condemnation will probably still be remembered by our readers because of the very impressive evidence for the prosectuion given by Canon Bayton, of Westminster, died, we understand, in Wandsworth Prison yesterday morning from syncope."—Extract from the *Times*, January 3, 1900.

FRANK HARRIS.

THE CHYMICAL JOUSTING OF
BROTHER PERARDUA
WITH THE SEVEN LANCES
THAT HE BRAKE

CARL HENTSCHEL, LTD. ENG., LONDON, E.C.

THE CHYMICAL JOUSTING OF
BROTHER PERARDUA
WITH THE SEVEN LANCES
THAT HE BRAKE

He slayeth Sir Argon le Paresseux.

Now Brother Perardua, though he was but a Zelator of our ancient Order, had determined in himself to perform the Magnum Opus, and to procure for himself one grain of the Powder, one minim of the Elixir, and the Tincture of Double Efficacy. Not fully did he yet comprehend the Mysterium of our Art, therefore impose he upon himsef the sevenfold regimen. For without the Bell of Electrum Magicum of Paracelsus how should the adept even give warning to the Powers of the Work of his entry thereunto?

Yet our brother, being of stout heart—for he had been a soldier in many distant lands—began right cheerfully. His head that was hoary with eld he crowned with five petals of white lotus, as if to signify the purity of his bodyt, and went forth into that place where is no field, nor any furrow therein; and there he sowed a scroll that had two and twenty seeds diverse.

He slayeth Sir Abjad the Saracen.

Nor for all his care and labour could he gather therefrom more than seven plants, that shone in the blackness; and each plant beareth a single blossom that hath seven petals—one would have thought them stars; for though they were not of a verity in themselves brilliant and flashing, yet so black was that wherein they grew that they seemed brighter than suns. And these were placed one above the other in a single line and straight, even according unto the seven centres of his intention that he bare about him in the hollow tube that hath thirty and two joints.

He slayeth Sir Amorex le Desirous.

These plants did our brother Perardua pluck, as the mystic rites ordain; and these did he heat furiously in his alembic, yet with vegetable heat alone, while he kept them ever moist, dropping upon them of his lunar water, whereof he had three and seventy minims left of the eight and seventy that his Father had given him; and these he had borne upon a camel through the desert unto this place where he now was, which is called the Oasis of the Lion, even as the whole Regimen that in the end he accomplished is in the form of a Lion.

Thus then his Lion waxed exceeding thirsty, and licked up all that dew. But the fire being equal thereunto, he was not discomforted.

He slayeth Sir Lionel the Warder of the Marches.

So now indeed he had wrought the first Matter to a pitch of excellence beyond the human; for without trouble was his tincture thus beautiful. First, it had the crown and horns of Alexander the mighty king; also it had wings of fine sapphire; its fore part was like the Lion, whereby indeed it partook of the highest Virtue, and its hinder quarters were as a bull's.

BROTHER PERARDUA

Moreover it stood upon the White Sphere and the Red Cube; and it is not possible for any Elixir to exceed this, unless it be by Our path and working.

He slayeth Sir Merlin the Wizard.

Yet our brother Perardua—and by now he was right skilful at the athanor!—determined to attain to that higher Projection. Therefore he subtly prepared a Red Dragon, or as some alchemists will have it, a Fiery Flying Serpent, whereby he should eat up that Sphinx of his, that he had nourished with such ingenium and care.

Now this Red Dragon hath seven fiery coils, proper to the seven silver stars. Also was his head right venemous and greedy, and eight flames were about it; for that Sphinx had two wings and four feet and two horns; but the Serpent is one, even as the King is one.

He slayeth the Great Dragon called Stooping or Twisted.

Now then is this work utterly burnt up and abolished in that tremendous heat that is in the mouth and belly of the Dragon; and that which cometh forth therefrom is in no wise that which went in. Yet are these twelve the children of those two-and-twenty. So when he had broken the cucurbirte, he find therein no trace of the seven, but a button of fused gold—as we say, for it is not gold....

Now this button hath twelve faces, and angles twenty-four salient and reentrant; and Our Egyptian brethren have called it the Pavement of the Firmament of Nu.

THE EQUINOX

He slayeth King Astur of the Arms Argent.

Now this metal is not in any wise like unto earthly metal; let the brethren well beware, for many false knaves be abroad. Three things be golden: the mineral gold of the merchant that is dross; the vegetable gold that groweth from the seed of the scroll by virture of the Lion; and the animal gold that cometh forth from the regimen of the Dragon, and this last is the sole marketable gold of the Philosopher. For, behold, an Arcanum! I charge you, keep secret this matter; for the vile brothers, could they divine it, would pervert it.

This mineral Gold cannot be changed into any other substance by any means.

This Vegetable Gold is fluidic; it must increase wonderfully and be fixed in the Perfection of the Sphinx.

But this our Animal Gold is to this mighty pitch unstable, that it can neither increase nor decrease, nor can it remain that which it is, or seemeth to be. For even as a drop of glass unequally cooled flieth at a touch into a myriad fine particles, so also at a touch this gold philosophical dissolveth his being, ofttimes with a great and terrible explosion, ofttimes so softly and subtly that no man may perceive it, be he never so acute, nay, as a needle for sharpness or for fineness as a spyglass of the necromancer!

Yet herein lieth the core of the matter that in this explosion aforesaid naught whatever is left either of the seven or the twelve or of the three Mother seeds that lie concealed therein. But in a certain mystical way the Other Ten are shadowed forth, though dimly, as if the Brazen Serpent had become a Sword of Lightning. Yet this is but a glyph; for in truth there is no link or bond between them.

BROTHER PERARDUA

For this Animal Gold is passed utterly away; there is not any button thereof, nor any feather of the Wings of the Sphinx, nor any mark of the Sower or of the Seed. But at that Lightning Flash all did entirely disappear, and the Cucurbite and the Alembic and the Athanor were shattered utterly... and there arose That which he had set himself to seek; yea, more! a grain of the Powder, and three minims of the Elixir, and Six drachms of the Tincture of Double Efficacy.

...Yet the brethren mocked him; for he had imperilled himself sore; so that unto this hour hath the name of Perardua been forgotten, and they that have need to speak of him say in right joyaunce *Non Sine Fulmine*.

THE LONELY BRIDE

"Blest among women," they say: I stand
    Here in the market-place,
And the crowd throngs by in this lonely land,
    Nor stays to heed my face.
My head is bowed down with the shame of my thought:
    Mine eyes grow hot with disgrace.
Oh the evil that men have wrought!

I was once a King's daughter,
    Back in the olden time,
They called me the Bride of Water:
    I went to the sea for her rhyme;
I went to the stars for their song of life,
    For then I was in my prime.
Now I am filled with strife.

I stare all day at the men that pass,
    And all that I see I crave;
There are simple-gatherers fresh from the grass,
    There are mariners brown from the wave,
There are merchants stout with tablets wide;
    There is many a fair young slave;
They call me The Lonely Bride.

THE EQUINOX

I was men's wonder the day I came;
    I was ruddy and gold and pale:
My eyes were light with a smouldering flame,
    On my lips was the untold tale,
And men, as they passed, gazed hard and long,
    And women looked scorn and bale.
Yea! I was fair and strong.

How should they know the thing I sought?
    I was rich and lovely and young,
Not young with the flame that the spring had wrought,
    But with fire from the summer sprung.
No man dared speak, but they longed to speak:
    Aye! Many a glance they flung.
But I stood with an unflushed cheek.

And only the strangers heed me now;
    I am but a statue cold.
Ah! could they see the pain in my brow,
    My heart that is growing old.
I may not summon them to my side,
    Or move my lips' stern fold.
I am The Lonely Bride.

But never a man doth dare to speak,
    And with burning heart I stand,
Till I feel the hot blood mount to my cheek,
    And a trembling shake my hand.
If they but knew of my need, my need,
    As I wait in love's barren land,
To me, to me would they speed.

THE LONELY BRIDE

Here in the market place they pass,
    Merchant and slave and thrall;
The dewy herb-gatherer from the grass,
    The steward from out the hall.
Ah! the weary waiting till one shall speak,
    Oh! then the spell will fall,
And I shall find what I seek.

VICTOR B. NEUBURG.

AT THE FORK OF THE ROADS

AT THE FORK OF THE ROADS

HYPATIA GAY knocked timidly at the door of Count Swanoff's flat. Hers was a curious mission, to serve the envy of the long lank melancholy unwashed poet whom she loved. Will Bute was not only a poetaster but a dabbler in magic, and black jealousy of a younger man and a far finer poet gnawed at his petty heart. He had gained a subtle hypnotic influence over Hypatia, who helped him in his ceremonies, and he had now commissioned her to seek out his rival and pick up some magical link through which he might be destroyed.

The door opened, and the girl passed from the cold stone dusk of the stairs to a palace of rose and gold. The poet's rooms were austere in their elegance. A plain gold-black paper of Japan covered the walls; in the midst hung an ancient silver lamp within which glowed the deep ruby of an electric lamp. The floor was covered with black and gold of leopards' skins; on the walls hung a great crucifix in ivory and ebony. Before the blazing fire lay the poet (who had concealed his royal Celtic descent beneath the pseudonym of Swanoff) reading in a great volume bound with vellum.

He rose to greet her.

"Many days have I expected you," he exclaimed, "many days have I wept over you. I see your destiny—how thin a thread links you to that mighty Brotherhood of the Silver Star whose trembling neophyte I am—how twisted and thick are the tentacles of the Black Octopus whom you now serve. Ah! wrench yourself away while you are yet linked with us: I would not that you sank into the Ineffable Slime. Blind and bestial are the worms of the Slime: come to me, and by the Faith of the Star, I will save you."

The girl put him by with a light laugh. "I came," she said, "but to chatter about clairvoyance—why do you threat me with these strange and awful words?"

"Because I see that to-day may decide all for you. Will you come with me into the White Temple, while I administer the Vows? Or will you enter the Black Temple, and swear away your soul?"

"Oh really," she said, "you are too silly—but I'll do what you like next time I come here."

"To-day your choice—to-morrow your fate," answered the young poet.

And the conversation drifted to lighter subjects.

But as she left she managed to scratch his hand with a brooch, and this tiny blood-stain on the pin she bore back in triumph to her master; he would work a strange working therewith!

* * * * *

Swanoff closed his books and went to bed. The streets were deadly silent; he turned his thoughts to the Infinite Silence of the Divine Presence, and fell into a peaceful sleep. No dreams disturbed him; later than usual he awoke.

How strange! The healthy flush of his cheek had faded: the hands were white and thin and wrinkled: he was so weak

AT THE FORK OF THE ROADS

that he could hardly stagger to the bath. Breakfast refreshed him somewhat; but more than this the expectation of a visit from his master.

The master came. "Little brother!" he cried aloud as he entered, "you have disobeyed me. You have been meddling again with the Goetia!"

"I swear to you, master!" He did reverence to the adept.

The new comer was a dark man with a powerful clean-shaven face almost masked in a mass of jet-black hair.

"Little brother," he said, "if that be so, then the Goetia has been meddling with you."

He lifted up his head and sniffed. "I smell evil;" he said, "I smell the dark brothers of iniquity. Have you duly performed the Ritual of the Flaming Star?"

"Thrice daily, according to your word."

"Then evil has entered in a body of flesh. Who has been here?"

The young poet told him. His eyes flashed. "Aha!" he said, "now let us Work!"

The neophyte brought writing materials to his master: the quill of a young gander, snow-white; virgin vellum of a young male lamb; ink of the gall of a certain rare fish; and a mysterious Book.

The master drew a number of incomprehensible signs and letters upon the vellum.

"Sleep with this beneath the pillow," he said, "you will awake if you are attacked; and whatever it is that attacks you, kill it! Kill it! Kill it! Then instantly go into your temple and assume the shape and dignity of the god

Horus, send back the Thing to its sender by the might of the god that is in you! Come! I will discover unto you the words and the signs and the spells for this working of magic art."

They disappeared into the little white room lined with mirrors which Swanoff used for a temple.

  *   *   *   *   *

Hypatia Gay, that same afternoon, took some drawings to a publisher in Bond Street. This man was bloated with disease and drink; his loose lips hung in an eternal leer; his fat eyes shed venom; his cheeks seemed ever on the point of bursting into nameless sores and ulcers.

He bought the young girl's drawings. "Not so much for their value," he explained, "as that I like to help promising young artists—like you, my dear!"

Her steely virginal eyes met his fearlessly and unsuspiciously. The beast cowered, and covered his foulness with a hideous smile of shame.

  *   *   *   *   *

The night came, and young Swanoff went to his rest without alarm. Yet with that strange wonder that denotes those who expect the unknown and terrible, but have faith to win through.

This night he dreamt—deliciously.

A thousand years he strayed in gardens of spice, by darling streams, beneath delightful trees, in the blue rapture of the wonderful weather. At the end of a long glade of ilex that reached up to a marble palace stood a woman, fairer than all the women of the earth. Imperceptibly they drew together—she was in his arms. He awoke with a start. A woman indeed lay in his arms and showered a rain of burning kisses on his face. She clothed him about with ecstasy; her touch waked the serpent of essential madness in him.

Then, like a flash of lightning, came his master's word to his memory—Kill it! In the dim twilight he could see the lovely face that kissed him with lips of infinite splendour, hear the cooing words of love.

"Kill it! My God! Adonai! Adonai!" He cried aloud, and took her by the throat. Ah God! Her flesh was not the flesh of woman. It was hard as india-rubber to the touch, and his strong young fingers slipped. Also he loved her—loved, as he had never dreamt that love could be.

But he knew now, he knew! And a great loathing mingled with his lust. Long did they struggle; at last he got the upper, and with all his weight above her drove down his fingers in her neck. She gave one gasping cry—a cry of many devils in hell—and died. He was alone.

He had slain the succubus, and absorbed it. Ah! With what force and fire his veins roared! Ah! How he leapt from the bed, and donned the holy robes. How he invoked the God of Vengeance, Horus the mighty, and turned loose the Avengers upon the black soul that had sought his life!

At the end he was calm and happy as a babe; he returned to bed, slept easy, and woke strong and splendid.

*   *   *   *   *

Night after night for ten nights this scene was acted and re-acted: always identical. On the eleventh day he received a postcard from Hypatia Gay that she was coming to see him that afternoon.

"It means that the material basis of their working is

exhausted," explained his master. "She wants another drop of blood. But we must put an end to this."

They went out into the city, and purchased a certain drug of which the master knew. At the very time that she was calling at the flat, they were at the boarding-house where she lodged, and secretly distributing the drug about the house. Its function was a strange one: hardly had they left the house when from a thousand quarter came a lamentable company of cats, and made the winter hideous with their cries.

"That" (chuckled the master) "will give her mind something to occupy itself with. She will do no black magic for our friend awhile!"

Indeed the link was broken; Swanoff had peace. "If she comes again," ordered the master, "I leave it to you to punish her."

*   *   *   *   *

A month passed by; then, unannounced, once more Hypatia Gay knocked at the flat. Her virginal eyes still smiled; her purpose was yet deadlier than before.

Swanoff fenced with her awhile. Then she began to tempt him.

"Stay!" he said, "first you must keep your promise and enter the temple!"

Strong in the trust of her black master, she agreed. The poet opened the little door, and closed it quickly after her, turning the key.

As she passed into the utter darkness that hid behind curtains of black velvet, she caught one glimpse of the presiding god.

It was a skeleton that sat there, and blood stained all its

bones. Below it was the evil altar, a round table supported by an ebony figure of a negro standing upon his hands. Upon the altar smouldered a sickening perfume, and the stench of the slain victims of the god defiled the air. It was a tiny room, and the girl, staggering, came against the skeleton. The bones were not clean; they were hidden by a greasy slime mingling with the blood, as though the hideous worship were about to endow it with a new body of flesh. She wrenched herself back in disgust. Then suddenly she felt it was alive! It was coming towards her! She shrieked once the blasphemy which her vile master had chosen as his mystic name; only a hollow laugh echoed back.

Then she knew all. She knew that to seek the left-hand path may lead one to the power of the blind worms of the Slime—and she resisted. Even then she might have called to the White Brothers; but she did not. A hideous fascination seized her.

And then she felt the horror.

Something—something against which nor clothes nor struggles were any protection—was taking possession of her, eating its way into her...

And its embrace was deadly cold.... Yet the hell-clutch at her heart filled her with a fearful joy. She ran forward; she put her arms round the skeleton; she put her young lips to its bony teeth, and kissed it. Instantly, as at a signal, a drench of the waters of death washed all the human life out of her being, while a rod as of steel smote her even from the base of the spine to the brain. She had passed the gates of the abyss. Shriek after shriek of ineffable agony burst from her tortured mouth; she writhed and howled in that ghastly celebration of the nuptials of the Pit.

Exhaustion took her; she fell with a heavy sob.

* * * * *

When she came to herself she was at home. Still that lamentable crew of cats miauled about the house. She awoke and shuddered. On the table lay two notes.

The first: "You fool! They are after me; my life is not safe. You have ruined me—Curse you!" This from the loved master, for whom she had sacrificed her soul.

The second a polite note from the publisher, asking for more drawings. Dazed and desperate, she picked up her portfolio, and went round to his office in Bond Street.

He saw the leprous light of utter degradation in her eyes; a dull flush came to his face; he licked his lips.

THE MAGICIAN
[TRANSLATED FROM ELIPHAZ LEVI'S VERSION OF THE FAMOUS HYMN]

O LORD, deliver me from hell's dark fear and gloom !
Loose thou my spirit from the larvæ of the tomb !
I seek them in their dread abodes without affright :
On them will I impose my will, the law of light.

I bid the night conceive the glittering hemisphere.
Arise, O sun, arise! O moon, shine white and clear !
I seek them in their dread abodes without affright:
On them will I impose my will, the law of light.

Their faces and their shapes are terrible and strange.
These devils by my might to angels I will change.
These nameless horrors I address without affright:
On them will I impose my will, the law of light.

These are the phantoms pales of mine astonied view
Yet none but I their blasted beauty can renew;
For to the abyss of hell I plunge without affright:
On them will I impose my will, the law of light.

THE SOLDIER AND THE HUNCHBACK
! AND ?

THE SOLDIER AND THE HUNCHBACK
! AND ?

"Expect seven misfortunes from the cripple, and forty-two from the one-eyed man; but when the hunchback comes, say 'Allah our aid.' "

ARAB PROVERB.

I

INQUIRY. Let us inquire in the first place: What is Scepticism? The word means looking, questioning, investigating. One must pass by contemptuously the Christian liar's gloss which interprets "sceptic" as "mocker"; though in a sense it is true for him, since to inquire into Christianity is assuredly to mock at it; but I am concerned to intensify the etymological connotation in several respects. First, I do not regard mere incredulity as necessary to the idea, though credulity is incompatible with it. Incredulity implies a prejudice in favour of a negative conclusion; and the true sceptic should be perfectly unbiassed.

Second, I exclude "vital scepticism." What's the good of anyfink? Expects (as we used to learn about "nonne?") the answer, "Why, nuffink!" and again is prejudice. Indolence is no virtue in a questioner. Eagerness, intentness, concentration, vigilance—all these I include in the connotation of "sceptic." Such questioning as has been called "vital scepticism" is but a device to avoid true questioning, and therefore its very antithesis, the devil disguised as an angel of light.

[Or *vice versâ*, friend, if you are a Satanist; 'is a matter of words—words—words. You may write x for y in your equations, so long as you consistently write y for x. They remain unchanged—and unsolved. Is not all our "knowledge" an example of this fallacy of writing one unknown for another, and then crowing like Peter's cock?]

I picture the true sceptic as a man eager and alert, his deep eyes glittering like sharp swords, his hands tense with effort as he asks, "What does it matter?"

I picture the false sceptic as a dude or popinjay, yawning, with dull eyes, his muscles limp, his purpose in asking the question but the expression of his slackness and stupidity.

This true sceptic is indeed the man of science; as Wells' "Moreau" tells us. He has devised some means of answering his first question, and its answer is another question. It is difficult to conceive of any question, indeed, whose answer does not imply a thousand further questions. So simple an inquiry as "Why is sugar sweet?" involves an infinity of chemical researches, each leading ultimately to the blank wall—what is matter? and an infinity of physiological researches, each (similarly) leading to the blank wall—what is mind?

Even so, the relation between the two ideas is unthinkable; causality is itself unthinkable; it depends, for one thing, upon experience—and what, in God's name, is experience?

THE SOLDIER AND THE HUNCHBACK

Experience is impossible without memory. What is memory? The mortar of the temple of the ego, whose bricks are the impressions. And the ego? The sum of our experience, may be. (I doubt it!) Anyhow, we have got values of y and z for x, and values of x and z for y—all our equations are indeterminate; all our knowledge is relative, even in a narrower sense than is usually implied by the statement. Under the whip of the clown God, our performing donkeys the philosophers and men of science run round and round in the ring; they have amusing tricks: they are cleverly trained; but they get nowhere.

I don't seem to be getting anywhere myself.

II

A fresh attempt. Let us look into the simplest and most certain of all possible statements. *Thought exists*, or if you will, *Cogitatur*.

Descartes supposed himself to have touched bed-rock with his *Cogito, ergo Sum*.

Huxley pointed out the complex nature of this proposition, and that it was an enthymeme with the premiss *Omnes sunt, qui cogitant* suppressed. He reduced it to *Cogito*; or, to avoid the assumption of an ego, *Cogitatur*.

Examining more closely this statement, we may still cavil at its form. We cannot translate it into English without the use of the verb to be, so, that, after all, existence is implied. Nor to we readily conceive that contemptuous silence is sufficient answer to the further query, "By whom is it thought?" The Buddhist may find it easy to image an act without an agent; I am not so clever. It may be possible for a sane man; but I should like to know more about his mind before I give a final opinion.

But apart from purely formal objections, we may still inquire: Is this *Cogitatur* true?

Yes; reply the sages; for to deny it implies thought. *Negatur* is only a sub-section of *Cogitatur*.

This involves, however, an axiom that the part is of the same nature as the whole; or (at the very least) an axiom that *A* is *A*.

Now, I do not wish to deny that *A* is *A*, or may occasionally be *A*. But certainly *A is A* is a very different statement to our original *Cogitatur*.

The proof of *Cogitatur*, in short, rests not upon itself but upon the validity of our logic; and if by logic we mean (as we should mean) the Code of the Laws of Thought, the irritating sceptic will have many more remarks to make: for it now appears that the proof that *thought exists* depends upon the truth of that which is thought, to say no more.

We have taken *Cogitatur*, to try and avoid the use of *esse*, but *A is A* involves that very idea, and the proof is fatally flawed.

Cogitatur depends on *Est*; and there's no avoiding it.

III

Shall we get on any better if we investigate this *Est*—Something is—Existence is—אהיה אשר אהיה?

What is Existence? The question is so fundamental that it

THE SOLDIER AND THE HUNCHBACK

finds no answer. The most profound meditation only leads to an exasperating sense of impotence. There is, it seems, no simple rational idea in the mind which corresponds to the word.

It is easy of course to drown the question in definitions, leading us to further complexity—but

> "Existence is the gift of Divine Providence,"
> "Existence is the opposite of Non-Existence,"

do not help us much!

The plain *Existence is Existence* of the Hebrews goes further. It is the most sceptical of statements, in spite of its form. Existence is just existence, and there's no more to be said about it; don't worry! Ah, but there is more to be said about it! Though we search ourselves for a thought to match the word, and fail, yet we have Berkeley's perfectly convincing argument that (so far as we know it) existence must mean *thinking existence* or *spiritual existence*.

Here then we find our *Est* to imply *Cogitatur*, and Berkeley's arguments are "irrefragable, yet fail to produce conviction" (Hume) because the *Cogitatur*, as we have shown, implies *Est*.

Neither of these ideas is simple; each involves the other. Is the division between them in our brain a proof of the total incapacity of that organ, or is there some flaw in our logic? For all depends on our logic; not upon the simple identity *A is A* only, but upon its whole structure from the question of simple propositions, enormously difficult from the moment when it occurred to the detestable genius that invented "existential import" to consider the matter, to that further complexity and contradiction, the syllogism.

IV

Thought is appears then (in the worst case possible, denial) as the conclusion of the premisses:
There is denial of thought.
(All) Denial of thought is thought.
Even formally, 'tis a clumsy monster. Essentially, it seems to involve a great deal beyond our original statement. We compass heaven and earth to make one syllogism; and when we have made it, it is tenfold more the child of mystery than ourselves.

We cannot here discuss the whole problem of the validity (the surface-question of the logical validity) of the syllogism; though one may throw out the hint that the doctrine of distributed middle seems to assume a knowledge of a Calculus of Infinites which is certainly beyond my own poor attainments, and hardly impregnable to the simple reflection that all mathematics is conventional, and not essential; relative, and not absolute.

We go deeper and deeper, then, it seems, from the One into the Many. Our primary proposition depends no longer upon itself, but upon the whole complex being of man, poor, disputing, muddle-headed man! Man with all his limitations and ignorance; man—man!

THE SOLDIER AND THE HUNCHBACK
V

We are of course no happier when we examine the Many, separately or together. They converge and diverge, each fresh hill-top of knowledge disclosing a vast land unexplored; each gain of power in our telescopes opening out new galaxies; each improvement in our microscopes showing us life minuter and more incomprehensible. A mystery of the mighty spaces between molecules; a mystery of the ether-cushions that fend off the stars from collision! A mystery of the fulness of things; a mystery of the emptiness of things! Yet, as we go, there grows a sense, an instinct, a premonition—what shall I call it?—that Being is One, and Thought is One, and Law is One—until we ask What is that One?

Then again we spin words—words—words. And we have got no single question answered in any ultimate sense.

What is the moon made of?

Science replies "Green Cheese."

For our one moon we now have two ideas.

Greenness, and *Cheese*.

Greenness depends on the sunlight, and the eye, and a thousand other things.

Cheese depends on bacteria and fermentation and the nature of the cow.

"Deeper, ever deeper, into the mire of things!"

Shall we cut the Gordian knot? shall we say "There is God"?

What, in the devil's name, is God?

If (with Moses) we picture Him as an old man showing us His back parts, who shall blame us? The great Question—*any* question is the great question—does indeed treat us thus cavalierly, the disenchanted Sceptic is too prone to think!

Well, shall we define Him as a loving Father, as a jealous priest, as a gleam of light upon the holy Ark? What does is matter? All these images are of wood and stone, the wood and stone of our own stupid brains! The Fatherhood of God is but a human type; the idea of a human father conjoined with the idea of immensity. Two for One again!

No combination of thoughts can be greater than the thinking brain itself; all we can think of God or say of Him, so long as our words represent thoughts, is less than the whole brain which thinks, and orders speech.

Very good: shall we proceed by denying Him all thinkable qualities, as do the heathen? All we obtain is mere negation of thought.

Either He is unknowable, or He is less than we are. Then, too, that which is unknowable is unknown; and "*God*" or "*There is God*" as an answer to our question becomes as meaningless as any other.

Who are we, then?

We are Spencerian Agnostics, poor silly, damned Spencerian Agnostics!

And there is an end of the matter.

VI

It is surely time that we began to question the validity of some of our data. So far our scepticism has not only knocked to pieces our tower of thought, but rooted up the foundation-

THE SOLDIER AND THE HUNCHBACK

stone and ground it into finer and more poisonous powder than that into which Moses ground the calf. These golden Elohim! Our calf-heads that brought us not out of Egypt, but into a darkness deeper and more tangible than any darkness of the double Empire of Asar.

Hume put his little ? to Berkeley's God-! ; Buddha his ? to the Vedic Atman-!—and neither Hume nor Buddha was baulked of his reward. Ourselves may put ? to our own ? since we have found no ! to put it to; and wouldn't it be jolly if our own second ? suddenly straightened its back and threw its chest out and marched off as ! ?

Suppose then we accept our scepticism as having destroyed our knowledge root and branch—is there no limit to its action? Does it not in a sense stultify itself? Having destroyed logic by logic—if Satan cast out Satan, how shall his kingdom stand?

Let us stand on the Mount, Saviours of the World that we are, and answer "Get thee behind me, Satan!" though refraining from quoting texts or giving reasons.

Oho! says somebody; is Aleister Crowley here?—Samson blinded and bound, grinding corn for the Philistines?

Not at all, dear boy!

We shall put all the questions that we can put—but we may find a tower built upon a rock, against which the winds beat in vain.

Not what Christians call faith, be sure! But what (possibly) the forgers of the Epistles—those eminent mystics!—meant by faith. What I call Samadhi!—and as "faith without works is dead," so, good friends, Samadhi is all humbug unless the practitioner shows the glint of its gold in his work in the world. If your mystic becomes Dante, well; if Tennyson, a fig for his trances!

But how does this tower of Samadhi stand the assault of Question-time?

Is not the idea of Samadhi just as dependent on all the other ideas—man, time, being, thought, logic? If I seek to explain Samadhi by analogy, am I not often found talking as if we knew all about Evolution, and Mathematics, and History? Complex and unscientific studies, mere straws before the blast of our hunchback friend!

Well, one of the buttresses is just the small matter of common sense.

The other day I was with Dorothy, and, as I foolishly imagined, very cosy; for her sandwiches are celebrated. It was surely bad taste on the part of Father Bernard Vaughan, and Dr. Torrey, and Ananda Metteyya, and Mr G.W. Foote, and Captain Fuller, and the ghost of Immanuel Kant, and Mr. Bernard Shaw, and young Neuburg, to intrude. But intrude they did; and talk! I never heard anything like it. Every one with his own point of view; but all agreed that Dorothy was non-existent, or if existent, a most awful specimen, that her buns were stale, and her tea stewed; *ergo*, that I was having a very poor time of it. Talk! Good God! But Dorothy kept on quietly and took no notice; and in the end I forgot about them.

Thinking it over soberly, I see now that very likely they were quite right: I can't prove it either way. But as a mere practical man, I intend taking the steamer—for my sins I am in Gibraltar—back to Dorothy at the earliest possible

THE SOLDIER AND THE HUNCHBACK

moment. Sandwiches of bun and German sausage may be vulgar even imaginary—it's the taste I like. And the more I munch, the more complacent I feel, until I go so far as to offer my critics a bite.

This sounds in a way like the "Interior Certainty" of the common or garden Christian; but there are differences.

The Christian insists on notorious lies being accepted as an essential part of his (more usually her) system; I, on the contrary, ask for facts, for observation. Under Scepticism, true, one is just as much a house of cards as the other; but only in the philosophical sense.

Practically, Science is true; and Faith is foolish.

Practically, $3 \times 1 = 3$ is the truth; and $3 \times 1 = 1$ is a lie; though, sceptically, both statements may be false or unintelligible.

Practically, Franklin's method of obtaining fire from heaven is better than that of Prometheus or Elijah. I am now writing by the light that Franklin's discovery enabled men to use.

Practically, "I concentrated my mind upon a white radiant triangle in whose centre was a shining eye, for 22 minutes and 10 seconds, my attention wandering 45 times" is a scientific and valuable statement. "I prayed fervently to the Lord for the space of many days" means anything or nothing. Anybody who cares to do so may imitate my experiment and compare his result with mine. In the latter case one would always be wondering what "fervently" meant and who "the Lord" was, and how many days made "many."

My claim, too, is more modest than the Christian's. He (usually she) knows more about my future than is altogether pleasant; I claim nothing absolute from my Samadhi—I know only too well the worthlessness of single-handed observations, even on so simple a matter as a boiling-point determination!—and as for his (usually her) future, I content myself with mere common sense about the probable end of a fool.

So that after all I keep my scepticism intact—and I keep my Samadhi intact. The one balances the other; I care nothing for the vulgar brawling of these two varlets of my mind!

VII

If, however, you would really like to know what might be said on the soldierly side of the question, I shall endeavour to oblige.

It is necessary if a question is to put intelligibly that the querent should be on the same plane as the quesited.

Answer is impossible if you ask: Are round squares triangular? or Is butter virtuous? or How may ounces go to the shilling? for the "questions" are not really questions at all.

So if you ask me Is Samadhi real? I reply: First, I pray you, establish a connection between the terms. What do you mean by Samadhi?

There is a physiological (or pathological; never mind now!) state which I call Samadhi; and that state is as real—in relation to man—as sleep, or intoxication, or death.

Philosophically, we may doubt the existence of all of these; but we have no grounds for discriminating between them—the Academic Scepticism is a wholesale firm, I hope!—and practically, I challenge you to draw valid distinctions.

All these are states of the consciousness of man; and if you seek to destroy one, all fall together.

VIII

I must, at the risk of appearing to digress, insist upon this distinction between philosophical and practical points of view, or (in Qabalistic language) between Kether and Malkuth.

In private conversation I find it hard—almost impossible—to get people to understand what seems to me so very simple a point. I shall try to make it exceptionally clear.

A boot is an illusion.

A hat is an illusion.

Therefore, a boot is a hat.

So argue my friends, not distributing the middle term.

But thus argue I.

All boots are illusions.

All hats are illusions.

Therefore (though it is not a syllogism), all boots and hats are illusions.

I add:

To the man in Kether no illusions matter.

Therefore: to the man in Kether neither boots nor hats matter.

In fact, the man in Kether is out of all relation to these boots and hats.

You, they say, claim to be a man in Kether (I don't). Why

then, do you not wear boots on your head and hats on your feet?

I can only answer that I the man in Kether ('tis but an argument) am out of all relation as much with feet and heads as with boots and hats. But why should I (from my exalted pinnacle) stoop down and worry the headed and footed gentleman in Malkuth, who after all doesn't exist for me, by these drastic alterations in his toilet? There is no distinction whatever; I might easily put the boots on his shoulders, with his head on one foot and his hat on the other.

In short, why not be a clean-living Irish gentleman, even if you do have insane ideas about the universe?

Very good, say my friends, unabashed, then why not stick to that? Why glorify Spanish gipsies when you have married a clergyman's daughter?

Why go about proclaiming that you can get as good fun for eighteenpence as usually costs men a career?

Ah! let me introduce you to the man in Tiphereth; that is, the man who is trying to raise his consciousness from Malkuth to Kether.

This Tiphereth man is in a devil of a hole! He knows theoretically all about the Kether point of view (or thinks he does) and practically all about the Malkuth point of view. Consequently he goes about contradicting Malkuth; he refuses to allow Malkuth to obsess his thought. He keeps on crying out that there is no difference between a goat and a God, in the hope of hypnotising himself (as it were) into that perception of their identity, which is his (partial and incorrect) idea of how things look from Kether.

This man performs great magic; very strong medicine. He

THE SOLDIER AND THE HUNCHBACK

really does find gold on the midden and skeletons in pretty girls.

In Abiegnus the Sacred Mountain of the Rosicrucians the Postulant finds but a coffin in the central shrine; yet that coffin contains Christian Rosencreutz who is dead and is alive for evermore and hath the keys of Hell and of Death.

Ay! your Tiphereth man, child of Mercy and Justice, looks deeper than the skin!

But he seems a ridiculous object enough both to the Malkuth man and to the Kether man.

Still, he's the most interesting man there is; and we all must pass through that stage before we get our heads really clear, the Kether-vision above the Clouds that encircle the mountain Abiegnus.

IX

Running and returning, like the Cherubim, we may now resume our attempt to drill our hunchback friend into a presentable soldier. The digression will not have been all digression, either; for it will have thrown a deal of light on the question of the limitations of scepticism.

We have questioned the Malkuth point of view; it appears absurd, be it agreed. But the Tiphereth position is unshaken; Tiphereth needs no telling that Malkuth is absurd. When we turn our artillery against Tiphereth, that too crumbles; but Kether frowns above us.

Attack Kether, and it falls: but the Yetziratic Malkuth is still there . . . . until we reach Kether of Atziluth and the

Infinite Light, and Space, and Nothing.

So then we retire up the path, fighting rear-guard actions; at every moment a soldier is slain by a hunchback; but as we retire there is always a soldier just by us.

Until the end. The end? Buddha thought the supply of hunchbacks infinite; but why should not the soldiers themselves be infinite in number?

However that may be, here is the point; it takes a moment for a hunchback to kill his man, and the further we get from our base the longer it takes. You may crumble to ashes the dream-world of a boy, as it were, between your fingers; but before you can bring the physical universe tumbling about a man's ears he requires to drill his hunchbacks so devilish well that they are terribly like soldiers themselves. And a question capable of shaking the consciousness of Samadhi could, I imagine, give long odds to one of Frederick's grenadiers.

It is useless to attack the mystic by asking him if he is quite sure Samadhi is good for his poor health; 'tis like asking the huntsman to be very careful, please, not to hurt the fox.

The ultimate Question, the one that really knocks Samadhi to pieces, is such a stupendous Idea that it is far more of a ! than all previous !'s together, for all its ? form.

And the name of that Question is Nibbana.

Take this matter of the soul.

When Mr. Judas McCabbage asks the Man in the Street why he believes in a soul, the Man stammers out that he has always heard so; naturally McCabbage has no difficulty in proving to him by biological methods that he has no soul; and with a sunny smile each passes on his way.

But McCabbage is wasted on the philosopher whose belief

THE SOLDIER AND THE HUNCHBACK

in a soul rests on introspection; we must have heavier metal; Hume will serve our turn, may be.

But Hume in his turn becomes perfectly futile, pitted against the Hindu mystic, who is in constant enjoyment of his new-found Atman. It takes a Buddha-gun to knock *his* castle down.

Now the ideas of McCabbage are banal and dull; those of Hume are live and virile; there is a joy in them greater than the joy of the Man in the Street. So too the Buddha-thought, Anatta, is a more splendid conception than the philosopher's Dutch-doll-like Ego, or the rational artillery of Hume.

This weapon, too, that has destroyed our lesser, our illusionary universes, ever revealing one more real, shall we not wield it with divine ecstasy? Shall we not, too, perceive the inter-dependence of the Questions and the Answers, the necessary connection of the one with the other, so that (just as $0 \times \infty$ is an indefinite) we destroy the absolutism of either ? or ! by their alteration and balance, until in our series ?!?!?!?...!?!?... we care nothing as to which may prove the final term, any single term being so negligible a quantity in relation to the vastness of the series? Is it not a series of geometrical progression, with a factor positive and incalculably vast?

In the light of the whole process, then, we perceive that there is no absolute value in the swing of the pendulum, though its shaft lengthen, its rate grow slower, and its sweep wider at every swing.

What should interest us is the consideration of the Point from which it hangs, motionless at the height of things! We are unfavourably placed to observe this, desperately clinging as we are to the bob of the pendulum, sick with our senseless swinging to and fro in the abyss!

We must climb up the shaft to reach that point—but—wait one moment! How obscure and subtle has our simile become! Can we attach any true meaning to the phrase? I doubt it, seeing what we have taken for the limits of the swing. True, it may be that the end of the swing is always 360° so that the !-point and the ?-point coincide; but that is not the same thing as having no swing at all, unless we make kinematics identical with statics.

What is to be done? How shall such mysteries be uttered?

Is this how it is that the true Path of the Wise is said to lie in a totally different plane from all his advance in the path of Knowledge, and of Trance? We have already been obliged to take the Fourth Dimension to illustrate (if not explain) the nature of Samadhi.

Ah, say the adepts, Samadhi is not the end, but the beginning. You must regard Samadhi as the normal state of mind which enables you to begin your researches, just as waking is the state from which you rise to Samadhi, sleep the state from which you rose to waking. And only from Sammasamadhi—continuous trance of the right kind—can you rise up as it were on tiptoe and peer through the clouds unto the mountains.

Now of course it is really awfully decent of the adepts to take all that trouble over us, and to put it so nicely and clearly. All we have to do, you see, is to acquire Samma-samadhi, and then rise on tiptoe. Just so!

But then there are the other adepts. Hark at him! Little brother, he says, let us rather consider that as the pendulum

THE SOLDIER AND THE HUNCHBACK

swings more and more slowly every time, it must ultimately stop, as soon as the shaft is of infinite length. Good! then it isn't a pendulum at all but a Mahalingam—The Mahalingam of Shiva (*Namo Shivaya namaha Aum!*) which is all I ever thought it was; all you have to do is to keep swinging hard—I know it's hook-swinging!—and you get there in the End. Why bother to swing? First, because you're bound to swing, whether you like it or not; second, because your attention is thereby distracted from those lumbar muscles in which the hook is so very firmly fixed; third, because after all it's a ripping good game; fourth, because you want to get on, and even to seem to progress is better than standing still. A treadmill is admittedly good exercise.

True, the question, "Why become an Arahat?" should precede, "How become an Arahat?" but an unbiassed man will easily cancel the first question with "Why not?"—the How is not so easy to get rid of. Then, from the standpoint of the Arahat himself, perhaps this "Why did I become an Arahat?" and "How did I become an Arahat?" have but a single solution!

In any case, we are wasting our time—we are as ridiculous with or Arahats as Herod the Tetrarch with his peacocks! We pose Life with the question Why? and the first answer is: To obtain the Knowledge and Conversation of the Holy Guardian Angel.

To attach meaning to this statement we must obtain that Knowledge and Conversation: and when we have done that, we may proceed to the next Question. It is no good asking it now.

"There are purse-proud penniless ones that stand at the door of the tavern and revile the guests."

THE EQUINOX

We attach little importance to the Reverend Out-at-Elbows, thundering in Bareboards Chapel that the rich man gets no enjoyment from his wealth.

Good, then. Let us obtain the volume entitled "The Book of the Sacred Magic of Abramelin the Mage"; or the magical writings of that holy illuminated Man of God, Captain Fuller, and carry out fully their instructions.

And only when we have succeeded, when we have put a colossal ! against our vital ? need we inquire whether after all the soldier is not going to develop spinal curvature.

Let us take the first step; let us sing:

> "I do not ask to see
> The distant path; one step's enough for me."

But (you will doubtless say) I pith your ? itself with another ?: Why question life at all? Why not remain "a clean-living Irish gentleman" content with his handicap, and contemptuous of card and pencil? Is not the Buddha's goad "Everything is sorrow" little better than a currish whine? What do I care for old age, disease, and death? I'm a man, and a Celt at that. I spit on your snivelling Hindu prince, emasculate with debauchery in the first place, and asceticism in the second. A weak, dirty, paltry cur, sir, your Gautama!

Yes, I think I have no answer to that. The sudden apprehension of some vital catastrophe may have been the exciting cause of my conscious devotion to the attainment of Adeptship—but surely the capacity was there, inborn. Mere despair and desire can do little; anyway, the first impulse of fear was the passing spasm of an hour; the magnetism of the path itself was the true lure. It is as foolish to ask me "Why

THE SOLDIER AND THE HUNCHBACK

do you adep?" as to ask God "Why do you pardon?" *C'est son métier*.

I am not so foolish as to think that my doctrine can ever gain the ear of the world. I expect than ten centuries hence the "nominal Crowleians" will be as pestilent and numerous a body as the "nominal Christians" are to-day; for (at present) I have been able to devise no mechanism for excluding them. Rather, perhaps, should I seek to find them a niche in the shrine, just as Hinduism provides alike for those capable of the Upanishads and those whose intelligences hardly reaches up to the Tantras. In short, one must abandon the reality of religion for a sham, so that the religion may be universal enough for those few who are capable of its reality to nestle in its breast, and nurse their nature on its starry milk. But we anticipate!

My message is then twofold; to the greasy *bourgeois* I preach discontent; I shock him, I stagger him, I cut away earth from under his feet, I turn him upside down, I give him hashish and make him run amok, I twitch his buttocks with the red-hot tongs of my Sadistic fancy—until he feels uncomfortable.

But to the man who is already as uneasy as St. Lawrence on his silver grill, who feels the Spirit stir in him, even as a woman feels, and sickens at, the first leap of the babe in her womb, to him I bring the splendid vision, the perfume and the glory, the Knowledge and Conversation of the Holy Guardian Angel. And to whosoever hath attained that height will I put a further Question, announce an further Glory.

It is my misfortune and not my fault that I am bound to deliver this elementary Message.

THE EQUINOX

"Man has two sides; one to face the world with,
One to show a woman that he loves her."

We must pardon Browning his bawdy jest; for his truth is ower true! But it is your own fault if you are the world instead of the beloved; and only see of me what Moses saw of God!

It is disgusting to have to spend one's life jetting dirt in the face of the British public in the hope that in washing it they may wash off the acrid grease of their commercialism, the saline streaks of their hypocritical tears, the putrid perspiration of their morality, the dribbling slobber of their sentimentality and their religion. And they don't wash it! ...

But let us take a less unpleasing metaphor, the whip! As some schoolboy poet repeatedly wrote, his rimes as poor as Edwin Arnold, his metre as erratic and as good as Francis Thompson, his good sense and frank indecency a match for Browning!

"Can't be helped; must be done—
So..."

Nay! 'tis a bad, bad rime.

And only after the scourge that smites shall come the rod that consoles, if I may borrow a somewhat daring simile from Abdullah Haji of Shiraz and the twenty-third Psalm.

Well, I would much prefer to spend my life at the rod; it is wearisome and loathsome to be constantly flogging the tough hide of Britons, whom after all I love. "Whom the Lord loveth He chasteneth, and scourgeth every son that He receiveth." I shall really be glad if a few of you will get it over, and come and sit on daddy's knee!

THE SOLDIER AND THE HUNCHBACK

The first step is the hardest; make a start, and I will soon set the hunchback lion and the soldier unicorn fighting for your crown. And they shall lie down together at the end, equally glad, equally weary; while sole and sublime that crown of thine (brother!) shall glitter in the frosty Void of the abyss, its twelve stars filling that silence and solitude with a music and a motion that are more silent and invisible than they; thou shalt sit throned on the Invisible, thine eyes fixed upon That which we call Nothing, because it is beyond Everything attainable by thought, or trance, thy right hand gripping the azure rod of Light, thy left hand clasped upon the scarlet scourge of Death; thy body girdled with a snake more brilliant than the Sun, its name Eternity; thy mouth curved moonlike in a smile, in the invisible kiss of Nuit, our Lady of the Starry Abodes; the body's electric flesh stilled by sheer might to a movement closed upon itself in the controlled fury of Her love—nay, beyond all these Images art thou (little brother!) who art passed from I and Thou, and He unto That which hath no Name, no Image....

Little brother, give me thy hand; for the first step is hard.

ALEISTER CROWLEY.

THE HERMIT

AN ATTACK ON BARBERCRAFT

AT last an end of all I hoped and feared!
Muttered the hermit through his elfin beard.

Then what art thou? the evil whisper whirred.
I doubt me sorely if the hermit heard.

To all God's questions never a word he said,
But simply shook his venerable head.

God sent all plagues; he laughed and heeded not;
Till people took him for an idiot.

God sent all joys; he only laughed amain,
Till people certified him as insane.

But somehow all his fellow-lunatics
Began to imitate his silly tricks.

And stranger still, their prospects so enlarged
That one by one the patients were discharged.

THE EQUINOX

God asked him by what right he interfered;
He only laughed into his elfin beard.

When God revealed Himself to mortal prayer
He gave a fatal opening to Voltaire.

Our hermit had dispensed with Sinai's thunder,
But on the other hand he made no blunder;

He knew (no doubt) that *any* axiom
Would furnish bricks to build some Donkeydom.

But!—all who urged that hermit to confess
Caught the infection of his happiness.

I would it were my fate to dree his weird;
I think that I will grow an elfin beard.

THE TEMPLE OF SOLOMON THE KING

To plead the organic causation of a religious state of mind, then, in refutation of its claim to possess superior spiritual value, is quite illogical and arbitrary, unless one have already worked out in advance some psycho-physical theory connecting spiritual values in general with determinate sorts of physiological change. Otherwise none of our thoughts and feelings, not even our scientific doctrines, not even our *dis*-beliefs, could retain any value as revelations of the truth, for every one of them without exception flows from the state of their possessor's body at the time.

It is needless to say that medical materialism draws in point of fact no such sweeping skeptical conclusion. It is sure, just as every simple man is sure, that some states of mind are inwardly superior to others, and reveal to us more truth, and in this it simply makes use of an ordinary spiritual judgment. It has no physiological theory of the production of these its favourite states, by which it may accredit them; and its attempt to discredit the states which it dislikes, by vaguely associating them with nerves and liver, and connecting them with names connoting bodily affliction, is altogether illogical and inconsistent.

PROF. WILLIAM JAMES.

And there was given me a reed like unto a rod: and the angel stood, saying, Rise, and measure the temple of God and the altar, and them that worship therein.—*Rev*. xi. 1.

PREFACE

THE QUESTION

AVE!

There must have been a time in the life of every student of the Mysteries when he has paused whilst reading the work or the life of some well-known Mystic, a moment of perplexity in which, bewildered, he has turned to himself and asked the question: "Is this one telling me the truth?"

Still more so does this strike us when we turn to any commentative work upon Mysticism, such as Récéjac's "Bases of the Mystic Knowledge," or William James's "Varieties of Religious Experience." In fact, so much so, that unless we are more than commonly sceptical of the wordy theories which attempt to explain these wordy utterances we are bound to clasp hands with the great school of medical-materialism, which is all but paramount at the present hour, and dismiss all such as have had a glimpse of something we do not see as *détraqués*, degenerates, neuropaths, psychopaths, hypochondriacs, and epileptics.

Well, even if we do, these terms explain very little, and in most cases, especially when applied to mystic states, nothing at all; nevertheless they form an excellent loophole out of which the ignorant may crawl when faced with a difficulty they have not the energy or wit to surmount.

THE EQUINOX

True, the utter chaos amongst all systems of magic and mysticism that has prevailed in the West during the last two thousand years, partially, if not entirely, accounts for the uncritical manner in which these systems have been handled by otherwise critical minds.

Even to-day, though many thousand years after they were first written down, we find a greater simplicity and truth in the ancient rituals and hymns of Egypt and Assyria than in the extraordinary entanglement of systems that came to life during the first five hundred years of Christian era. And in the East, from the most remote antiquity to the present day, scientific systems of illuminism have been in daily practice from the highest to the lowest in the land; though, as we consider, much corrupted by an ignorant priestcraft, by absurd superstitions and by a science which fell to a divine revelation in place of rising to a sublime art.

In the West, for some fifteen hundred years now, Christianity has swayed the minds of men from the Arctic seas to the Mediterranean. At first but one of many small excrescent faiths, which sprang up like fungi amongst the superb *débris* of the religions of Egypt, Babylonia, and Greece, it was not long before (on account of its warlike tenets and the deeply magical nature of its rites*) it forced its head and then its arms above the shoulders of its weaker brothers; and when once in a position to strike, so thoroughly bullied all com-petitors that the few who inwardly stood outside the Church, to save the

---

* Primitive Christianity had a greater adaptability than any other contemporary religion of assimilating to itself all that was more particularly pagan in polytheism; the result being that it won over the great masses of the people, who then were, as they are now, inherently conservative.

bruised skins of the faiths they still held dear, were, for self-preservation, bound to clothe them in the tinsel of verbosity, in wild values and extravagant symbols and cyphers; the result being that chaos was heaped upon chaos, till at last all sense became cloaked in a truculent obscurantism. Still, by him who has eyes will it be seen that through all this darkness there shone the glamour of a great and beautiful Truth.

Little is it to be wondered then, in these present shallow intellectual days, that almost any one who has studied, or even heard of, the theories of any notorious nobody of the moment at once relegates to the museum or the waste-paper basket these theories and systems, which were once the very blood of the world, and which in truth are so still, though few suspect it.

Truth is Truth; and the Truth of yesterday is the Truth of to-day, and the Truth of to-day is the Truth of to- morrow. Our quest, then, is to find Truth, and to cut the kernel from the husk, the text from the comment.

To start from the beginning would appear the proper course to adopt; but if we commence sifting the shingle from the sand with the year 10,000 B.C. there is little likelihood of our ever arriving within measurable distance of the present day. Fortunately, however, for us, we need not start with any period anterior to our own, or upon any subject outside of our own true selves. But two things we must learn, if we are ever to make ourselves intelligible to others, and these are, firstly an alphabet, and secondly a language whereby to express our thoughts; for without some definite system of expression our only course is to remain silent, lest further confusion be added to the already bewildering chaos.

THE EQUINOX

It will be at once said by any one who has read as far as this: "I lay you whatever odds you name that the writer of this book will prove to be the first offender!" And with all humility will we at once plead guilty to this offence. Unfortunately it is so, and must at first be so; yet if in the end we succeed in creating but the first letter of the new Alphabet we shall not consider that we have failed; far from it, for we shall rejoice that, the entangled threshold having been crossed, the goal, though distant, is at last in sight.

In a hospital a chart is usually kept for each patient, upon which may be seen the exact progress, from its very commencement, of the case in question. By it the doctor can daily judge the growth or decline of the disease he is fighting. On Thursday, let us say, the patient's temperature in 100°; in the evening he is given a cup of beef-tea (the patient up to the present having been kept strictly on milk diet); on the following morning the doctor finds that his temperature has risen to 102°, and at once concludes that the fever has not yet sufficiently abated for a definite change of diet to be adopted, and, "knocking off" the beef-tea, down drops the temperature.

Thus, if he be a worthy physician, he will study his patient, never overlooking the seemingly most unimportant details which can help him to realise his object, namely, recovery and health.

Not only does this system of minute tabulation apply to cases of disease and sickness, but to every branch of healthy life as well, under the name of "business"; the best business man being he who reduces his special occupation in life from "muddle" to "science."

In the West religion alone has never issued from chaos;

and the hour, late though it be, has struck when without fear or trembling adepts have arisen to do for Faith what Copernicus, Kepler, and Newton did for what is vulgarly known as "Science." And as Faith, growing old before its day, held back Science with a cruel hand, so let us now, whilst Science is still young, step briskly forward and claim our rights, lest if we halt we too shall find the child of the Morning once again strangled in the maw of a second Night.

Now, even to such as are still mere students in the mysteries, it must have become apparent that there are moments in the lives of others, if not in their own, which bring with them an enormous sense of inner authority and illumination; moments which created epochs in our lives, and which, when they have gone, stand out as luminous peaks in the moonlight of the past. Sad to say, they come but seldom, so seldom that often they are looked back upon as miraculous visitations of some vastly higher power beyond and outside of ourselves. But when they do come the greatest joys of earth wither before them like dried leaves in the fire, and fade from the firmament of our minds as the stars of night before the rising sun.

Now, if it were possible to induce these states of ecstasy or hallucination, or whatever we care to call them, at will, so to speak, we should have accomplished what was once called, and what is still known as, the Great Work, and have discovered the Stone of the Wise, that universal dissolvent. Sorrow would cease and give way to joy, and joy to a bliss quite unimaginable to all who have not as yet experienced it.

St. John of the Cross, writing of the "intuitions" by which God reaches the soul, says:

"They enrich us marvellously. A single one of them may be sufficient to abolish at a stroke certain imperfections of which the soul during its whole life has vainly tried to rid itself, and to leave it adorned with virtues and loaded with supernatural gifts. A single one of the intoxicating consolations may reward it for all the labours undergone in its life—even were they numberless. Invested with an invincible courage, filled with an impassioned desire to suffer for its God, the soul then is seized with a strange torment—that of not being allowed to suffer enough."*

In the old days, when but a small portion of the globe was known to civilised man, the explorer and the traveller would return to his home with weird, fantastic stories of long-armed hairy men, of impossible monsters, and countries of fairy-like wonder. But he who travels now and who happens to see a gorilla, or a giraffe, or perchance a volcano, forgets to mention it even in his most casual correspondence! And why? Because he has learnt to understand that such things are. He has named them, and, having done so, to him they cease as objects of interest. In one respect he gives birth to a great truth, which he at once cancels by giving birth to a great falsehood; for his reverence, like his disdain, depends but on the value of a name.

Not so, however, the adept; for as a zoologist does not lose

---

* "Œuvres," ii. 320. Prof. William James writes: "The great Spanish mystics, who carried the habit of ecstasy as far as it has often been carried, appear for the most part to have shown indomitable spirit and energy, and all the more so for the trances in which they indulged."

Writing of St. Ignatius, he says: "St. Ignatius was a mystic, but his mysticism made him assuredly one of the most powerful practical human engines that ever lived" ("The Varieties of Religious Experience," p. 413).

his interest in the simian race because he has learnt to call a long-armed hairy man a gorilla; so he, by learning to explain himself with clearness, and to convey the image of his thoughts with accuracy to the brain of another, is winnowing the wheat from the chaff, the Truth from the Symbol of Truth.

Now when St. John of the Cross tells us that a single vision of God may reward us for all the labours of this life, we are at perfect liberty, in these tolerant days, to cry "Yea!" or "Nay!" We may go further: we may extol St. John to the position of a second George Washington, or we may call him "a damned liar!" or, again, if we do not wish to be considered rude, a "neuropath," or some other equally amiable synonym. But none of these expressions explains to us very much; they are all equally vague—nay (curious to relate!), even mystical—and as such appertain to the Kingdom of Zoroaster, that realm of pure faith: *i.e.*, faith in St. John, or faith in something opposite to St. John.

But now let us borrow from Pyrrho—the Sceptic, the keen-sighted man of science—that word "WHY," and apply it to our "Yea" and our "Nay," just as a doctor questions himself and the patient about the disease; and we shall very soon find that we are being drawn to a logical conclusion, or at least to a point from which such a conclusion becomes possible.* And from this spot the toil of the husbandman must not be condemned until the Season arrives in which the tree he has

---

* "In the natural sciences and industrial arts it never occurs to any one to try to refute opinions by showing up their author's neurotic constitution. Opinions here are invariably tested by logic and by experiment, no matter what may be their author's neurological type. It should be no otherwise with religious opinions."—"The Varieties of Religious Experience," pp. 17, 18.

planted bears fruit; then by its fruit shall it be known, and by its fruit shall it be judged.*

This application of the word "Why" is the long and short of what has been called Scientific Illuminism,† or the science of learning how not to say "Yes" until you know that it *is* YES, and how not to say "No" until you know that it *is* NO. It is the all-important word of our lives, the corner- stone of the Temple, the keystone of the arch, the flail that beats the grain from the chaff, the sieve through which Falsehood passes and in which Truth remains. It is, indeed, the poise of the balance, the gnomon of the sun-dial; which, if we learn to read aright, will tell us at what hour of our lives we have arrived.

Through the want of it kingdoms have fallen into decay and by it empires have been created; and its dreaded foe is of necessity "dogma."

---

* "Dr. Maudsley is perhaps the cleverest of the rebutters of supernatural religion on grounds of origin. Yet he finds himself forced to write ('Natural Causes and Supernatural Seemings,' 1886, pp. 256, 257):

" 'What right have we to believe Nature under any obligation to do her work by means of complete minds only? She may find an incomplete mind a more suitable instrument for a particular purpose. It is the work that is done, and the quality in the worker by which it was done, that is alone of moment; and it may be no great matter from a cosmical standpoint if in other qualities of character he as singularly defective—if indeed he were hypocrite, adulterer, eccentric, or lunatic. ... Home we come again, then, to the old and last resort of certitude,—namely the common assent of mankind, or of the competent by instruction and training among mankind.'

"In other words, not its origin, but *the way in which it works on the whole*, is Dr. Maudsley's final test of a belief. This is our own empiricist criterion; and this criterion the stoutest insisters on supernatural origin have also been forced to use in the end."—"The Varieties of Religious Experience," pp. 19, 20.

To put it vulgarly, "the proof of the pudding is in the eating," and it is sheer waste of time to upbraid the cook before tasting of his dish.

† Or Pyrrho-Zoroastrianism.

THE TEMPLE OF SOLOMON THE KING

Directly a man begins to say "Yes" without the question "Why?" he becomes a dogmatist, a potential, if not an actual liar. And it is for this reason that we are so bitterly opposed to and use such scathing words against the present-day rationalist* when we attack him. For we see he is doing for Darwin, Huxley, and Spencer what the early Christian did for Jesus, Peter, and Paul; and that is, that he, having already idealised them, is now in the act of apotheosising them. Soon, if left unattacked, will *their* word become THE WORD, and in the place of the "Book of Genesis" shall we have the "Origin of Species," and in the place of the Christian accepting as Truth the word of Jesus shall we have the Rationalist accepting as Truth the word of Darwin.

But what of the true man of science? say you; those doubting men who silently work in their laboratories, accepting no theory, however wonderful it may be, until theory has given birth to fact. We agree—but what of the Magi? answer we; the few fragments of whose wisdom which escaped the Christian flames will stand in the eyes of all men as a wonder. It was the Christians who slew the magic of Christ, and so will it be, if they are allowed to live, the Rationalists who will slay the magic of Darwin; so that four hundred years hence perchance will some disciple of Lamarck

---

* "We have to confess that the part of it [mental life] of which rationalism can give an account is relatively superficial. It is the part that has the *prestige* undoubtedly, for it has the loquacity, it can challenge you for proofs, and chop logic, and put you down with words. But it will fail to convince or convert you all the same, if your dumb intuitions are opposed to its conclusions. If you have intuitions at all, they come from a deeper level of your nature than the loquacious level which rationalism inhabits."—"The Varieties of Religious Experience," p. 73.

be torn to pieces in the rooms of the Royal Society by the followers of Haeckel, just as Hypatia, that disciple of Plato, was torn to pieces in the Church of Christ by followers of St. John.

We have nothing to say against the men of science, we have nothing to say against the great Mystics—all hail to both! But such of their followers who accepted the doctrines of either the one or the other as a dogma we here openly pronounce to be a bane, a curse, and a pestilence to mankind.

Why assume that only one system of ideas can be true? And when you have answered this question there will be time enough to assume that all other systems are wrong. Start with a clean sheet, and write neatly and beautifully upon it, so that others can read you aright; do not start with some old palimpsest, and then scribble all over it carelessly, for then indeed others will come who will of a certainty ready you awry.

If Osiris, Christ, and Mahomet were mad, then indeed is madness the key to the door of the Temple. Yet if they were only called mad for being wise beyond the sane, then ask you why their doctrines brought with them the crimes of bigotry and the horrors of madness? And our answer is, that though they loved Truth and wedded Truth, they could not explain Truth; and their disciples therefore had to accept the symbols of Truth for Truth, without the possibility of asking "Why?" or else reject Truth altogether. Thus it came about that the greater the Master the less was he able to explain himself, and the more obscure his explanations the darker became the minds of his followers. It was the old story of the light that blinded the darkness. You can teach a bushman to add one to one, and he may after some teaching grasp the idea of "two"; but do not try to teach him the

THE TEMPLE OF SOLOMON THE KING

differential calculus! The former may be compared to the study of the physical sciences, the latter to that of the mental; therefore all the more should we persevere to work out correctly the seemingly most absurd, infinitesimal differences, and perchance one day, when we have learnt how to add unit to unit, a million and a millionth part of a unit will be ours.

We will now conclude this part of our preface with two long quotations from Prof. James's excellent book; the first of which, slightly abridged, is as follows:

"It is the terror and beauty of phenomena, the 'promise' of the dawn and of the rainbow, the 'voice' of the thunder, the 'gentleness' of the summer rain, the 'sublimity' of the stars, and not the physical laws which these things follow, by which the religious mind still continues to be most impressed; and just as of yore the devout man tells you that in the solitude of his room or of the fields he still feels the divine presence, and that sacrifices to this unseen reality fill him with security and peace.

"Pure anachronism! says the survival-theory;—anachronism for which deanthropomorphization of the imagination is the remedy required. The less we mix the private with the cosmic, the more we dwell in universal in impersonal terms, the truer heirs of Science we become.

"In spite of the appeal which this impersonality of the scientific attitude makes to a certain magnanimity of temper, I believe it to be shallow, and I can now state my reason in comparatively few words. That reason is that, so long as we deal with the cosmic and the general, we deal only with the symbols of reality, but *as soon as we deal with the private and personal phenomena as such, we deal with realities in the completest sense of the term.* I think I can easily make clear what I mean by these words.

"The world of our experience consists at all times of two parts, an objective and a subjective part, of which the former may be incalculably more extensive than the latter, and yet the latter can never be omitted or suppressed. The objective part is the sum total of whatsoever at any given time we may be thinking of, the subjective part is the inner 'state' in which the thinking comes to pass. What we think of may be enormous—the cosmic times and spaces, for example— whereas the inner state may be the most fugitive and paltry activity of mind. Yet the cosmic objects, so far as the experience yields them, are but ideal pictures of something whose existence we do not inwardly possess, but only point at outwardly, while the inner state is our very experience itself; its reality and that of our experience are one. A conscious field *plus* its object as felt or thought of *plus* an attitude towards the object *plus* the sense of a self to whom the attitude belongs—such a concrete bit of personal experience may be a small bit, but it is a solid bit as long as it lasts; not hollow, not a mere abstract element of experience, such as the 'object' is when taken all alone. It is a *full* fact, even though it be an insignificant fact; it is of the *kind* to which all realities whatsoever must belong; the motor currents of the world run through the like of it; it is on the line connecting real events with real events. That unshareable feeling which each one of us has of the pinch of his individual destiny as he privately feels it rolling out on fortune's wheel may be disparaged for its egotism, may be sneered at as unscientific, but it is the one thing that fills up the measure of our concrete actuality, and any would-be existence that should lack such a feeling, or its analogue, would be a piece of reality only half made up.

"If this be true, it is absurd for science to say that the egotistic elements of experience should be suppressed. The axis of reality runs solely through the egotistic places—they are strung upon it like so many beads. To describe the world with all the various feelings of the individual pinch of destiny, all the various spiritual attitudes, left out from the description—they being as describable as anything else— would be something like offering a printed bill of fare as the equivalent for a solid meal. Religion makes no such blunders.... A bill of fare with one real raisin on it instead of the word 'raisin' and one real egg instead of the word 'egg' might be an inadequate meal, but it would at least be a commencement of reality. The contention of the survival-theory that we ought to stick to non-personal elements exclusively seems like saying that we ought to be satisfied forever with reading the naked bill of fare.... It does not follow, because our ancestors made so many errors of fact and mixed them with their religion, that we should therefore leave off being religious at all. By being religious we establish ourselves in possession of ultimate reality at the only points at which reality is given us to guard. Our responsible concern is with our private destiny after all."*

"We must next pass beyond the point of view of merely subjective utility, and make inquiry into the intellectual content itself.

"First, is there, under all the discrepancies of the creeds, a

---

* "The Varieties of Religious Experience," pp. 498-501.

common nucleus to which they bear their testimony unanimously?

"And second, ought we to consider the testimony true?

"I will take up the first question first, and answer it immediately in the affirmative. The warring gods and formulas of the various religions do indeed cancel each other, but there is a certain uniform deliverance in which religions all appear to meet. It consists of two parts:

"(1) An uneasiness; and

"(2) Its solution.

"1. The uneasiness, reduced to its simplest terms, is a sense that there is *something wrong about us* as we naturally stand.

"2. The solution is a sense that *we are saved from the wrongness* by making proper connection with the higher powers.

"In those more developed minds which alone we are studying, the wrongness takes a moral character, and the salvation takes a mystical tinge. I think we shall keep well within the limits of what is common to all such minds if we formulate the essence of their religious experience in terms like these:

"The individual, so far as he suffers from his wrongness and criticises it, is to that extent consciously beyond it, and in at least possible touch with something higher, if anything higher exist. Along with the wrong part there is thus a better part of him, even though it may be but a most helpless germ. With which part he should identify his real being is by no means obvious at this stage; but when Stage 2 (the stage of solution or salvation) arrives, the man identifies his real being with the germinal higher part of himself; and does

THE TEMPLE OF SOLOMON THE KING

so in the following way: *He becomes conscious that this higher part is conterminous and continuous with a* MORE *of the same quality, which is operative in the universe outside of him, and which he can keep in working touch with, and in a fashion get on board of and save himself when all his lower being has gone to pieces in the wreck"**

These last few lines bring us face to face with the subject of this volume, viz.:—

FRATER P.

To enter upon a somewhat irrelevant matter, this is what actually happened to the complier of this book:

For ten years he had been a sceptic, in that sense of the word which is generally conveyed by the terms infidel, atheist, and freethinker; then suddenly, in a single moment, he withdrew all the scepticism with which he had assailed religion, and hurled it against freethought itself; and as the former had crumbled into dust, so now the latter vanished in smoke.

In this crisis there was no sickness of soul, no division of self; for he simply had turned a corner on the road along which he was travelling and suddenly became aware of the fact that the mighty range of snow-capped mountains upon which he had up to now fondly imagined he was gazing was after all but a great bank of clouds. So he passed on smiling to himself at his own childlike illusion.

Shortly after this he became acquainted with a certain brother of the Order of A∴ A∴; and himself a little later became an initiate in the first grade of that Order.

In this Order, at the time of his joining it, was a certain

---

* "The Varieties of Religious Experience", pp. 507, 508.

brother of the name of P., who had but just returned from China, and who had been six years before sent out by the Order to journey through all the countries of the world and collect all knowledge possible in the time which touched upon the mystical experiences of mankind. This P. had to the best of his ability done, and though he had only sojourned in Europe, in Egypt, India, Ceylon, China, Burma, Arabia, Siam, Tibet, Japan, Mexico, and the United States of America, so deep had been his study and so exalted had been his understanding that it was considered by the Order that he had collected sufficient material and testimony whereon to compile a book for the instruction of mankind. And as Frater N.S.F. was a writer of some little skill, the diaries and notes of Frater P. were given to him and another, and they were enjoined to set them together in such a manner that they would be an aid to the seeker in the mysteries, and would be as a tavern on a road beset with many dangers and difficulties, wherein the traveller can find good cheer and wine that strengtheneth and refresheth the soul.

It is therefore earnestly hoped that this book will become as a refuge to all, where a guide may be hired or instructions freely sought; but the seeker is requested—nay, commanded—with all due solemnity by the Order of the A∴ A∴ to accept nothing as Truth until he has proved it so to be, to his own satisfaction and to his own honour.

And it is further hoped that he may, upon closing this book, be somewhat enlightened, and, even if as through a glass darkly, see the great shadow of Truth beyond, and one day enter the Temple.

So much for the subject; now for the object of this volume:

THE TEMPLE OF SOLOMON THE KING
THE AUGOEIDES.*

"Lytton calls him Adonai in 'Zanoni,' and I often use this name in the note-books.

"Abramelin calls him Holy Guardian Angel. I adopt this:

"1. Because Abramelin's system is so simple and effective.

"2. Because since *all* theories of the universe are absurd it is better to talk in the language of one which is patently absurd, so as to mortify the metaphysical man.

"3. Because a child can understand it.

"Theosophists call him the Higher Self, Silent Watcher, or Great Master.

"The Golden Dawn calls him the Genius.

"Gnostics say the Logos.

"Zoroaster talks about uniting all these symbols into the form of a Lion—see Chaldean Oracles.†

"Anna Kingsford calls him Adonai (Clothed with the Sun). Buddhists call him Adi-Buddha—(says H. P. B.)

"The Bhagavad-Gita calls him Vishnu (chapter xi.).

"The Yi *K*ing calls him "The Great Person."

"The Qabalah calls him Jechidah.

"We also get metaphysical analysis of His nature, deeper and deeper according to the subtlety of the writer; for this

---

* From a letter of Fra P.

† "A similar Fire flashingly extending through the rushings of Air, or a Fire formless whence cometh the Image of a Voice, or even a flashing Light abounding, revolving, whirling forth, crying aloud. Also there is the vision of the fire-flashing Courser of Light, or also a Child, borne aloft on the shoulders of the Celestial Steed, fiery, or clothed with gold, or naked, or shooting with the bow shafts of Light, and standing on the shoulders of the horse; then if thy meditation prolongeth itself, thou shalt unite all these symbols into the Form of a Lion."

vision—it is all one same phenomenon, variously coloured by our varying Ruachs*—is, I believe, the first and the last of all Spiritual Experience. For though He is attributed to Malkuth,† and the Door of the Path of His overshadowing, He is also in Kether (Kether is in Malkuth and Malkuth in Kether —"as above, so beneath"), and the End of the "Path of the Wise" is identity with Him.

"So that while he is the Holy Guardian Angel, He is also Hua‡ and the Tao.§

"For since Intra Nobis Regnum de∥ all things are in Ourself, and all Spiritual Experience is a more of less complete Revelation of Him.

"Yet it is only in the Middle Pillar¶ that His manifestation is in any way perfect.

"The Augoedes invocation is the whole thing. Only it is so difficult; one goes along through all the fifty gates of Binah** at once, more or less illuminated, more or less deluded. But the First and the Last is this Augoeides Invocation."

THE BOOK

This Book is divided into four parts:

---

* Ruach: the third form, the Mind, the Reasoning Power, that which possesses the Knowledge of Good and Evil.

† Malkuth: the tenth Sephira.

‡ The supreme and secret title of Kether.

§ The great extreme of the Yi King.

∥ I.N.R.I.

¶ Or "Mildness," the Pillar on the right being that of "Mercy," and that on the left "Justice." These refer to the Qabalistic Tree of Life.

** Binah: the third Sephira, the Understanding. She is the Supernal Mother, as distinguished from Malkuth, the Inferior Mother. (Nun) is attributed to the Understanding; its value is 50. *Vide* 'The Book of Concealed Mystery," sect. 40.

THE TEMPLE OF SOLOMON THE KING

    I. The Foundations of the Temple.
   II. The Scaffolding of the Temple.
  III. The Portal of the Temple.
  IV. The Temple of Solomon the King.

Three methods of expression are used to enlighten and instruct the reader:

    (*a*) Pictorial symbols.
    (*b*) Metaphorically expressed word-pictures.
    (*c*) Scientifically expressed facts.

The first method is found appended to each of the four Books, balancing, so to speak, Illuminism and Science.

The second method is found almost entirely in the first Book and the various pictures are entitled:*

The Black Watch-tower, or the Dreamer.
The Miser, or the Theist.
The Spendthrift, or the Pantheist.
The Bankrupt, or the Atheist.
The Prude, or the Rationalist.
The Child, or the Mystic.
The Wanton, or the Sceptic.
The Slave, or he who stands before the veil of the Outer Court.
The Warrior, or he who stands before the veil of the Inner Court.
The King, or he who stands before the veil of the Abyss.
The White Watch-tower, or the Awakened One.

---

* Nine pictures between Darkness and Light, or eleven in all. The union of the Pentagram and the Hexagram is to be noted; also the eleven-lettered name ABRAHADABRA; 418; Achad Osher, or One and Ten; the Eleven Averse Sephiroth; and Adonai.

The third method is found almost entirely in the second Book.

The third and fourth Books of this essay consist of purely symbolic pictures. For the Key of the Portal the neophyte must discover for himself; and until he finds the Key the Temple of Solomon the King must remain closed to him.

Vale!

BOOK I
The foundations of the Temple
of
SOLOMON THE KING
and
The nine cunning Craftsmen who
laid them between the
Watch-towers of
Night & Day.

And from that place are cast out all the Lords who are the exactors of the debts of mankind, and they are subjugated.

The Greater Holy Assembly, xx. 440.

THE BLACK WATCH-TOWER

WHO has not, at some period during his life, experienced that strange sensation of utter bewilderment on being awakened by the sudden approach of a bright light across the curtained threshold of slumber; that intoxicating sense of wonderment, that hopeless inability to to open wide the blinded eyes before the dazzling flame which has swept night into the corners and crannies of the dark bedchamber of sleep?

Who, again, has not stepped from the brilliant sunlight of noon into some shadowy vault, and, groping along its dark walls, has found all there to be but as the corpse of day wrapped in a starless shroud of darkness?

Yet as the moments speed by the sight grows accustomed to the dazzling intruder; and as the blinding, shimmering web of silver which he has thrown around us melts like a network of snow before the awakening fire of our eyes, we perceive that the white flame of bewilderment which had but a moment ago enwrapped us as a mantle of lightnings, is, but in truth, a flickering rushlight fitfully expiring in an ill-shapen socket of clay. And likewise in the darkness, as we pass along the unlit arches of the vault, or the lampless recesses which, toad-like, squat here and there in the gloom, dimly at first do the mouldings of the roof and the cornices of the walls creep forth; and then, as the twilight becomes more certain, do they twist and writhe into weirdly shapen arabesques, into fanciful figures, and contorted faces; which, as we advance, bat-like flit into the depths of a deeper darkness beyond.

Stay!—and but for a moment hurry back, and bring with you that little rushlight we left spluttering on the mantel-shelf of sleep. Now all once again vanishes, and from the floor before us jut up into the shadowland of darkness the stern grey walls of rock, the age-worn architraves, the clustered columns, and all the crumbling capitols of Art, where the years alone sit shrouded slumbering in their dust and mould—a haunting memory of long-forgotten days.

O dreamland of wonder and mystery! like a tongue of gold wrapped in a blue flame do we hover for a moment over the Well of Life; and then the night-wind rises, and wafts us into the starless depths of the grave. We are like gnats hovering in the sunbeams, and then the evening falls and we are gone: and who can tell whither, and unto what end? Whether to the City of Eternal Sleep, or to the Mansion of the Music of Rejoicing?

O my brothers! come with me! follow me! Let us mount the dark stairs of this Tower of Silence, this Watch-tower of Night; upon whose black brow no flickering flame burns to guide the weary wanderer across the mires of life and through the mists of death. Come, follow me! Grope up these age-worn steps, slippery with the tears of the fallen, and bearded with the blood of the vanquished and the salt of the agony of failure. Come, come! Halt not! Abandon all! Let us ascend. Yet bring with ye two things, the flint and the steel—the

THE TEMPLE OF SOLOMON THE KING

slumbering fire of Mystery, and the dark sword of Science; that we may strike a spark, and fire the beacon of Hope which hangs above us in the brasier of Despair; so that a great light may shine forth through the darkness, and guide the toiling footsteps of man to that Temple which is built without hands, fashioned without iron, or gold, or silver, and in which no fire burns; whose pillars are as columns of light, whose dome is as a crown of effulgence set betwixt the wings of Eternity, and upon whose altar flashes the mystic eucharist of God.

THE MISER

"GOD." What a treasure-house of wealth lies buried in that word! what a mine of precious stones!—Ptah, Father of Beginnings, he who created the Sun and the Moon; Nu, blue, starry lady of Heaven, mistress and mother of the gods; Ea, Lord of the Deep; Istar—"O Thou who art set in the sky as a jewelled circlet of moonstone"; Brahma the golden, Vishnu the sombre, and Siva the crimson, lapped in seas of blood. Everywhere do we find Thee, O Thou one and awful Eidolon, who as Aormuzd once didst rule the sun-scorched plains of Euphrates, and as Odin the icy waves and the shrieking winds, round the frozen halls of the North.

Everywhere!—everywhere! And yet now Thou art again God, nameless to the elect—O Thou vast inscrutable Pleroma built in the Nothingness of our imagination!—and to the little ones, the children who play with the units of existence, but a myriad-named doll a cubit high, a little thing to play with—or else: an ancient, bearded Father, with hair as white as wool, and eyes like flames of fire; whose voice is as the sound of many waters, in whose right hand tremble the seven stars of Heaven, and out of whose mouth flashes forth a flaming sword of fire. There dost Thou sit counting the orbs of Space, and the souls of men: and we tremble before Thee, worshipping, glorifying, supplicating, beseeching; lest perchance Thou cast us back into the furnace of destruction, and place us not among the gold and silver of Thy treasury.

True, Thou hast been the great Miser of the worlds, and the Balances of Thy treasure-house have weighed out Heaven and Hell. Thou hast amassed around Thee the spoil of the years, and the plunder of Time and of Space. All is Thine, and we own not even the breath of our nostrils, for it is but given us on the usury of our lives.

Still from the counting-house of Heaven Thou hast endowed us with a spirit of grandeur, an imagination of the vastness of Being. Thou hast taken us out of ourselves, and we have counted with Thee the starry hosts of night, and unbraided the tangled tresses of the comets in the fields of Space. We have walked with Thee at Mamre, and talked with Thee in Eden, and listened to Thy voice from out the midst of the whirlwind. And at times Thou hast been a Father unto us, a joy, strong as a mighty draught of ancient wine, and we have welcomed Thee!

But Thy servants—those self-seeking, priestly usurers—See! how they have blighted the hearts of men, and massed the treasure of Souls into the hands of the few, and piled up the coffers of the Church. How they racked from us the very emblems of joy, putting out our eyes with the hot irons of extortion, till every pound of human flesh was soaked as a thirsty sponge in a well of blood: and life became a hell, and men and women went singing, robed in the *san-benito* painted with flames and devils, to the stake; to seek in the fire the God of their forefathers—that stern Judge who with sworded hand was once wont to read out the names of the living from the Book of Life, and exalt the humble on the golden throne of tyrants.

Yet in these ages of crucifix, of skull, and of candle; these ages of *auto-da-fé* and *in pace*; these ages when the tongue jabbered madness and the brain reeled in delirium, and the bones were split asunder, and the flesh was crushed to pulp, was there still in the darkness a glamour of truth, as a great and scarlet sunset seen through the memory of years. Life was a shroud of horror, yet it was life! Life! life in the awful hideous grandeur of gloom, until death severed the dull red thread with a crooked sword of cruel flame. And Love, a wild, mad ecstasy, broken-winged, fluttering before the eyeless sockets of Evil, as the souls of men were bought and sold and bartered for, till Heaven became a bauble of the rich, and Hell a debtor's dungeon for the poor. Yet amongst those rotting bones in the *oubliette*, and in those purple palaces of papal lust, hovered that spirit of life, like a golden flame rolled in a cloud of smoke over the dark altar of decay.

Listen: "Have you got religion? . . . Are you saved? . . . Do you love Jesus?" . . . "Brother, God can save you. . . . Jesus is the sinner's friend. . . . Rest your head on Jesus . . . dear, dear Jesus!" Curse till thunder shake the stars! curse till this blasphemy is cursed from the face of heaven! curse till the hissing name of Jesus, which writhes like a snake in a snare, is driven from the kingdom of faith! Once "Eloi, Eloi, Lama Sabachthani" echoed through the gloom from the Cross of Agony; now Jerry McAuley, that man of God, ill-clothed in cheap Leeds shoddy, bobbing in a tin Bethel, bellows, "Do you love Jesus?" and talks of that mystic son of Him who set forth the sun and the moon, and all the hosts of

THE TEMPLE OF SOLOMON THE KING

Heaven, as if he were first cousin to Mrs. Booth or to Aunt Sally herself.

Once man in the magic land of mystery sought the elixir and the balsam of life; now he seeks "spiritual milk for American babes, drawn from the breasts of both Testaments." Once man, in his frenzy, drunken on the wine of Iacchus, would cry to the moon from the ruined summit of some temple of Zagraeus, "Evoe ho! Io Evoe!" But now instead, "Although I was quite full of drink, I knew that God's work begun in me was not going to be wasted!"

Thus is the name of God belched forth in beer and bestial blasphemy. Who would not rather be a St. Besarion who spent forty days and nights in a thorn-bush, or a St. Francis picking lice from his sheepskin and praising God for the honour and glory of wearing such celestial pearls in his habit, than become a smug, well-oiled evangelical Christian genteel-man, walking to church to dear Jesus on a Sabbath morning, with Prayer-book, Bible, and umbrella, and a three-penny-bit in his glove?

THE SPENDTHRIFT

"ARCADIA, night, a cloud, Pan, and the moon." What words to conjure with, what five shouts to slay the five senses, and set a leaping flame of emerald and silver dancing about us as we yell them forth under the oaks and over the rocks and myrtle of the hill-side. "Bruised to the breast of Pan"—let us flee church, and chapel, and meeting-room; let us abandon this mantle of order, and leap back to the heaths, and the marshes, and the hills; back to the woods, and the glades of night! back to the old gods, and the ruddy lips of Pan!

How the torches splutter in the storm, pressing warm kisses of gold on the gnarled and knotted trunks of the beech trees! How the fumigation from musk and myrrh whirls up in an aromatic cloud from the glowing censer!—how for a time it greedily clings to the branches, and then is wafted to the stars! Look!—as we invoke them, how they gather round us, these Spirit of Love and of Life, of Passion, of Strength, and of Abandon—these sinews of the manhood of the World!

O mystery of mysteries! "For each one of the Gods is in all, and all are in each, being ineffably united to each other and to God; because each, being a super-essential unity, their conjunction with each other is a union of unities." Hence each is all; thus Nature squanders the gold and silver of our understanding, till in panic frenzy we beat our head on the storm-washed boulders and the blasted trunks, and shout forth, "Io . . . Io . . . Io . . . Evoe! Io . . . Io!" till the glades thrill as with the music of syrinx an sistrum, and our souls are rent asunder on the flaming horns of Pan.

Come, O children of the night of Death, awake, arise! See, the sun is nodding in the West, and no day-spring is at hand in this land of withered dreams; for all is dull with the sweat of gloom, and sombre with the industry of Evil! Wake! O wake! Let us hie to the summits of the lonely mountains, for soon a sun will arise in us, and then their white peaks will become golden and crimson and purple as the breasts of a mighty woman swollen with the blood and milk of a new life. There, amongst those far-off hills of amethyst, shall we find the fair mistress of our heart's desire—that bountiful Mother who will clasp us to her breast.

Yours are the boundless forests, and the hills, and the far-off purple of the horizon. Call, and they shall answer you; ask, and they shall shower forth on you the hoarded booty of the years, and all the treasure of the ages; so that none shall be in need, and all shall possess all in the longing for all things. Come, let us shatter the vault of Circumstance and the walls of the dungeon of Convention, and back to Pan in the tangled brakes, and to the subtle beauty of the Sorceress, and to the shepherd-lads—back to the white flocks on the hill-side, back to Pan—to Pan—to Pan! Io! to Pan.

Under the mistletoe and the oak there is no snickering of the chapel-pew, no drawing-room grin of lewd desire, no smacking of wanton lips over the warm flesh and the white skin of life; but a great shout of joyous laughter arises, which sways the winds from their appointed courses, and rattles down the dead branches from the leafy boughs overhead: or, all is solemn and still as a breathless night; for here life is ever manly in turmoil as in repose.

Here there is no barter, no usury, no counting of the gains and losses of life; and the great Sower leaps over the fields like a madman, casting forth the golden grain amongst the briars, and on the rocks, as well as between the black furrows of the earth; for each must take its chance, and battle to victory in manliness and strength. Here there is neither sect nor faction: live or die, prosper or decay! So the great live, and the little ones go back to the roots of life. Neither is their obedience outside the obedience which is born of Necessity; for here there is no support, no resting on others—ploughshares are beaten into swords, and spindles are fashioned into the shafts of arrows, and the winds shriek through our armour as we battle for the strength of the World.

The rain falleth upon the deserts as upon the fertile valleys; and the sun shineth upon the blue waters as upon the verdant fields; and the dew heedeth not where it sleepeth, whether on the dung-hill, or betwixt the petals of the wild rose; for all is lavish in this Temple of the World, where on the throne of inexhaustible wealth sits the King of Life, tearing the jewels from his golden throat, and casting them out to the winds to be carried to the four corners of the Earth. There is no thrift here, no storing up for the morrow; and yet there is no waste, no wantonness, for all who enter this Treasure-house of Life become one with the jewels of the treasury.

Words! . . . words! . . . words! They have shackled and chained you, O children of the mists and the mountains; they have imprisoned you, and walled you up in the dungeon of a lightless reason. Fancy has been burnt at the stake of Fact; and the imagination cramped in the irons of tort and quibble. O vanity of vain words! O cozening, deceitful art! Nimbly do the great ones of to-day wrestle with the evil-smelling breath of their mouths, twisting and contorting it into beguilements, bastardising and corrupting the essence of things, sucking as a greedy vampire the blood from your hearts, and breathing into your nostrils the rigid symbols of law and of order, begotten on the death-bed of their understanding.

O children of Wonder and of Fancy, fly to the wild woods whilst yet there is time! Back to the mysteries of the shadowy oaks, to the revolt of imagination, to the insurrection of souls, to the moonlit festivals of love: back where the werewolf lurks, and the moonrakes prowl. Back, O back to the song of life, back to the great God Pan! And there, wrapped in your goat-skins, drink with the shepherds of Tammuz out of the skin of a suckling yet unborn, and ye shall become as the silver-gleaming waters of Istar—pure and bright! Speed, for he is the divine king of the fauns and the satyrs, the dryads and the oreads; the Lord of the Crowns; the Decider of Destiny; the God who prospers all above and beneath! And tarry not, lest as ye wander along the shore of the Ionian Sea ye hear a voice of lamentation crying, "Great Pan is dead!"

THE BANKRUPT

"O WHERE are the terraced gardens of Babylon, with their mighty groves towering up amongst the clouds? O where is the sun-god of Rhodes, whose golden brow was wont to blush with the first fire of dawn, whilst yet the waters at his feet were wrapped in the mists of night? O where is the Temple of Ephesus, and those who cried unto Diana? O where is the gleaming eye of Pharos that shone as a star of hope over the wild waters of the sea? Children of monsters and of gods, how have ye fallen! for a whirlwind hath arisen and swept through the gates of Heaven, and rushed down on the kingdoms of Earth, and as a tongue of consuming flame hath it licked up the handicrafts of man and cloaked all in the dust of decay. A yoke hath been laid on the shoulders of the ancient lands; and where once the white feet of Semiramis gleamed amongst the lilies and roses of Babylon there now the wild goats leap, and browse the sparse rank grass which sprouts in tufts from the red and yellow sand-heaps, those silent memorial mounds which mark the spot where once stood palaces of marble, and of jasper, and of jade. O woe! O woe! for all is dust and ruin; the flood-gates of the years have been opened, and Time has swept away as a mighty wind the embattled castles of kings

THE TEMPLE OF SOLOMON THE KING

with the mud-daubed huts of shepherds. Merodach has gone, and so has Ea, and no longer doth Istar flame in the night, or cast down her kisses on the sparkling goblets in the palace of Belshazzar. Isis, dark-veiled, hath departed, and Nu no longer uplifteth the Sun-bark with the breath of dawn. O Amen, bull fair of face, where is thy glory? Thebes is in ruins! O Lord of joy, O mighty one of diadems! The Sekhet crown has fallen from thy brow, and the strength of thy life hath departed, and thine eyes are as the shrouded shadows of night. Olympus is but a barren hill, and Asgard a land of sullen dreams. Alone in the desert of years still crouches the Sphinx, unanswered, unanswerable, inscrutable, age-worn, coeval with the æons of eld; even facing the east and thirsting for the first rays of the rising sun. She was there when Cheops and Khephren builded the pyramids, and there will she sit when Yahveh has taken his appointed seat in the silent halls of Oblivion.

The fool hath said in his heart, "There is no God!" Yet the wise man has sat trembling over the ruins of the past, and has watched with fearful eyes the bankruptcy of Splendour, and all the glory of man fall victim to the usury of Time.

O God, what art Thou that Thou dost abandon the kingdoms of this world, as a wanton woman her nightly lovers; and that they depart from Thee, and remember and regret Thee not? Yet thou art so vast that I cannot grasp Thee; Time flees before Thee, and Space is as a bauble in thine hands. O monstrous vacancy of vastness! Thou surpassest me, and I am lost in the contemplation of Thy greatness.

The old gods slew Ymer the giant; and from his blood they poured out the seas; and from his flesh they dug the land; and the rocks were fashioned out of his bones; and Asgard, fair dwelling-house of gods, was builded from the brows of his eyes; and from his skull was wrought the purple vault of Immensity; and from his brains were woven the fleecy clouds of heaven. But thou art more than Ymer; Thy feet are planted deeper than the roots of Igdrasil, and the hair of Thine head sweepeth past the helm of thought. Nay, more, vastly more; for Thou art bloodless, and fleshless, and without bones; Thou (O my God!) art nothing—nothing that I can grasp can span Thee. Yea! nothing art Thou, beyond the Nothingness of the Nothingness of Eternity!

Thus men grew to believe in NO-GOD, and to worship NO-GOD, and to be persecuted for NO-GOD, and to suffer and to die for NO-GOD. And now they torture themselves for him, as they had of yore gashed themselves with flints at the footstool of God His Father; and to the honour of His name, and as a proof of His existence, have they not built up great towers of Science, bastions of steam and of flame, and set a-singing the wheels of Progress, and all the crafts and the guiles and the artifices of Knowledge? They have contained the waters with their hands; and the earth they have set in chains; and the fire they have bound up as a wisp of undried straw; even the winds they have ensnared as an eagle in a net;—yet the Spirit liveth and is free, and they know it not, as they gaze down from their Babel of Words upon the soot-grimed fields, and the felled forests, and the flowerless banks of their rivers of mud, lit by the sun which glows red through the hooded mists of their magic.

Yet he who gazeth into the heavens, and crieth in a loud voice, "There is NO-GOD," is as a prophet unto mankind; for he is as one drunken on the vastness of Deity. Better to have no opinion of God than such an opinion as is unworthy of Him. Better to be wrapped in the black robe of unbelief than to dance in the stinking rags of blasphemy. So they learnt to cry, "For the children, belief and obedience; for us men, solitude"—the monarchy of Mind, the pandemoniacal majesty of Matter!

"A Bible on the centre-table in a cottage pauperises the monarchical imagination of man"; but a naked woman weeping in the wilderness, or singing songs of frenzy unto Istar in the night, from the ruined summit of Nineveh, invoking the elemental powers of the Abyss, and casting the dust of ages about her, and crying unto Bel, and unto Assur, and unto Nisroch, and smiting flames from the sun-scorched bones of Sennacherib with the age-worn sword of Sharezer and Adrammelech, is a vision which intoxicates the brain with the sparkling wine of imagination, and sets the teeth a-rattling in the jaws, and the tongue a-cleaving to the palate of the mouth.

But the book-men have slain the Great God, and the twitterers of words have twisted their squeaking screws into his coffin. The first Christians were called Atheists; yet they believed in God: the last Christians are called Theists; yet they believe not in God. So the first Freethinkers were called Atheists; yet they believed in NO-GOD: and the last Freethinkers will be called Theists; for they will believe not in NO-GOD. Then indeed in these latter days may we again find the Great God, that God who liveth beyond the twittering of man's lips, and the mumblings of his mouth.

Filled with the froth of words, have these flatulent fools

argued concerning God. Not as the bard sung of Ymer; but as the cat purrs to the strangling mouse: "Since God is First Cause, therefore he possesses existence *a se*; therefore he must be both necessary and absolute, and cannot be determined by anything else." Nevertheless these wise doctors discuss him as if he were a corpse on the tables of their surgeries, and measure his length with their foot-rules, and stretch and lop him to fit the bed of their Procrustean metaphysic. Thus he is absolutely unlimited from without, and unlimited also from within, for limitation is non-being, and God is being itself, and being is all-things, and all-things is no-thing. And so we find Epicurus walking arm in arm, from the temple of windy words, with Athanasius, and enter the market-place of life, and the throng of the living—that great tongueless witness of God's bounty; and mingle with the laughing boys, showering rose-leaves on Doris and Bacchis, and blowing kisses to Myrtale and Evardis.

God or No-God—so let it be! Still the Sun rises and sets, and the night-breeze blows the red flames of our tourches athwart the palm-trees, to the discomfiture of the stars. Look! —in the distance between the mighty paws of the silent Sphinx rests a cubical temple whose god has been called Ra Harmakhis, the Great God, the Lord of the Heaven, but who in truth is nameless and beyond name, for he is the Eternal Spirit of Life.

Hush—the sistrum sounds from across the banks of the dark waters. The moon rises, and all is as silver and mother-of-pearl. A shepherd's pipe shrills in the distance—a kid has strayed from the fold.... O stillness ... O mystery of God ... how soft is Thy skin ... how fragrant is Thy breath! Life as a strong wine flames through me. The frenzy of resistance, the rapture of the struggle—ah! the ecstasy of Victory. . . . The very soul of life lies ravished, and the breath has left me. . . . A small warm hand touches my lips—O fragrance of love! O Life! . . . Is there a God?

THE PRUDE

A FLY once sat upon the axle-tree of a chariot, and said: "What a dust do I raise!" Now a swarm of flies has come—the fourth plague of Egypt is upon us, and the land is corrupted by reason of their stench. The mighty ones are dead, the giants are no more, for the sons of God come not in unto the daughters of men, and the world is desolate, and greatness and renown are gone. To-day the blue blow-flies of decay sit buzzing on the slow-rolling wheel of Fortune, intoxicated on the dust of the dead, and sucking putrefaction from the sinews of the fallen, and rottenness from the charnel-house of Might.

O Reason! Thou hast become as a vulture feasting off the corpse of a king as it floats down the dark waters of Acheron. Nay! not so grand a sight, but as an old, wizened woman, skaldy and of sagging breast, who in the solitude of her *latrina* cuddles and licks the oleograph of a naked youth. O Adonis, rest in the arms of Aphrodite, seek not the hell-fouled daughter of Ceres, who hath grown hideous in the lewd embrace of the Serpent-God, betrayer of the knowledge of good and of evil. Behold her bulging belly and her shrivelled breasts, full of scale and scab—"bald, rotten, abominable!" Her tears no longer blossom into the anemones of Spring; for their purity has left them, and they are become as the bilge which poureth forth from the stern of a ship full of hogs. O! Eros, fly, speed! Await not the awakening oil to scorch Thy cheek, lest Thou discover that Thy darling has grown hideous and wanton, and that in the place of a fair maiden there slimeth a huge slug fed of the cabbage-stalks of decay.

O Theos! O Pantheos! O Atheos! Triple God of the brotherhood of warriors. Evoe! I adore Thee, O thou Trinity of might and majesty—Thou silent Unity that rulest the hearts of the great. Alas! that men are dead, their thrones of gold empty, and their palaces of pearl fallen into ruin! Grandeur and Glory have departed, so that now in the Elysian fields the sheep of woolly understanding nibble the green turnip-tops of reason and the stubble in the reaped cornfields of knowledge. Now all is rational, virtuous, smug, and oily. Those who wrestled with the suns and the moons, and trapped the stars of heaven, and sought God on the summits of the mountains, and drove Satan into the bowels of the earth, have swum the black waters of Styx, and are now in the halls of Asgard and the groves of Olympus, amongst the jewels of Havilah and the soft-limbed houris of Paradise. They have left us, and in their stead have come the carrion kites, who have usurped the white thrones of their understanding, and the golden palaces of their wisdom.

Let us hie back to the cradle of Art and the swaddling bands of Knowledge, and watch the shepherds, among the lonely hills where the myrtle grows and the blue-bells ring out the innocence of Spring, learning from their flocks the mysteries of life. . . . A wolf springs from the thicket, and a lamb lies sweltering in its blood; then an oaken cudgel is

THE EQUINOX

raised, and Hermas has dashed out the brains from betwixt those green, glittering eyes. There now at his feet lie the dead and the dying; and man wonders at the writhing of the entrails and the bubbling of the blood. See! now he gathers in his flock, and drives them to a dark cavern in the sloping side of the mountain; and when the moon is up he departs, speeding to his sister the Sorceress to seek of her balsams and herbs wherewith to stanch his wound and to soothe the burning scratches of the wolf's claws. There under the stars, whilst the bats circle around the moon, and the toad hops through the thicket, and the frogs splash in the mere, he whispers to her, how green were the eyes of the wild wolf, how sharp were his claws, how white his teeth and then, how the entrails wriggled on the ground, and the pink brains bubbled out their blood. Then both are silent, for a great awe fills them, and they crouch trembling amongst the hemlock and the foxgloves. A little while and she arises, and, pulling her black hood over her head, sets out alone through the trackless forest, here and there lit by the moon; and, guided by the stars, she reaches the city.

At a small postern by the tower of the castle known as the "lover's gate" she halts and whistles thrice, and then, in shrill, clear notes as of some awakened night-bird, calls: "Brother, brother, brother mine!" Soon a chain clanks against the oaken door, and a bolt rumbles back in its staple, and before her in his red shirt and his leathern hose stands her brother the Hangman. And there under the stars she whispers to him, and for a moment he trembles, looking deep into her eyes; then he turns and leaves her. Presently there is a creaking of chains overhead—an owl, awakened from the gibbet above, where it had been blinking perched on the shoulder of a corpse, flies shrieking into the night.

Soon he returns, his footsteps resounding heavily along the stone passage, and in his arms he is carrying the dead body of a young man. "*Hé,* my little sister," he pants, and for a moment he props his heavy load up against the door of the postern. Then these two, the Sorceress and the Hangman, silently creep out into the night, back into the gloom of the forest, carrying between them the slumbering Spirit of Science and Art sleeping in the corse of a young man, whose golden hair streams gleaming in the moonlight, and around whose white throat glistens a snake-like bruise of red, of purple, and of black.

There under the oaks by an age-worn dolmen did they celebrate their midnight mass. . . . "Look you! I must needs tell you, I love you well, as you are to-night; you are more desirable than ever you have been before . . . you are built as a youth should be. . . . Ah! how long, how long have I loved you! . . . But to-day I am hungry, hungry for you! . . ."

Thus under the Golden Bough in the moonlight was the host uplifted, and the Shepherd, and the Hangman, and the Sorceress broke the bread of Necromancy, and drank deep of the wine of witchcraft, and swore secrecy over the Eucharist of Art.

Now in the place of the dolmen stands the hospital, and where the trilithons towered is built the "Hall of Science." Lo! the druid has given place to the doctor; and the physician has slain the priest his father, and with wanton words ravished the heart of his mother the sorceress. Now instead of the mystic circle of the adepts we have the great "Bosh-Rot" school of Folly. Miracles are banned, yet still at the word of man do the halt walk, and the lame rise up and run. The devils have been banished, and demoniacal possession is no more, yet now the most lenient of these sages are calling it "hystero-demonopathy"—what a jargon of unmusical syllables! Saul, when he met God face to face on the dusty road of Damascus, is dismissed with a discharging lesion of the occipital cortex; and George Fox crying, "Woe to the bloody city of Lichfield!" is suffering from a disordered colon; whilst Carlyle is subject to gastro-duodenal catarrh. Yet this latter one writes: "Witchcraft and all manner of Spectre-work, and Demonology, we have now named Madness, and Diseases of the Nerves; seldom reflecting that still the new question comes upon us: What is Madness, what are Nerves?"—Indeed, what is Madness, what are Nerves?

Once, when a child, I was stung by a bee whilst dancing through the heather, and an old shepherd met me, and taking a black roll of tobacco from a metal box, he bit off a quid and, chewing it, spat it on my leg, and the pain vanished. He did not spend an hour racking through the dictionary of his brain to find a suitable "itis" whereby to allay the inflammation, and then, having carefully classified it with another, declared the pain to be imaginary and myself to be an hysterio-monomaniac suffering from apiarian illusions!

To-day Hercules is a sun-myth, and so are Osiris and Baal; and no may can raise his little finger without some priapic pig shouting: "Phallus . . . phallus! I see a phallus! O what a phallus!" Away with this church-spire sexuality, these atavistic obstetrics, these endless survivals and hypnoid states, and all these orchitic superficialities! Back to the fruits of life and the treasure-house of mystery!

Let us leap beyond the pale of these pedantic dictionary *proxenetes* and this shuffling of the thumbed cards of Reason. Let us cease gnawing at this philosophic ham-bone, and abandon the thistles of rationalism to the tame asses of the Six-penny Cult, and have done with all this pseudo-scientce, this logic-chopping, this levelling loquacity of loons, louts, lubbers, and lunatics!

O Thou rationalistic Boreas, how Thou belchest the sheep and with the flatulence of windy words! Away with the ethics and morals of the schoolmen, those prudish pedants whose bellies are swollen with the overboiled spinach of their sploshy virtues; and cease rattling the bread-pills of language in the bladder of medical terminology! The maniac's vision of horror is better than this, even the shambles clotted with blood; for it is the blood of life; and the loneliness of the distant heath is as a cup of everlasting wine compared with the soapsuds of these clyster-mongers, these purge-puffed prudes, who loose forth on us an evil-smelling gas from their cabbage-crammed duodenary canals.

Yea! it shall pass by, this gastro-epileptic school of neurological maniacs; for in a little time we shall catch up with this moulting ostrich, and shall slay him whilst he buries his occipital cortex under the rubbish-heap of discharging lesions. Then the golden tree of life shall be replanted in Eden, and we little children shall dance round it, and shall banquet under the stars, feasting off the abandon of the wilderness and the freedom of the hills. Artists we shall become, and in the storm shall we see a woman weeping; and in the lightning and the thunder the sworded warrior who crushes her to his shaggy breast. Away with laws and labours. . . . Lo! in the groves of Pan the dance catches us up, and whirls us onward! O how we dash aside the goblets and the wine-skins, and how the tangled hair of our heads is blown amongst the purple clusters of the vine that clambers along the branches of the plane-trees in the Garden of Eros!

But yet for a little while the mystic child of Freedom must sit weeping at the footstool of the old prude Reason, and spell out her windy alphabets whilst she squats like a toad above her, dribbling, filled with lewd thoughts and longings for the oleograph of the naked youth and the stinking secrecy of her *latrina!*

THE CHILD

UNDER the glittering horns of Capricornus, when the mountains of the North glistened like the teeth of the black wolf in the cold light of the moon, and when the broad lands below the fiery girdle of many-breasted Tellus blushed red in the arms of the summer sun, did Miriam seek the cave below the cavern, in which no light had ever shone, to bring forth the Light of the World. And on the third day she departed from the cave, and, entering the stable of the Sun, she placed her child in the manger of the Moon. Likewise was Mithras born under the tail of the Sea-Goat, and Horus, and Krishna—all mystic names of the mystic Child of Light.

I am the Ancient Child, the Great Disturber, the Great Tranquilliser. I am Yesterday, To-day, and To-morrow. My name is Alpha and Omega—the Beginning and the End. My dwelling-house is built betwixt the water and the earth; the pillars thereof are of fire, and the walls are of air, and the roof above is the breath of my nostrils, which is the spirit of the life of man.

I am born as an egg in the East, of silver, and of gold, and opalescent with the colours of precious stones; and with my Glory is the beast of the horizon made purple and scarlet, and orange, and green, many-coloured as a great peacock caught up in the coils of a serpent of fire. Over the pillars of Æthyr do I sail, as a furnace of burnished brass; and blasts of fire pour from my nostrils, and bathe the land of dreams in the radiance of my Glory. And in the west the lid of mine Eye drops— down smites the Night of reckoning and destruction, that night of the slaughter of the evil, and of the overthrow of the wicked, and the burning of the damned.

Robed in the flames of my mouth, I compass the heavens, so that none shall behold me, and that the eyes of men shall be spared the torture of unutterable light. "Devourer of Millions of Years" is my name; "Lord of the Flame" is my name; for I am as an eye of Silver set in the heart of the Sun. Thou spreadest the locks of thine hair before thee, for I burn thee; thou shakest them about thy brow, so that thine eyes may not be blinded by the fire of my fury. I am He who was, who is, and who will be; I am the Creator, and the Destroyer, and the Redeemer of mankind. I have come as the Sun from the house of the roaring of lions, and at my coming shall there be laughter, and weeping, and singing, and gnashing of teeth. Ye shall tread upon the serpent and the scorpion, and the hosts of your enemies shall be as chaff before the sickle of your might: yet ye must be born in the cavern of darkness and be laid in the manger of the moon.

Lo! I am as a babe born in a crib of lilies and roses, and wrapped in the swaddling bands of June. Mine hands are delicate and small, and my feet are shod in flame, so that they touch not the kingdoms of this earth. I arise, and leave the cradle of my birth, and wander through the valleys, and over the hills, across the sun-scorched deserts of day, and through the cool groves of night. Everywhere, everywhere, I find myself, in the deep pools, and in the dancing streams, and in the many-coloured surface of the mere: there I am white and wonderful, a child of loveliness and of beauty, a child to entice songs from the wild rose, and kisses from the zephyrs of dawn.

Herod would have slain me, and Kansa have torn me with his teeth of fire; but I eluded them, as a flame hidden in a cloud of smoke, and took refuge in the land of Ptah and sought sanctuary in the arms of Seb. There were the glories of Light revealed to me, and I became as a daughter of Ceres playing in the poppied fields of yellow corn: yet still as a sun-limbed bacchanal I trampled forth the foaming must from the purple grapes of Bacchus, and breathing it into the leaven of life, caused it to ferment, and bubble forth as the Wine of Iacchus. Then with the maiden, who was also myself, I partook of the Eucharist of Love—the corn and the wine, and became one.

Then there came unto me a woman subtle and beautiful to behold, whose breasts were as alabaster bowls filled with wine, and the purple hair of whose head was as a dark cloud on a stormy night. Dressed in a gauze of scarlet and gold, and jewelled with pearls and emeralds and magic stones, she, like a spider spun in a web of sunbeams and blood, danced before me, casting her jewels to the winds, and naked she sang to me: "O lover of mine heart, thy limbs are as chalcedony, white and round, and tinged with the mingling blush of the sapphire, the ruby, and the sard. Thy lips are as roses in June; and thine eyes as amethysts set in the vault of heaven. O! come kiss me, for I tremble for thee; fill me with love, for I am consumed by the heat of my passion; say me, O slay me with kisses, burn me in the fire of thy kingdom, O slay me with the sword of thy rapture!"

Then I cried unto her in a loud voice saying: "O Queen of the lusts of flesh! O Queen of the lands haunted by satyrs! O Mistress of Night! O Mother of the mysteries of birth and death! Who art girt in the flames of passion, and jewelled with emerald, and moonstone, and chrysoleth. Lo! on thy brow burns the star-sapphire of heaven, thy girdle is as the serpent of Eden, and round thine ankles chatter the rubies and garnets of hell. Hearken, O Lilith! O Sorceress of the blood of life! My lips are for those who suckle not Good, and my kisses for those who cherish not Evil. And my kingdom is for the children of light who trample under foot the garment of shame, and rend from their loins the sackcloth of modesty. When Two shall be One, then shalt thou be crowned with a crown neither of gold nor of silver, nor yet of precious stones; but as with a crown of fire fashioned in the light of God's glory. Yea! when my sword falleth, then that which is without shall be like unto that which is within; then tears shall be as kisses, and kisses as tears; then all shall be leavened and made whole, and thou shalt find in thine hand a sceptre, neither of lilies nor of gold, but a sceptre of light, yea! a sceptre of the holiness and loveliness of light and of glory!"

O Children of the land of Dreams! O ye who would cross the bar of sleep, and become as Children of Awakenment and Light. Woe unto you! for ye cleanse outside the cup and the platter; but within they are full of uncleanness. Ye are soaked in the blood of corruption, and choked with the vomit of angry words. Close your eyes, O ye neophytes in the mysteries of God, lest ye be blinded, and cry out like a man whose sight has been smitten black by a burning torch of tar. O Children of Dreams! plough well the fields of night, and prepare them for the Sower of Dawn. Heed lest the golden corn ripen and ye be not ready to pluck the swollen ears, and feast, and become as Bezaleel, filled with a divine spirit of wisdom, and understanding, and knowledge—a cunning worker in gold, and in silver, and in brass, in scarlet, in purple, and in blue.

But woe unto ye who tarry by the wayside, for the evening is at hand; to-day is the dawn, tomorrow the night of weeping. Gird up your loins and speed to the hills; and perchance on the way under the cedars and the oaks ye meet God face to face and know. But be not downcast if ye find not God in the froth or the dregs of the first cup: drink and hold fast to the sword of resolution—onwards, ever onwards, and fear not!

Devils shall beset the path of the righteous, and demons, and all the elemental spirits of the Abyss. Yet fear not! for they add grandeur and glory to the might of God's power. Pass on, but keep thy foot upon their necks, for in the region whither thou goest, the seraph and the snake dwell side by side.

Sume lege. Open the Book of THYSELF, take and read. Eat, for this is thy body; drink, for this is the blood of thy redemption. The sun thou seest by day, and the moon thou beholdest by night, and all the stars of heaven that burn above thee, are part of thyself—are thyself. And so is the bowl of Space which contains them, and the wine of Time in which they float; for these two are part of thyself—are Thyself. And God also who casteth them forth from the coffers of his treasury. He, too, though thou knowest it not, is part of thyself—is THYSELF. All is in thee, and thou art in all, and separate existence is not, being but a net of dreams wherein the dreamers of night are ensnared. Read, and thou becomest; eat and drink, and thou art.

Though weak, thou art thine own master; listen not to the babblers of vain words, and thou shalt become strong. There is no revelation except thine own. There is no understanding except thine own. There is no consciousness apart from thee, but that it is held feodal to thee in the kingdom of thy Divinity. When thou knowest thou knowest, and there is none other beside thee, for all becometh as an armour around thee, and thou thyself as an invulnerable, invincible warrior of Light.

Heed not the pedants who chatter as apes among the treetops; watch rather the masters, who in the cave under the cavern breathe forth the breath of life.

One saith to thee:

"Abandon all easy, follow the difficult; eat not of the best, but of the most distasteful; pander not to thy pleasures, but feed well thy disgusts; console not thyself, but seek the waters of desolation; rest not thyself, but labour in the depths of the night; aspire not to things precious, but to things contemptible and low."

But I say unto thee: heed not this vain man, this blatherer of words! For there is Godliness in ease, in fine dishes, and in pleasures, in consolations, in rest, and in precious things.

So if in thyself thou findest a jewelled goblet, I say unto

thee, drink from it, for it is the cup of thy salvation; seek not therefore a dull bowl of heavy lead!

Yet another saith unto thee:

"Will not anything, will nothing; seek not for the best, but for the worst. Despise thyself; slander thyself; speak lightly of thyself."

And again:

"To enjoy the taste for all things, then have no taste for anything."

"To know all things; then resolve to possess nothing."

"To be all; then, indeed be willing to be naught."

But I say unto thee: this one is filed like a fool's bladder with wind and a rattling of dried peas; for he who wills everything, is he who seeks of the best; for he who honours himself, he who prides himself most; and he who speaks highly of himself, is he who also shall reign in the City of God.

"To have no taste for anything, then enjoy the taste of all things.

"To resolve to possess nothing, then possess all things.

"To be naught, then indeed be all."

Open the book of Thyself in the cave under the cavern and read it by the light of thine own understanding, then presently thou shalt be born again, and be placed in the manger of the Moon in the stable of the Sun.

For, children! when ye halt at one thing, ye cease to open yourselves to all things. For to come to the All, ye must give up the All, and likewise possess the All. Verily ye must destroy all things and out of No-thing found and build the Temple of God as set up by Solomon the King, which is placed between Time and Space; the pillars thereof are

Eternity, and the walls Infinity, and the floor Immortality, and the Roof—but ye shall know of this hereafter! Spoil thyself if so thou readest thyself; but if it is written adorn thyself, then spare not the uttermost farthing, but deck thyself with all the jewels and gems of earth; and from a child playing with the sands on the sea-shore shalt thou become God, whose footstool is the Abyss, and from whose mouth goeth forth the sword of the salvation and destruction of the worlds, and in whose hand rest the seven stars of heaven.

THE WANTON

THERE is a woman, young, and beautiful, and wise, who grows not old as she dances down the centuries: she was in the beginning, and she will be in the end, ever young, ever enticing, and always inscrutable. Her back is to the East and her eyes are towards the night, and in her wake lieth the world. Wherever she danceth, there man casteth the sweat from his brow and followeth her. Kings have fled their thrones for her; priests their temples; warriors their legions; and husbandmen their ploughs. All have sought her; yet ever doth she remain subtle, enticing, virginal. None have known her save those little ones who are born in the cave under the cavern; yet all have felt the power of her sway. Crowns have been sacrificed for her; gods have been blasphemed for her; swords have been sheathed for her; and the fields have lain barren for her; verily! the helm of man's thoughts has been cloven in twain by the magic of her voice. For like some great spider she has enticed all into the silken meshes of her web, wherein she hath spun the fair cities of the world, where sorrow sits tongueless and laughter abideth not; and tilled the fertile plains, where innocence is but as the unopened book of Joy. Yet it is she also who hath led armies into battle; it is she who hath brought frail vessels safely across the greedy ocean; it is she who hath enthroned priests, crowned kings, and set the sword in the hand of the warrior; and it is she who hath helped the weary slave to guide his plough through the heavy soil, and the miner to rob the yellow gold from the bowels of the earth. Everywhere will you find her dancing down empires, and weaving the destiny of nations. She never sleeps, she never slumbers, she never rests; ever wakeful, day and night, her eyes glisten like diamonds as she danceth on, the dust of her feet burying the past, disturbing the present, and clouding the future. She was in Eden, she will be in Paradise!

I followed her, I abandoned all for her; and now I lie, as a fevered man, raving in the subtle web of her beauty.

Lo! there she stands swaying between the gates of Light and Darkness under the shadow of the Three of the Knowledge of Good and Evil, whose fruits are death; yet none that have not tasted thereof can tell whether they be sweet or bitter to the tongue. Therefore all must pluck and eat and dream. But when the time cometh for the mystic child to be born, they shall awake, and with eyes of fire behold that on the summit of the mountain in the centre of the garden there groweth the Tree of Life.

Now round the trunk of the Tree and the lower branches thereof there twines a woman, wild, wanton, and wise; whose body is as that of a mighty serpent, the back of which is vermilion, and the belly of red-gold; her breasts are purple, and from her neck spring three heads.

And the first head is as the head of a crownéd priestess, and is of silver, and on her brow is set a crown of pearls, and her eyes are as blue as the sapphire; but upon perceiving man they turn green and yellow as the water of a troubled sea; and her mouth is as a moonstone cleft in twain, in which lurks a tongue born of flame and water.

And on beholding her, I cried to her in a loud voice, saying: "O Priestess of the Veil who art throned between the Pillars of Knowledge and Ignorance, pluck and give me of the fruit of the Tree of Life that I may eat thereof, so that my eyes shall be opened, and that I become as a god in understanding, and live for ever!"

Then she laughed subtly, and answered me saying: "Understanding, O fool that art so wise, is Ignorance. Fire licketh up water, and water quencheth fire; and the sword which one man fleeth from, another sheatheth in his breast. Seek the Crown of Truth, and thou shalt be shod with the sandals of Falsehood; unclasp the girdle of Virtue, and thou shalt be wrapped in the shroud of Vice."

And, when she had finished speaking, she wove from her lips around me a net-work of cloud and of flame; and in a subtle song she sang to me: "In the web of my tongue hast thou been caught; in the breath of my mouth shalt thou be snared. For Time shall be given unto thee wherein to seek all things; and all things shall be thy curse, and thine understanding shall be as the waves of the sea ever rolling onwards to the shore from whence they came; and when at the height of their majesty shall their pride and dominion be dashed against the rocks of Doubt, and all thy glory shall become as the spume and the spray of shattered waters, blown hither and thither by the storm."

Then she caught me up in the web of her subtleties and breathed into my nostrils the breath of Time; and bore me to the Abyss, where all is as the darkness of Doubt, and there she strangled me with the hemp and the silk of the abominations and arrogance of mine understanding.

And the second head is as the head of a young woman veiled with a veil as clear as rock crystal, and crowned with a crown fashioned in the shape of a double cube around which is woven a wreath of lilies and ivy. And her countenance is as that of Desolation yet majestic as an Empress of Earth, who possessing all things yet cannot find a helpmeet worthy to possess her; and her eyes are as opals of light; and her tongue as an arrow of flame.

And on beholding her I cried in a loud voice saying: "O Princess of the Vision of the Unknown, who art throned as a sphinx between the hidden mysteries of Earth and Air, give me of the fruit of the Tree of Life that I may eat thereof, so that mine eyes shall be opened, and I may become as a god in understanding, and live for ever!"

And when I had finished speaking she wept bitterly and answered me saying: "Verily if the poor man trespass within the palace gate, the king's dogs shall be let loose so that they may tear him in pieces. Also, if the king seek shelter in the hut of the pauper the louse taketh refuge in his hair, and heedeth not his crown nor his cap of ermine and gold. Now, thou, O wise man who art so foolish, askest for Understanding; yet how shall it be given unto him who asketh for it, for in the giving it it ceaseth to be, and he who asketh of me is unworthy to receive. Wouldst thou enter the king's palace in rags and beg crumbs of his bounty? Take heed lest, the king perceiving thee not, his knaves set the hounds upon thee, so that even the rags that thou possessest are torn from thee: or, even should the kind cast his eyes on thee, that he be not overcome with fury at the presumption of thine offence, and order thee to be stripped naked and beaten from his garden with staves back to the hovel whence thou camest. And being a king, if thou seekest knowledge and understanding in a beggar's hut, thou shalt become as an abode of vermin, and a prey to hunger and thirst, and thy limbs shall be bitten by cold and scorched with fire, and all thy wealth will depart from thee and thy people will cast thee out and take away thy crown. Yet there is hope for the beggar and the king, and the balances which sway shall be adjusted, and the sun shall drink up the clouds, and the clouds shall swallow the sun, and there shall be neither darkness nor light. Pledge thy pride and it will become but the habitations of vermin, pledge thy humility and thou shalt be cast out naked to the dogs."

Then when she had finished speaking she bared her breast to me, and it was as the colour of the vault of heaven at the rising of the sun; and she took me in her arms and did caress me, and her tongue of fire crept around and about me as the hand of a sly maid. Then I drank in the breath of her lips, and it filled me as with the spirit of dreams and of slumber, so that I doubted that the stars shone above me, and that the rivers flowed at my feet. Thus all became as a vast Enigma to me, a riddle set in the Unknowability of Space.

Then in a subtle voice she sang to me: "I know not who thou art, or whence thou camest; whether from across the snowy hills, or from over the plains of fire. Yet I love thee; for thine eyes are as the blue of still waters, and thy lips ruddy as the sun in the West. Thy voice is as the voice of a shepherd at even, calling together his flock in the twilight. Thy breath is as the wind blown from across a valley of musk; and thy loins are lusty as red coral washed from the depths of the sea. Come, draw nigh unto me, O my love: my sister ensnared thee with her subtle tongue, she gave thee to suck from the breasts of Time: come, I will give thee more than she, for I will give unto thee as an inheritance my body, and thou shalt fondle me as a lover, and as a reward for thy love will I endow thee with all the realms of Space—the motes in the sunbeam shall be thine, and the starry palaces of night, all shall be thine even unto the uttermost depths of Infinity." So she possessed me, and I her.

And the third head is as the head of a woman neither young nor old, but beautiful and compasionate; and on her forehead is set a wreath of Cypress and Poppies fastened by a winged cross. And her eyes are as star-sapphires, and her mouth is as a pearl, and on the lips crouches the Spirit of Silence.

And on beholding her I cried to her in a loud voice, saying: "O Thou Mother of the Hall of Truth! Thou who art both sterile and pregnant, and before whose judgment-seat tremble the clothed and the naked, the righteous and the unjust, give me of the fruit of the Tree of Life, that I may eat thereof so that mine eyes shall be opened, and that I become as a god in understanding, and live forever!"

Then I stood before her listening for her answer, and a great shaking possessed me, for she answered not a word; and the silence of her lips rolled around me as the clouds of night and overshadowed my soul, so that the Spirit of life left me. Then I fell down and trembled, for I was alone.

THE SLAVE

THE blue vault of heaven is red and torn as the wound of a tongueless mouth; for the West has drawn her sword, and the Sun lies sweltering in his blood. The sea moans as a passionate bridegroom, and with trembling lips touches the swelling breasts of night. Then wave and cloud cling together, and as lovers who are maddened by the fire of their kisses, mingle and become one.

Come, prepare the feast in the halls of the Twilight! Come, pour out the dark wine of the night, and bring in the far-sounding harp of the evening! Let us tear from our burning limbs the dusty robes of the morning, and, naked, dance in the silver radiance of the moon. Voices echo from the darkness, and the murmur of many lips lulls the stillness of departing day, as a shower in springtime whispering amongst the leaves of the sprouting beech trees. Now the wolves howl outside, and the jackals call from the thicket; but none heed them, for all inside is as the mossy bank of a sparkling streamlet—full of softness and the flashing of many jewels.

O where art thou, my loved one, whose eyes are as the blue of the far-off hills? O where art thou whose voice is as the murmur of distant waters? I stretch forth mine hands and

THE EQUINOX

feel the rushes nodding in the wind; I gaze through the shadows, for the night mist is rising from the lake; but thee I cannot find. Ah! there thou art by the willow, standing between the bulrush and the water-lily, and thy form is as a shell of pearl caught up by the waves in the moonlight. Come, let us madden the night with our kisses! Come, let us drink dry the vats of our passion! Stay! Why fleest thou from me, as the awakened mist of the morning before the arrows of day? Now I can see thee no more; thou art gone, and the darkness hath swallowed thee up. O wherefore hast thou left me, me who loved thee, and wove kisses in thine hair? Behold, the Moon hath followed thee! Now I see not the shadows of the woods, and the lilies in the water have become but flecks of light in the darkness. Now they mingle and melt together as snow-flakes before the sun, and are gone; yea! the stars have fled the skies, and I am alone.

How cold has grown the night, how still! O where art thou! Come, return unto me, that I stray not in vain; call unto me that I lose not my way! Lighten me with the brightness of thine eyes, so that I wander not far from the path and become a prey to the hunger of wild beasts!

I am lost; I know not where I am; the mossy mountains have become as hills of wind, and have been blown far from their appointed places; and the waving fields of the valleys have become silent as the land of the dead, so that I hear then not, and know not whither to walk. The reeds whisper not along the margin of the lake; all is still; heaven has closed her mouth and there is no breath in her to wake the slumber of desolation. The lilies have been sucked up by the greedy waters, and now night sleeps like some mighty serpent gorged on the white flesh and the warm blood of the trembling maidens of dawn, and the wild youths of the noontide.

O my dove, my loved one! Didst thou but approach as a wanderer in the wilderness, thine hair floating as a raiment of gold about thee, and thy breasts lit with the blush of the dawn! Then would mine eyes fill with tears, and I would leap towards thee in the madness of my joy; but thou comest not. I am alone, and tremble in the darkness like the bleached bones of a giant in the depths of a windy tomb.

There is a land in which no tree groweth, and where the warbling of the birds is as a forgotten dream. There is a land of dust and desolation, where no river floweth, and where no cloud riseth from the plains to shade men's eyes from the sand and the scorching sun. Many are they who stray therein, for all live upon the threshold of misery who inhabit the House of joy. There wealth taketh wing as a captive bird set free, and fame departeth as a breath from fainting lips; love playeth the wanton, and the innocence of youth is but as a cloak to cover the naked hideousness of vice; health is not known, and joy lies corrupted as a corpse in the grave; and behind all standeth the great slave master called Death, all-encompassing with his lash, all-desolating in the naked hideousness and the blackness wherewith he chastiseth.

"I looked on all the works that my hands had wrought, and behold all was vanity and vexation of spirit." Yea! all are of dust, and turn to dust again, and the dead know not anything. Health has left me, wealth has departed from me, those whom I love have been taken from me, and now Thou

(O my God!) hast abandoned me, and cast me out, and setting a lock upon Thy lips hast stopped Thine ears with wax and covered Thine eyes with the palms of Thine hands, so that Thou seest me not, nor hearest me, nor answerest unto my bitter cry. Thus I am cast out from Thy presence and sit alone as one lost in a desert of sand, and cry unto Thee, thirsting for Thee, and then deny Thee and curse Thee in my madness, until death stop the blasphemies of my lips with the worm and the dust of corruption, and I am set free from the horror of this slavery of sorrow.

I am alone, yea! alone, sole habitant of this kingdom of desolation and misery. Hell were as Paradise to this solitude. O would that dragons came from out the deep and devoured me, or that lions tore me asunder for their food; for their fury would be as milk and honey unto the bitterness of this torture. O cast unto me a worm, that I may no longer be alone, and that in its writhings on the sand I read Thine answer to my prayer! Would I were in prison that I might hear the groans of the captives; would I were on the scaffold that I might listen to the lewd jests of bloody men! O would I were in the grave, wound in the roots of the trees, eyeless gazing up into the blackness of death!

Between the evening and the morning was I born, like a mushroom I sprang up in the night. At the breast of desolation was I fed, and my milk was as whey, and my meat as the bitterness of aloes. Yet I lived, for God was with me; and I feared, for the devil was at hand. I did not understand what I needed, I was afraid, and fear was as a pestilence unto my soul. Yet was I intoxicated and drunken on the cup of life, and joy was mine, and reeling I shrieked blasphemies to the storm. Then I grew sober, and diced with mine understanding, and cheated mine heart, and lost my God, and was sold into slavery, and became as a coffin-worm unto the joy of my life. Thus my days grew dark, and I cried unto myself as my spirit left me: "O what of to-day which is as the darkness of night? O what then of to-morrow which is as the darkness of Eternity? Why live and tempt the master's lash?" So I sought the knife at my girdle to sunder the thread of my sorrow; but courage had taken flight with joy, and my hand shook so that the blade remained in its sheath. Then I cried unto myself: "Verily why should I do aught, for life itself hath become unto me as a swordless scabbard"—so I sat still and gloomed into the darkness.

THE WARRIOR

THERE is an indifference which overleaps satisfaction; there is a surrender which overthrows victory, there is a resignation which shatters the fetters of anxiety, a relaxation which casts to the winds the manacles of despair. This is the hour of the second birth, when from the womb of the excess of misery is born the child of the nothingness of joy. *Solve!* For all must be melted in the crucible of affliction, all must be refined in the furnace of woe, and then on the anvil of strength must it be beaten out into a blade of gleaming joy. *Coagula!*

Weep and gnash your teeth, and sorrow sits crowned and exultant; therefore rise and gird on the armour of utter desolation! Slay anger, strangle sorrow, and drown despair; then a joy shall be born which is beyond love or hope, endurable, incorruptible. Come heaven, come hell! Once the Balances are adjusted, then shall the night pass away, and desire and sorrow vanish as a dream with the breath of the morning.

The war of the Freedom of Souls is not the brawling of slaves in the wine-dens, or the haggling of the shopmen in the market-place; it is the baring of the brand of life, that unsheathing of the Sword of Strength which lays all low before the devastation of its blade. Life must be held in contempt—the life of self and the life of others. Here there must be no weakness, no sentiment, no reason, no mercy. All must taste of the desolation of war, and partake of the blood of the cup of death. O! warriors, ye cannot be too savage, to barbarous, too strong. On, O storm-blown sons of the fire of life! Success is your password; destruction is your standard; Victory is your reward!

Heed not the shrieking of women, or the crying of little children; for all must die, and not a stone must be left standing in the city of the World, lest darkness depart not. Haste! bring flint and steel, light the match, fire the thatch of the hovel and the cedar rafters of the palace; for all must be destroyed, and no man must delay, or falter, or turn back, or repent. Then from the ashes of Destruction will rise the King, the birthless and the deathless one, the great monarch who shall shake from his tangled beard the blood of strife, and who shall cast from his weary hand the sword of desolation.

Yea! from out the night flashes a sword of flame, from out the darkness speeds an arrow of fire!

I am alone, and stand at the helm of the barque of Death, and laugh at the fury of the waves; for the prow of my laughter smiteth the dark waters of destruction into a myriad jewels of unutterable and uttermost joy!

I am alone, and stand in the centre of the desert of Sorrow, and laugh at the misery of earth: for the music of my laughter whirleth the sands of desolation into a golden cloud of unutterable and uttermost joy!

I am alone, and stand on the storm cloud of life, and laugh at the shrieking of the winds; for the wings of my laughter sweep away the web of outer darkness, and reveal the stars of unutterable and uttermost joy!

I am alone, and stand on the flames of the mountains of pleasure, and laugh at the fire of rapture; for the breath of my laughter bloweth the bright flames into a pillar of unutterable and uttermost joy.

I am alone, and stand amongst the ghosts of the dead, and laugh at the shivering of the shades, for the heart of my laughter pulseth as a mighty fountain of blood clothing the shadows of night with the spirit of unutterable and uttermost joy!

I am alone, yea alone, one against all; yet in my sword have I all things; for in it lives the strength of my might, and if joy come not at my beckoning, then joy shall be slain as a disobedient slave, and if sorrow depart not at my command, then shall sorrow speed through the valley of death as a foe that passeth not his neck beneath the yoke.

In the bastion of mine imagination lie all the munitions of my might; and from the tower of my resolution do I sweep away the stars, and pour forth fire and water on the world of laughter and weeping. I cannot be despoiled, for none can approach me; I cannot be succoured, for I am far beyond the path of man's help. Yet neither would I if I could; for if I could, I would not; and if I would, I could not; for I have become as a giant amongst men, strong as he can only be who has feasted on the agony of life, and drunken of the cup of the sorrow of death, and towered above all things.

Laugher is mine, not the laughter of bitterness, nor the laughter of jest; but the laughter of strength and of life. I live like a mighty conquering Lord and all things are mine.

THE TEMPLE OF SOLOMON THE KING

Fair groves and gardens, palaces of marble and fortresses of red sandstones; and the coffers of my treasury are filled with gold and silver and precious stones; and before my path the daughters of pleasure dance with unbraided tresses, scattering lilies and roses along my way. Life is a joy indeed, a rapture of clinging lips and of red wine, which flows in beads along the bronze and purple tresses, and then like rubies of blood finds refuge between the firm white breasts of maddened maidenhood.

Hark! ... What is that, the yelping of a dog? No, it is the death-cry of a man! ... Ay! the biting of sharp swords, and the shrieking of many women. Ho! the feast has indeed begun, the rabble have broken in, scythes glisten in the torchlight and tables are overturned; wine is gulped down by filthy mouths, and spilt and mingled with the blood of the slaughtered children of Eros, so that the banquet of love has become the shambles of death. ...

Now all is still and the rose has given birth to the poppy, and the bronze tresses of the revellers lie motionless as snakes gorged on clotted blood, and shimmer wantonly in the moonlight between discovered limbs and disemboweled entrails. Soon the quivering maggots, which once were the brains of men, will lick up the crumbs of the feast in the temple of love, and the farce will be ended.

I rise from the corpse of her I kissed, and laugh; for all is beautiful, more beautiful still; for I create from the godless butchery of fiends the overpowering grandeur of death. There she stands before me, rose-limbed, crimson-lipped, with breast of scarlet flame, her tresses floating about her like a cloud of ruby fire, and the tongue which creepeth from her lips is as a carbuncle wet with the strong blood of warriors. I laugh, and in the frenzy of my exultation she is mine; and on that soft bed of bloody corpses do I beget on her the laughter of the scorn of war, the joy of the contempt of sorrow.

Life is a horror, a writhing of famished serpents, yet I care not, for I laugh. The deserts awe me not, neither do the seas restrain the purpose of my mirth. Life is as prisoner in a dungeon, still I laugh; for I, in my strength, have begotten a might beyond the walls of prisons; for life and death have become one to me—as little children gambolling on the sands and splashing in the wavelets of the sea. I laugh at their pretty play, and upon the billows of my laughter do I build up the Kingdom of the Great in which all carouse at one table. Here virgins mingle with courtesans, and the youth and the old man know neither wisdom nor folly.

I have conquered the deserts and the forests, the valleys and the mountains, the seas and the lands. My palace is built of fire and water, of earth and of air, and the secret place within the sanctuary of my temple is as the abode of everlasting mirth. All is love, life, and laugher; death and decay are not: all is joy, purity, and freedom; all is as the fire of mystery; all is all; for my kingdom is known as the City of God.

The slave weepeth, for he is alone; O be not slaves unto yourselves, lashing your backs with the sorrows of your own begetting. But rather become strong in the widowhood of your joy, and evoke from the horror of your seclusion the morion of the victory of resolution, and from the misery of your loneliness, the sword of the destruction of desire. Then shall ye turn your faces towards the West, and stride after the night of desolation, and on the cup of the sunset shall ye become strong as warriors fed on the blood of bulls, and shall step out past the morning and the night in the manliness of might, to the conquest of thyself, and to the usurpation of the Throne of God!

THE KING

THE King is the undying One; he is the life and the master of life; he is the great living image of the Sun, the Sun, and the begetter of the Sun. He is the Divine Child, the God-begotten One, and the Begetter of God. He is the potent bull, the jewelled snake, the fierce lion. He is the monarch of the lofty mountains, and the lord of the woods and forests, the indweller of the globes of flame. As a royal eagle he soars through the heavens, and as a great dragon he churns up the waters of the deep. He holds the past between his hands as a casket of precious stones, the future lies before him clear as a mirror of burnished silver, and to-day is as an unsheathed dagger of gold at his girdle.

As a slave who is bold becomes a warrior, so a warrior who is fearless becomes a king, changing his battered helm of strength for a glittering crown of light; and as the warrior walks upright with the fearlessness of disdain in his eyes, so does the king walk with bowed head, finding love and beauty wherever he goeth, and whatever he doeth is true and lovely, for having conquered his self, he ruleth over his self by love alone, and not by the laws of good and evil, neither proudly nor disdainfully, neither by justice nor by mercy. Good and Evil is not his, for he hath become as an Higher Intelligence, as an Art enshrined in the mind; and in his kingdom actions no longer defile, and whatever his heart inclineth him to do, that he doeth purely and with joy. And as the countenance of a singer may be ruddy or white, fair or dark, nevertheless, the redness or the whiteness, the fairness or the darkness, affect not the song of his lips, or the rapture of his music; similarly, neither does man-made virtue and vice, goodness and wickedness, strength and weakness, or any of the seeming opposites of life, affect or control the actions of the King; for he is free-born from the delusions and the dream of opposites, and sees things as they are, and not as the five senses reflect them on the mirror of the mind.

Now he who would become as a king unto himself must not renounce the kingdoms of this world, but must conquer the lands and estates of others and usurp their thrones. Should he be poor he must aim at riches without forfeiting his poverty; should he be rich he must aim at possessing poverty as well, without taking one farthing from the coffers of his treasury. The man of much estate must aim at possessing all the land, until there is no kingdom left for him to conquer. The Unobtainable must be obtained, and in the obtaining of it is to be found the Golden Key of the Kingdom of Light. The virgin must become as the wanton, yet though filled with all the itchings of lust, she must in no wise forfeit the purity of her virginity; for the foundations of the Temple are indeed set between Day and Night, and the Scaffolding thereof is as an arch flung between Heaven and Hell. For if she who is a virgin become but as a common strumpet, then she indeed falls and rises not, becoming in her fall but a clout in the eyes of all men, a foul rag wherewith to sop up the lusts of flesh. So, verily, if she who being a courtesan, becometh as an untouched virgin, she shall be considered as a thing of naught, being both sterile and loveless; for what profit shall she be to this world who is the mother of unfruitfulness? But she who is both crimson and white, a twisted pillar of snow and fire, soothing where she burneth, and comforting where she chilleth, she shall be held as queen amongst women; for in her all things are found, and as an inexhaustible well of water around whose mouth grows the wild apricot, in which the bees set their sweet hives, she shall be both food and drink to the hearts of men: a well of life unto this world, yea! a goodly tavern wherein cool wine is sold, and good cheer is to be had, and where all shall be filled with the joyaunce of love.

Thus shall men attain to the unity of the crown and become as kings unto themselves. But the way is long and hilly and beset with many pitfalls, and it traverses a foul and a wild country. Indeed we see before us the towers and the turrets, the domes and the spires, the roofs and the gables, glittering beyond the purple of the horizon, like the helmets and spears of an army of warriors in the distance. But on approaching we find that the blue of the sky-line encompasses a dark wood wherein are all things unmindful of the Crown, and where there is darkness and corruption, and where lives the Tyrant of the World clothed in a robe of fantastic desires. Yet it is here that the Golden Key has been lost, where the hog, the wolf, the ape, and the bearded goat hold revel. Here are set the pavilions of dreams and the tented encampments of sleep, in which are spread the tables of demons, and where feast the wantons and the prudes, the youths and the old men, and all the opposites of virtue and of vice. But he who would wear the crown must find the key, else the door of the Palace remains closed, for none other than he can open it for him. And he who would find the Key of Gold must seek it here in the outer court of the World, where the flatterers, and the parasites, and the hypocrites, buzz like flies over the fleshpots of life.

Now he who enters the outer court sees set before him many tables and couches, at which with swollen veins revel the sons of the gluttony of life. Here men, in their furious love of greed, stuff their jaws with the luxuries of decay, which a little after go to the dunghill; and vomit their sour drink on one another as a certain sign of their good fellowship. Here they carouse together drunkenly as in a brothel filling the world with the noise of cymbal and drum, and the loud-sounding instruments of delusion, and with shouts of audacious shame. Here are their ears and eyes pleasantly titillated by the sound of the hissing of the frying-pans, and the sight of the bubbling of stews; and courting voracity, with necks stretched out, so that they may sniff up the wandering steam of the dishes, they fill their swollen bellies with things perishable, and drink up the gluttonies of life. Yet he who would partake of the Banquet of Light must pass this way and sojourn a while amongst these animals, who are so filled with swinish itchings and unbridled fornications that they perceive not that their manger and their dunghill lie side by side as twins in one bed. For a space he must listen to the hiccuping of those who are loaded with wine, and the snorting of those who are stuffed with food, and must watch these lecherous beasts who insult the name of man rolling in their offal, gambolling, and itching with a filthy prurience after the mischievous delights of lewdness, drunkenly groping amongst the herds of long-haired boys and short-skirted girls, from whom they suck away their beauty, as milk from the udders of a goat. He must dwell for a time with these she-apes, smeared with white paint, mangled, daubed, and plastered with the "excrement of crocodiles" and the "froth of putrid humours," who are known as women. Disreputable hags who keep up old wives' whispering over their cups, and who, as filthy in body as in mind, with unbridled tongues clatter wantonly as they giggle over their sluttish whisperings, shamelessly making with their lips sounds of lewdness and fornication. And wanton young dabs with mincing gait swing their bodies here and there amongst the men, their faces smeared with the ensnaring devices of wily cunning. Winking boldly and babbling nonsense they cackle loudly, and like fowls scratching the dunghill seek the dirt of wealth; and having found it, pass their way to the gutter and the grave loaded with gold like a filthy purse.

O seeker! All this must thou bear witness to, and become a partaker in, without becoming defiled or disgusted, and without contempt or reverence; then of a certain shalt thou find the Golden Key which turneth the bolt of evil from the staple of Good, and which openeth the door which leadeth unto the Palace of the King, wherein is the Temple. For when thou hast discovered Beauty and Wisdom and Truth in the swollen veins, in the distended bellies, in the bubbling lips, in the lewd gambollings, in the furious greed, the wanton whisperings, the sly winkings, and all the shameless nonsense of the Outer Court, then indeed shalt thou find that the Key of gold is only to be found in the marriage of wantonness and chastity. And taking it thou shalt place it in the lock of cherubic fire which is fashioned in the centre of the door of the King's house, which is built of ivory and ebony and studded with jet and silver; and the door shall open for a time as if a flame had been blown aside, and thou shalt see before thee a table of pearl on which are set the hidden waters and the secret bread of the Banquet of Light. And thou shalt drink and eat and become bright as a stream of molten silver; and, as the light of the body is the eye, so shalt thy true self become as an eye unto thee, and see all things, even the cup of the third birth; and, taking it, thou shalt drink from the cup the eucharist of Freedom, the wine of which is more fragrant than the sweet-scented grapes of Thrace, or the musk- breathing vines of Lesbos, and is sweeter than the vintage of Crete, and all the vineyards of Naxos and Egypt. And thou shalt be anointed with sweet-smelling nards, and unguent made from lilies and cypress, myrtle and amaranth, and of myrrh and cassia well mixed. And in thine hair shall be woven rose-leaves of crimson light, and the mingling loveliness of lilies and violets, twined as the dawn with night. And about thee shall waft a sweeter fragrance than the burning of frankincense, and storax, and lign-aloes; for it is the breath of the Temple of God. Then shalt thou step into the King's Palace, O warrior! and a voice more musical than the flute of ivory and the psaltery of gold, clear as a bell of mingled metals in the night, shall call unto thee, and thou shalt follow it to the throne which is as a perfect cube of flaming gold set in a sea of whiteness; and then shalt thou be unrobed of sleep and crowned with the silence of the King—the silence of song, of thought, and of reason, that unthinkable silence of the Throne.

THE WHITE WATCH-TOWER

CHAOS and ancient night have engulfed me; I am blind. I crouch on the tower of uttermost silence awaiting the coming of the armies of the dawn.

O whence do I come, where am I, O whither do I go? For I sit maddened by the terrors of a great darkness.... What do I hear? Words of mystery float around me, a music of voices, a sweetness, as of the scent of far burning incense; yea! I see, I hear, I am caught up on the wings of song. Yet I doubt, and doubt that I doubt... I behold!

See! the night heaves as a woman great with child, and the surface of the black waters shimmers as the quivering skin of one in the agony of travail.... The horizon is cleft and glows like a womb of fire, the hosts of the night are scattered, I am born, and the stars melt like flakes of snow before mine eyes....

Lo! there she stands, born in maturity, shaken from out the loins of the darkness, as a rainbow from the purple jars of the thunder. Her hair is as a flood of dancing moon-beams, woven with golden ears of corn, and caught up by flashing serpents of malachite and emerald. On her forehead shines the crescent moon, pearl-like, and softly gleaming with the light of an inner light. Her garment is as a web of translucent silver, glistening white and dew-like, now rippling with all the colours of the rainbow, now rushing into flames crimson and gold, as the petals of the red-rose, woven with poppy, and crocus, and tulips. And around her, as a cloud of irradiant mystery gleaming with darkness, and partly obscuring the softness of her form, sweeps a robe, woven of a network of misty waters, and flashing with a myriad stars of silver; and in its midst, as a great pearl of fire drawn from the depths of the seas, a full moon of silver trembles glowing with beams of opalescent light—mystic and wonderful. In her right hand she holds a sistrum, and chimes forth the music of the earth, and in her left an asp twisted to the prow of a boat of gold, wherein lie the mysteries of heaven.

Then clear and sweet as the breath of the hillside, I heard a voice, as of the winds across a silver harp, saying:

I am the Queen of the heavenly ones, of the Gods, and of the Goddesses, united in one form. I am She who was, who is, and will be; my form is one, my name is manifold; under the palm-trees, and in the deserts, in the valleys, and on the snowy mountains, mankind pays me homage, and thunders forth praises to my name. Yet I am nameless in the deep, as amongst the lightsome mountains of the sky. Some call me Mother of the Gods, some Aphrodite of the seas of pearl, some Diana of the golden nets, some Proserpina Queen of Darkness, some Hecate mistress of enchantments, some Istar of the boat of night, some Miriam of the Cavern, and others yet again Isis, veiled mother of Mystery.

I am she who cometh in unto all men, and if not here, then shalt thou behold Me amidst the darkness of Acheron, and as Queen in the palaces of Styx. I am the dark night that bringeth forth the bright day; I am the bright day that swalloweth up the dark night; that bright day that hath been begotten by the ages, and conceived in the hearts of men; that dawn in which storms shall cease their roaring, and the billows of the deep shall be smoothed out like a sheet of molten glass.

Then I was carried away on the wings of rapture, and in the strength of my joy I leapt from the tower of Night; but as I fell, she caught me, and I clung to her and she became as a Daughter of this world, as a Child of God begotten in the heart of man. And her hair swept around and about me, in clouds of gold, and rolled over me, as sunbeams poured out from the cups of the noon. Her cheeks were bright with a soft vermilion of the pomegranate mingling with the whiteness of the lily. Her lips were half open, and her eyes were deep, passionate, and tremulous, as the eyes of the mother of the human race, when she first struggled in the strong arms of man; for I was growing strong in her strength, I was becoming a worthy partner of her glory.

Then she clung to me, and her breath left her lips like gusts of fire mingled with the odours of myrtle; and in mine arms she sang unto me her bridal song:

"Come, O my dear one, my darling, let us pass from the land of the plough to the glades and the groves of delight! There let us pluck down the clustered vine of our trembling, and scatter the rose-leaves of our desire, and trample the purple grapes of our passion, and mingle the foaming cups of our joy in the glittering chalice of our love. O! love, what fountains of rapture, what springs of intoxicating bliss well up from the depths of our being, till the foaming wine jets forth hissing through the flames of our passion—and splashes into immensity, begetting a million suns.

"I have watched the dawn, golden and crimson; I have watched the night all starry-eyed; I have drunk up the blue depths of the waters, as the purple juice of the grape. Yet, alone in thine eyes, do I find the delights of my joy, and in thy lips the vintage of my love.

"The flowers of the fields have I gazed on, and the gay plumage of the birds, and the distant blue of the mountains; but they all fade before the blush of thy cheeks; and as the ruby goblet of the Sun is drained by the silver lips of night, so are they all swallowed up in the excess of thy beauty.

"I have breathed in the odour of roses and the fragrance of myrtle, and the sweet scent of the wild jessamine. I have drunk in the breath of the hillside, and the perfume of the woods and the seas; yet thy breath is more fragrant than they, it is sweeter still, it intoxicateth me and filleth me with joy, as a rich jar of wine found in the depths of a desert of salt—I have drunk deep and am bewildered with love.

"I have listened to the lark in the sky, to the curlew, and to the nightingale in the thicket, and to all the warblers of the woods, to the murmur of the waters and to the singing of the winds; yet what are they to the rapture of thy voice? which echoes in the valley of my breast, and trills through the depths of my being.

"I have tasted the juice of the peach, and the sweetness of honey and milk; but the wine of thy lips is strong as the aromatic vintage of Egypt, and sweet as the juice of the date-palms in the scented plains of Euphrates: Ay! let me drink till I reel bewildered with kisses and pleasure . . . O my love! . . . my love! . . . O my love!"

Then I caught up her song and cried: "Yea! O Queen of the Night, O arrow of brightness drawn from the quiver of the moon! O Thou who hast ensnared me in the meshes of thine hair, and caught me up on the kisses of thy mouth; O thou who hast laid aside thy divinity to take refuge in mine arms, listen!

"I have drunk deep of the flagons of passion with the white-veiled virgins of Vesta, and the crimson-girdled daughters of Circe, and the drowsy-eyed maidens of Ind. I have woven love with the lithe girls of Hellas, and the subtle-limbed women of Egypt whose fingers are created to caress; all the virgins of Assyria, and the veiled beauties of Arabia, have been mine; yet amongst them all have I not found one to compare to a lash on the lid of thine eye. O Thou art as the wine of ecstasy, a thousand times more delicious than all these. Ah! but what is this languor which cleaves to me? My strength has left me; my soul has mingled with thine; I am not, and yet I am. Is it Thy weakness that I feel?"

"Nay, O lover, for it is only at the price of the illusion of my strength that thou hast given me the pleasure of unity which I have tasted in thine arms. Beauty has conquered me and drunk up the strength of my might; I am alone, and all things are mine in the mystery of my loneliness.

"*Evoe!* life burns in the brasier of love as a ruby flame in a sapphire bowl. I am dead, yet I live for ever!"

Arise, O sleeper, for the night of loneliness hath rolled up the hangings of her couch, and my heart is burning like a sun of molten brass; awake before the Beast riseth and enter the sanctuary of Eden and defile the children of dawn. Thou Child-Man, cast off the cloak of dreams who before thy sleep wast enraptured with the strength of love. Fair and fresh didst thou come from the woods when the world was young, with breast like the snowy hills in the sunlight, and thine hair as a wind-ravished forest of oak, and thine eyes deep and still as the lakes of the mountains. No veil covered thee, and thou didst revel naked in the laughter of the Dawn, and under the kisses of mid-day didst thou leap with the sun, and the caressing hands of night laid thee to rest in the cradle of the moon. Thoughts did not tempt thee, Reason played not the prude with thee, nor imagination the wanton. Radiant child that thou art, thou didst grow in the light that shone from thine eyes, no shadow of darkness fell across thy path: thy love was strong and pure—bright as the stars of night, and deep as the echoing depths of hills of amber, and emerald, and vermilion.

Awake! tear from thy limbs the hempen ropes of darkness, arise!—fire the beacon of the awakenment of the nations, and night shall heave as an harlot great with child, and purity shall be born of corruption, and the light shall quiver through the darkness, an effulgence of opals like the beams of many colours irradiated from the L. V. X.

Through the night of reckoning hast thou passed, and thy path hath been wound around the land of darkness under the clouds of sleep. Thou hast cleft the horizon as a babe the womb of its mother, and scattered the gloom of night, and shouted in thy joy: "Let there be light!" Now that thou has seized the throne, thou shalt pass the portals of the tomb and enter the Temple beyond.

THE TEMPLE OF SOLOMON THE KING

There thou shalt stand upon the great watch-tower of Day, where all is awakenment, and gaze forth on the kingdom of the vine and the land of the houses of coolness. Thou shalt conquer the Empire of the Sceptre, and usurp the Kingdom of the Crown, for thou art as a little child, and none shall harm thee, no evil form shall spring up against thee. For Yesterday is in thy right hand, and To-morrow in thy left, and To-day is as the breath of thy lips.........

I am the Unveiled One standing between the two horizons, as the sun between the arms of Day and Night. My light shineth upon all men, and none can do me harm, neither can the sway of my rule be broken. I am the Unveiled one and the Unveiler and the Re-veiler; the world lieth below me and before me, and in the brilliance of mine eyes crouch the images of things that be. Space I unroll as a scroll, and Time chimeth from mine hand as the voice of a silver bell. I ring out the birth and the death of nations, and when I rise worlds pass away as feathers of smoke before the hurricane......

Yet, O divine Youth who has created thyself! What art thou? Thou art the birthless and the deathless one, without beginning and without end! Thou paintest the heavens bright with rays of pure emerald light, for thou art Lord of the beams of Light. Thou illuminest the two lands with rays of turquoise and beryl, and sapphire, and amethyst; for Lord of Love, Lord of Life, Lord of Immensity, Lord of Everlastingness is thy name. Thou hast become as a tower of Effulgence, whose foundations are set in the hearts of me, yea! as a mountain of chrysoleth slumbering in the Crown of Glory! whose summit is God!

[Book II "The Scaffolding" will appear in No. 2.]

THE HERB DANGEROUS

I. The Pharmacy of Hashish. By E. WHINERAY, M.P.S.
II. The Psychology of Hashish. With an attempt at a new classification of the mystic states of mind known to me, with a plea for Scientific Illuminism. By OLIVER HADDO.
III. The Poem of Hashish. By CHARLES BAUDELAIRE. (Translated.)
IV. Selections illustrating the Psychology of Hashish, from "The Hashish-Eater." By H. S. LUDLOW.

A PHARMACEUTICAL STUDY
OF CANNABIS SATIVA
(BEING A COLLATION OF FACTS AS KNOWN AT THE PRESENT DATE)

CANNABIS INDICA was introduced into England by O'Shaughnessy, and the first extract was made by the late Mr. Peter Squire, the well-known pharmacist of Oxford Street. According to the "British Pharmacopeia" the official variety may consist of the flowering or fruiting tops; and is frequently of inferior quality, seeing that the fruiting tops yield less resin.

According to the "Journal" of the Chemical Society's Transactions, the important constituent is a resin. The active principle is stated to be a red oil, Cannabinol, which is liable to be come oxidised and inert.

Its medicinal properties are sedative, anodyne, hypnotic and antispasmodic. It has been used with success in migraine and delirium, neuralgia, pain of the last stages of phthisis and in acute mania, also in menorrhagia and dysmenorrhoea. ("Squire's Companion," Page 167, 1904 edition.)

It does not produce constipation or loss of appetite; on the contrary it restores the appetite which had been lost by chronic opium or chloral drinking. (1889, *Lancet*, vol. 1. page 65.)

Dr. Martindale remarks that recently the Cannabis imported had more toxic effects than formerly (this in spite of the fact that a high export duty has been placed upon the drug); it has indeed been stated that toxic symptoms have been produced by doses of the extract within the official limits. According to the "British Pharmacopeia" the dose is $\frac{1}{4}$ to 1 grain. The *Lancet* vol. i, page 1042 (1908), records two interesting cases of toxic symptoms caused by taking overdoses of the tincture.

Antidotes for Cannabis poisoning are the stomach-pump or emetics followed by stimulating draughts of brandy and water or strong coffee, vegetable acids, such as lemon juice or vinegar.

Dr. Robert Hooper in his "Lexicon Medicum" (page 315), published in 1848, says: "Cannabis Indica is a variety of hemp much used in the East as an excitant. The Hindoos call it *Bangue*, the Arabs *Hasheesh*, the Turks *Malach*.

"The leaves are chewed or smoked like those of tobacco and an intoxicating liquor is prepared from them. This plant is also used by the Hottentots who call it *Dacha*.

The following article by Mr. David Hooper, F.C.S., F.L.S. (Curator of the Botanical Gardens at Calcutta) read at the last meeting of the British Pharmaceutical Conference at Aberdeen, throws a certain amount of light on to the commercial side of the question. At the close of the discussion Mr. D. B. Dott, an eminent Scottish Pharmacist, remarked that Professor Stockman had refuse to investigate the drug, s it was useless. Mr. Edmund White, Ph.C., considered that the deterioration of the drug was due to enzymes, and suggested careful storage to preclude enzymic activity.

A PHARMACEUTICAL STUDY

CHARAS OF INDIAN HEMP
BY DAVID HOOPER, F.C.S., F.L.S.

Although "charas" has been properly described as "a foul and crude drug, the use of which is properly excluded from civilised medicine," it is imported into British India to the value of £120,000 per annum, a total exceeding the combined value of all the other medicinal imports, so that it is an article which deserves more than passing notice. Indian hemp (Cannabis Sativa), when grown in the East, secretes an intoxicating resinous matter on the upper leaves and flowering spikes, the exudation being marked in plants growing throughout the Western Himalayas and Turkestan, where charas is prepared as a commercial article. Formerly it was cultivated in fields in Turkestan, but now it is grown as a border around other crops (such as maize), the seeds of both being sown at the same time. A sticky exudation (white when damp and greyish when dry) is found on the upper parts of the plant before the flowers show, and in April and May, when the plants attain a height of 4 or 5 ft. and the seeds ripen, the Cannabis is gathered, after reaping the crops, and stored in a cool, dry place. When dry the powdery resinous substance can be detached by even slight shaking, the dust being collected on a cloth. In some districts the plants are cut close to the roots, suspended head downwards, and the dust or *gard* shaken from them and collected on sheets placed on the floor. The leaves, seeds, etc., are picked out, and sand, etc., separated by passing through a fine sieve, the powder being collected and stored in cloth or skin bags, when it is ready for export. In some villages the charas or extract is made up into small balls, which are collected by the middleman.

On reaching British territory all charas is weighed before the nearest magistrate, by whom it is sealed, a certificate of weight swigned by the Deputy Commissioner being given to the owner. The trader, before leaving the district, obtains a permit allowing him to take the drug to a special market. The zamindars of Chinese Turkestan are the vendors of the drug, the importers being Yarkhandis or Ladakhis, who dispose of it at Hoshiapur and Amritsar principally, returning with piece-goods, or Amritsar merchants who trade with Ladakh. The drug in this way reaches the chief cities of the Punjab during September and October. Thence it is distributed over the Central and United Provinces as far as Bombay and Calcutta, and is used everywhere for smoking. Charas, though a drug, plays the part of money to a great extent in the trade that is carried on at Ladakh, the price of the drug depending on the state of the market, and any fluctuations causing a corresponding increase or decrease in the value of the goods for which it is bartered. The exchange price of charas thus gives rise to much gambling. A pony-load (two pais or three maunds) sells for Rs. 40 or Rs. 50, the cost of transport to Hoshiapur (the chief Punjab depot) is Rs. 100, and there it fetches from Rs. 30 to Rs. 100 per maund. Retail dealers sell small quantities at a price that works out at Rs. 200 to Rs. 500 per maund. Five years ago the Kashgar growers, encouraged by the high prices, sowed a large crop and reaped a bumper harvest, only to find the market already overstocked and prices on the Leh Exchange fallen from Rs. 60 to RS. 30 per maund. The following are

A PHARMACEUTICAL STUDY

the imports of charas from Ladakh and Kashmir between 1904 and 1907:

	1904-5	1905-6	1906-7
Cwt.	2818	2446	2883
Value	Rs. 12,13,860	Rs. 18,39,960	Rs. 22,90,560

Small quantities of charas are made, chiefly for local consumption, in the Himalayan districts of Nepal, Kumaon, and Garhwal, and in Baluchistan. Samples of Baluchistan charas made in the Sarawan division of the Kalat State have been sent to the Indian Museum by Mr. Hughes-Buller.

The following is the mode of preparation.

"The female 'bhang' plants are reaped when they are waist high and charged with seed. The leaves and seeds are separated and half dried. They are then spread on a carpet made of goat's hair, another carpet is spread over them and slightly rubbed. The dust containing the narcotic principle falls off, and the leaves, etc., are removed to another carpet and again rubbed. The first dust is the best quality, and is known as *nup;* the dust from the second shaking is called *tahgalim,* and is of inferior quality. A third shaking gives *gania,* of still lower quality. Each kind of dust is made unto small balls called *gabza,* and kept in cloth bags. The first quality is recognised by the ease with which it melts."

The local rates per tola are: for first quality 2a.5p., second quality 1a.7p., and third quality 11p. Small quantities of charas find their way from Thibet into British and Native Garhwal, and a little is prepared in Simla and Kashmir; while other sources are Nepal and the hill districts of Almora and Garhwal. In preparing Nepal charas, the ganja-plant is squeezed between the palms of the hands, and the sticky resinous substance scraped off. *Momea,* black wax-like cakes, valued at Rs. 10 per seer, and *Shahjehani,* sticks containing portions of leaf, valued at Rs. 3 per seer, are the two kinds of Nepal charas, a few maunds being exported annually to Lucknow and Cawnpore. No charas is made in the plains of India, except a small quantity in Gwalior, the Bengal ganja yielding no charas in all the handling it undergoes in the process of perparation—thus emphasising the fact that the intoxicating secretion is developed in plants growing where the altitude and climate are suitable, as in the Himalayas and Turkestan.

Adulterations.—Aitchison in 1874 stated that no charas of really good quality ever came to Leh, the best charas in the original balls being sent to Bokhara and Kokan. He said the chief adulterant is the mealy covering of the fruits of the wild and cultivated Trebizond date (*Eloeagnus hortensis*). The impression in the United Provinces and the Punjab is that the Yarkhand drug is sophisticated, and a preference is given in some quarters to the Nepal and other Himalayan forms, which command a higher price. The Special Assistant in Kashgar declares there is no advantage in increasing the weight, as when dealers in India buy the drug they test it, otherwise they would pay a heavy duty on the adulterant as well as on the charas itself; so no exporter at present would spoil his charas by adding extraneous substances.

Mr. Hooper added descriptions of samples, namely: Kashgar charas, Yarkhand charas, Baluchistan charas, Gwalior charas, Kumaon charas, Garhwal charas, Nepal charas and Momea charas, from Simla.

Chemical Examination.—The table of analyses appended is taken from the author's report to the Indian Hemp Drug

A PHARMACEUTICAL STUDY

Commission of 1893-4, but a few recent analyses have been added:

Description of Charas	Extract, Alcoholic	Vegetable Matter	Ash Soluble	Sand	Volatile Matter
Yarkhand	40.0	18.2	23.9	11.4	6.5
Amballa "Mashak"	42.7	12.9	12.4	28.2	5.8
Amritsar "Bhara"	38.1	14.9	10.8	29.8	6.4
" "Mashak"	46.5	12.6	10.0	27.3	3.6
Delhi Dust, 12a.	42.4	17.9	9.8	25.9	4.0
" 11. 1a.	42.6	18.8	11.1	23.2	4.3
" "Mashak" 11. 9a.	41.1	11.3	10.7	29.5	7.4
Bombay	36.1	20.2	11.8	27.3	4.6
Gwalior	43.3	27.7	8.2	17.7	3.1
Kumaon (wild)	22.4	52.0	9.2	7.4	9.1
" (cult.)	34.2	46.3	9.0	3.0	7.5
Garhwal	41.9	37.0	7.9	5.5	7.7
Almora	36.9	40.5	10.5	4.6	7.5
Nepal	44.6	35.1	8.2	6.5	5.6
" "Shahjehani"	44.4	37.7	9.6	4.1	4.2
Simla "Momea" . .	37.0	32.0	12.3	9.3	9.4
Baluchistan (1) 1903	22.4	19.9	14.8	38.6	4.3
" (2) "	22.0	35.2	20.8	15.1	6.9
" (3) 1905	24.2	16.0	13.3	39.3	7.2
" (4) " . .	26.0	24.1	9.6	31.0	9.3
" (5) "	24.9	27.3	11.5	25.8	10.5
Kashgar (1)	40.2	21.1	9.2	16.8	12.7
" (2)	40.9	16.3	9.9	20.5	12.4
" (3)	48.1	15.6	8.2	16.1	12.0

According to Fluckiger and Hanbury, charas yields one-fourth to one- third of its weight of amorphous resin, and it has been stated that good samples yield 78 per cent. of resin. It will be seen above that the average yield in the North Indian samples is 40 per cent., the highest being from Kashgar and the lowest from Baluchistan and from Kumaon wild plants, the last-named corresponding to a good sample of ganja.

Physiological Values.—Captain J. F. Evans. I.M.S., Chemical Examiner to the Government of Bengal, also gave results of his physiological tests in the Indian Hemp Drug Commission's Proceedings for 1893-4. His experiments were made with alcoholic extracts, and only one sample --- Amritsar best charas --- approached in definite physiological effects the extract, taken as a standard, prepared from Bengal ganja. The following are the values compared with that of Amritsar mashak, designated as 32:

Amritsar Mashak.	32	Bombay	4
Delhi Mashak	24	Amballa Mashak	2
Amballa Mashak.	23	Delhi dust	2
Garhwal.	21	Kumaon wild	1
Delhi dust (2nd)	20	Kumaon cultivated	1
Amritsar Bhara	19	Gwalior	1

so that the best Amritsar charas is thirty-two times as potent as the Gwalior product, the latter from plants grown in the plains, while the amount of alcoholic extract bears no relation to the physiological activity of the drug.

Professor Greenish in his well-known work on *Materia Medica* says the Cannabis Indica is an annual dioecious herb indigenous to Central and Western Asia, but largely cultivated in temperate countries for its strong fibres (hemp) and its oily seed (hemp-seed) and in tropical countries also for the resinous secretions which it there produces. The secretion possesses very valuable and powerful medicinal properties; but it is not produced in the plant when grown in temperate climates; on the other hand the fibre of the plant under the latter condition is much stronger than that of the tropical plant.

The hemp plant grown in India differs, however, in certain

A PHARMACEUTICAL STUDY

particulars from that grown in Europe; and the plant was formerly considered a distinct species and named Cannabis Indica, but this opinion is now abandoned.

The cultivation of hemp for its seed and fibre dates from very remote periods. It was used as an intoxicant by the Persians and Arabians in the eleventh and twelfth centuries and probably much earlier, but was not introduced into European medicine until the year 1838. For medicinal use it is grown in the districts of Bogra and Rajshaki to the North of Calcutta and westward, thence through central India to Gujerat. Very good qualities of the drug are purchased in Madras, but the European market is chiefly supplied with inferior grades from Ghalapur.

The pistillate plants by which alone the resin is secreted in any quantity are pruned to produce flowering branches, the tops of these flowering branches are collected, allowed to wilt, and then pressed by treading them under the feet into more or less compact masses. This forms the drug known as "ganjah," or (on the London market) Guaza.

The larger leaves are collected separately; when dried they are known as "bhang."

During the manipulations to which the plant is subjected in preparing the drug, a certain quantity of the resin is separated; it is collected and forms the drug known as "charas" (Churrus). Charas is also prepared by rubbing ganjah between the hands or by men in leather garments brushing against the growing plants, in any case separating part of the active adhesive resin; hence the official description limits the drug to that from which the resin has not been removed.

All these forms of the drug are largely used in India for producing an agreeable form of intoxication; ganjah and charas are smoked, while bhang is used to prepare a drink or sweetmeat.

The drug has a powerful odour, but is almost devoid of taste.

Numerous attempts have been made to isolate the active constituent of Indian hemp; it is not possible here to do more than allude to the chief late ones.

In 1881 Siebold and Bradbury isolated a thick yellowish oily liquid which they termed *Cannabinine* and their results were confirmed in 1884 by Warden and Waddell.

In 1894 Robert separated a dark red syrupy mass possessing intoxicating properties and in 1896 Wood, Spivey, and Easterfield obtained from charas under reduced pressure certain inactive terpenes and a viscous resin *Cannabinol* which when warmed melts to an oily liquid. Cannabinol when taken internally induces delirium and sleep, and, as far as at present known, is the intoxicating constituent of Indian hemp.

In addition to this principle Matthew Hay in 1883 obtained colourless crystals of an alkaloid *tetano-cannabine* which in physiological action resembled strychnine.

Cannabis Indica was formerly used as a hypnotic and anodyne but is uncertain in its action.

It is administered in mania and hysteria as an anodyne and antispasmodic.

Mr. E. M. Holmes, F.L.S., Curator of the Pharmaceutical Society's Museum, writing on the subject of Cannabis Indica says "The Dervishes make a preparation by macerating the resinous type in almond oil and give a small quantity of it in soup to produced prolonged sleep."

A PHARMACEUTICAL STUDY

A strong dose of Cannabis produces curious hallucinations abolishing temporarily the ideas of time and distance; but the ordinary drug as imported is never the current crop, which the Hindoos keep for their own use. The active principle Cannabinol (as far as is known) rapidly oxidises and loses its properties so that if a really active preparation is required, it is best to get it made in India, using absolute alcohol and the fresh tops, or recently made charas, which, being a solid mass, does not readily oxidise.

Before closing it might be well to notice in detail the final investigations made by Messrs. Wood, Spivey, and Easterfield.

The following is re-printed from the "Proceedings of the Chemical Society" for 1897-8, and is to be found on page 66.

CANNABINOL

"The Authors have continued their examination of Cannabinol, the toxic resinous constituent of Indian Hemp (Trans. 1896, 69, 539).

"The substance boils with slight decomposition at about 400° its absorption spectrum shows no characteristic bands, its vapour-density at the temperature of boiling Sulphur corresponds with the formula $C_{18}H_{24}O_2$ already assigned to the compound.

"An account is given of the reaction of Cannabinol with Acetic Anhydride, benzoyl Chloride and phosphoric Anhydride; the results indicate that one hydroxyl group is present. In the case of Acetic Anhydride or Acetyl chloride, however, a crystalline compound melting at 75° is one of the products of the reaction. The Authors assign the formula $C_{15}H_{18}O_2$ to this compound. The same compound has recently been described by Dunstan and Henry (Proc. 1898, 14, 44, Feb. 17), who ascribe the formula $C_{18}H_{22}OAc$ to it, fuming hydriodic Acid gives no methyl or ethyl iodide when boiled with Cannabinol. Reduction with hydrodic Acid in sealed tubes produces a hydro-carbon, $C_{10}H_{20}$.

"By long boiling with or without dehydrating agents a hydro-carbon $C_{10}H_{16}$ is formed.

"Oxidation with aqueous chromic acid, alkaline or acid permanganate or dilute nitric acid is accompanied by the production of a caproic acid, lower fatty acids being probably produced at the same time. The action of fuming nitric acid upon cannabinol dissolved in cold glacial acetic acid removes one carbon atom as carbonic anhydride, and produces a red amorphous substance which gives numbers on analysis agreeing with the formula $C_{17}H_{20}N_2O_6$.

"This substance when boiled with nitric acid yields a light-red substance $C_{17}H_{20}N_2O_8$ which upon further oxidation yields among other substances a yellow acid crystalline compound $C_{13}H_{15}N_2O_5$, which forms sparingly soluble crystalline sodium, ammonium and silver salts and is probably a dinitrophenol, and a compound $C_{11}H_{11}NO_4$, the properties of which agree closely with those of the oxycannabin of Bolas and Francis (*Chemical News* 1871, 24, 77).

"This compound has the properties of a nitro-lactone, as has already been shown by Dunstan and Henry.

"Corresponding crystalline potassium and silver Salts have been prepared and analysed. The name Cannabinic Acid is proposed for the unnitrated parent oxy-acid.

A PHARMACEUTICAL STUDY

"Amido-Cannabinolactone, $C_{11}H_{11}O_2NH_2$ is obtained in colourless crystals melting at 119° when the nitro-lactone is reduced either by hydriodic acid, or by tin and hydrochloric acid.

"The base is readily re-crystallised from hot water, its salts cannot be recrystalised from water without decomposition; the hydriodide and the platinochloride have been analysed."

In a later paper read before the Chemical Society Messrs. Wood, Spivey, and Easterfield (Proc. Chem. Soc. 1897-8, page 184) say:

"The oily lactone prepared from nitrocannabinolactone (oxycannabin) is shown to be a metatolybutyrlactone, oxycannabin being the corresponding nitroderivative.

"By the oxidation of Cannabinolactone a lactonic acid is produced which on fusion with potash yields isophthalic acid. Nitrocannabinolactonic acid is obtained by oxidising oxycannabin either by nitric acid in sealed tubes or by potassium permanganate. The volatile fatty acids produced on oxidising Cannabinol by nitric acid are shown to be normal butyric (Dunstan and Henry, Proc. Chem. Soc. 1898, 14, 44) normal valeric and normal caproic acids, Valeric acid being formed in largest amount."

Through the courtesy of Messrs. Parke, Davis and Co., manufacturing chemists of London and Detroit, Michigan, U.S.A., we are enabled to reproduce a clear pharmacological study of the drug by E. M. Houghton, Ph.C., M.D.; and H. C. Hamilton, M.S. (Excerpt from an article in the *American Journal of Pharmacy* for January 1908.)

From several samples of Cannabis Americana fluid

extracts and solid extracts were prepared according to the U.S.P., and were tested upon animals for physiological activity.

The method of assay, which has previously been called to the attention of this Society, is that which one of us (Houghton) devised and has employed for the past twelve years. This method consists essentially in the careful observation of the physiological effects produced upon dogs from the internal administration of the preparation of the drug under test. It is necessary in selecting the test animals to pick out those that are easily susceptible to the action of the Cannabis, since dogs as well as human beings vary considerably in their reaction to the drug. Also, preliminary tests should be made upon the animals before they are finally selected for test purposes, in order that we may know exactly how they behave under given conditions. After the animals have been finally selected and found to respond to the standard test dose, 0.01 Gm. per kilo, they are set aside for this particular work, care being taken to have them well fed, well housed, and in every way kept under the best sanitary conditions. Usually we have found it desirable to keep two or more of the approved animals on hand at all times, so there may not be delay in testing samples as they come in.

In applying the test, the standard dose (in form of solid extract for convenience) is administered internally in a small capsule. The dog's tongue is drawn forward between the teeth with the left hand and the capsule placed on the back part of the tongue with the right hand. The tongue is then quickly released and the capsule is swallowed with ease. In order that the drug may be rapidly absorbed, food should be withheld for twenty-four hours before the test and an efficient cathartic given if needed.

Within a comparatively short time the dog begins to show the characteristic action of the drug. There are three typical effects to be noticed from active extracts on susceptible animals: first a stage excitability, then a stage of inco-ordination, followed by a period of drowsiness. The first of these is so dependent on the characteristics of the dog used that it is of little value for judging the activity of the drug, while with only a few exceptions the second, or the stage of inco-ordination, invariably follows in one or two hours; the dog loses control of its legs and of the muscles supporting its head, so that when nothing occurs to attract its attention its head will droop, its body sway, and, when severely affected, the animal will stagger and fall, the intoxication being peculiarly suggestive and striking.

Experience is necessary on the part of the observer to determine just when the physiological effects of the drug begin to manifest themselves, since there is always, as in the case of many chemical tests, a personal factor to be guarded against. When an active extract is given to a susceptible animal, in the smallest dose that will produce any perceptible effect, one must watch closely for the slightest trace of incoordination, lack of attention, or drowsiness. It is particularly necessary for the animals to be confined in a room there nothing will excite them, since when their attention is drawn to anything of interest the typical effect of the drug may disappear.

The influence of the test dose of the unknown drug is carefully compared with that of the same dose of the standard preparation administered to another test dog at the same time and under the same conditions.

Finally, when the animals become drowsy, the observations are recorded and the animals are returned to their quarters.

The second day following, the observations upon the two dogs are reversed, *i.e.*, the animal receiving the test dose of the unknown receives a test dose of the known, and *vice versa*, and a second observation is made. If one desires to make a very accurate quantitative determination, it is advisable to use, not two dogs, but four or five, and to study the effects of the test dose of the unknown specimen in comparison with the test dose of the known, making several observations on alternate days. If the unknown is below standard activity, the amount should be increased until the effect produced is the same as for the test dose of the standard. If the unknown is above strength, the test dose is diminished accordingly. From the dose of the unknown selected as producing the same action as the test dose of the standard, the amount of dilution or concentration necessary is determined. The degree of accuracy with which the test is carried out will depend largely upon the experience of the observer and the care he exercises.

Another point to be noted in the use of dogs for standardising Cannabis is that, although they never appear to lose their susceptibility, the same dogs cannot be used indefinitely for accurate testing. After a time they become so accustomed to the effects of the drug they refuse to stand on their feet, and so do not show the typical inco-ordination which is its most characteristic and constant action.

Previous to the adoption of the physiological test over twelve years ago, we were often annoyed by complaints of physicians that certain lots of drugs were inert; in fact some hospitals, before accepting their supplies of hemp preparations, asked for samples in order to make rough tests upon their patients before ordering. Since the adoption of the test we have not had a well-authenticated report of inactivity, although many tons of the various preparations of Cannabis Indica have been tested and supplied for medicinal purposes.

At the beginning of our observations careful search of the literature on the subject was made to determine the toxicity of the hemp. Not a single case of fatal poisoning have we been able to find reported, although often alarming symptoms may occur. A dog weighting 25 pounds received an injection of two ounces of an active U.S.P. fluid extract in the jugular vein with the expectation that it would certainly be sufficient to produce death. To our surprise the animal, after being unconscious for about a day and a half, recovered completely. This dog received, not alone the active constituents of the drug, but also the amount of alcohol contained in the fluid extract. Another dog received about 7 grammes of Solid Extract Cannabis with the same result. We have never been able to give an animal a sufficient quantity of a U.S.P. or other preparation of the Cannabis (Indica Americana) to produce death.

There is some variation in the amount of extractive obtained, as would be expected from the varying amount of stems, seeds, etc., in the different samples. Likewise there is a certain amount of variation in the physiological action, but in every case the administration of 0.01 gramme of the extract per kilo body weight, has elicited the characteristic symptoms in properly selected animals.

THE EQUINOX

The repeated tests we have made convince us that Cannabis Americana properly grown and cured is fully as active as the best Indian drug.

Furthermore, we have placed our quantities of fluid extract and solid extract of Cannabis Americana in the hands of experienced clinicians, and from eight of these men, who are all large users of the drug, we have received reports which state that they are unable to determine any therapeutic difference between the Cannabis Americana and the Cannabis Indica.

CONCLUSIONS

1. The method, outlined in the paper, for determining the physiological activity of Cannabis Sativa by internal administration to especially selected dogs, has been found reliable when the standard dose of extract 0.01 gramme per kilo body weight, is tested on animals, the effects being noted by an experienced observe in comparison with the effects of the same quantity of a standard preparation.

2. Cannabis Sativa, when grown in various localities of the United States and Mexico, is found to be fully as active as the best imported Indian-grown Cannabis Sativa, as shown by laboratory and clinical tests.

Much has been written relative to the comparative activity of Cannabis Sativa grown in different climates (Cannabis Indica, Mexicana and Americana). It has been generally assumed that the American-grown drug was practically worthless therapeutically, and that Cannabis Sativa grown in India must be used if one would obtain physiologically active preparations.

A PHARMACEUTICAL STUDY

Furthermore, it has been claimed that the best Indian drug is that grown especially for medicinal purposes, the part used consisting of the flowering tops of the unfertilised female plants, care being taken during the growing of the drug to weed out the male plants. According to our experience, this is an erroneous notion, as we have repeatedly found that the Indian drug which contains large quantities of seed is fully as active as the drug which consists of the flowering tops only, provided the seed be removed before percolation.

Several years ago we began a systematic investigation of American-grown Cannabis Sativa. Samples from a number of localities were obtained and carefully investigated. From these samples fluid and solid extracts were prepared according to the Pharmacopoeial method, and carefully tested upon animals for physiological activity, and eventually they were standardised by physiological methods. Repeated tests have convinced us that Cannabis Americana properly grown and cured is fully as active as the best Indian drug, while on the other hand we have frequently found Indian Cannabis to be practically inert.

Before marketing preparations of Cannabis Americana, however, we placed specimens of the fluid and solid extracts in the hands of experienced clinicians for practical test; and from these men, all of whom had used large quantities of Cannabis Indica in practice, we have received reports which affirm that they have been unable to determine any therapeutic difference between Cannabis Americana and Cannabis Indica. We are, therefore, of the opinion that Cannabis Americana, will be found equally as efficient as, and perhaps more uniformly reliable than Cannabis Indica obtained from abroad, since it is evident that with a source of supply at our very doors proper precautions can be taken to obtain crude drug of the best quality.

The proper botanical name of the drug under consideration is Cannabis Sativa. The Indian plant was formerly supposed to be a distinct species *per se*, but botanists now consider the two plants to be identical. The old name of Cannabis Indica, however, has been retained in medicine. Cannabis Indica simply means Cannabis Sativa grown in the Indies, and Cannabis Americana means Cannabis Sativa grown in America. Its introduction into Western medicine dates from the beginning of the last century, but it has been used as an intoxicant in Asiatic countries from time immemorial, and under the name of "hashish," "bhang," "ganja," or "charas," is habitually consumed by upwards of two hundred millions of human beings.

The physiological action of Cannabis Americana is precisely the same as that of Cannabis Inidca. The effects of this drug are said to be due chiefly to its action upon the central nervous system. It first produces a state of excitement similar to that of the initial stage of acute alcoholism. This excitement of the motor areas and other lower centres in the brain, according to W. E. Dixon, of the University of Cambridge, "is not the result of direct stimulation of these, but is due to depression of the highest and controlling centres. At all events there is a depression of the highest centres, and this is shown by diminished efficiency in the performance of mental work, by inability to concentrate attention, and by feeble judgment." In lower animals the effects of Cannabis Indica resemble those in man, and present the same variations. A stage of exaltation with increased movements is sometimes present, and is followed by depression, lassitude and sleep. Reflex excitability is first increased and then diminished. Cannabis Indica differs from opium in producing no disturbance of digestion and no constipation. The heart is generally accelerated in man when the drug is smoked. Its intravenous injection into animals slows the pulse, partly through inhibitory stimulation and partly through direct action upon the heart muscle. The pupil is generally somewhat dilated. Death from acute poisoning is extremely rare, and recovery has occurred after enormous doses. The continued abuse of hashish by natives of the East sometimes leads to mania and dementia, but does not cause the same disturbance of nutrition that opium does; and the habitual use of small quantities, which is almost universal in some Eastern countries, does not appear to be detrimental to health.

Cannabis Americana is employed for the same medicinal purposes as Cannabis Indica, which is frequently used as a hypnotic in cases of sleeplessness, in nervous exhaustion, and as a sedative in patients suffering from pain. Its greatest use has perhaps been in the treatment of various nervous and mental diseases, although it is found as an ingredient in many cough mixtures. In general, Cannabis Americana can be used when a mild hypnotic or sedative is indicated, as it is said not to disturb digestion, and it produces no subsequent nausea and depression. It is of use in cases of migraine, particularly when opium in contra-indicated. It is recommended in paralysis agitans to quiet the tremors, in spasm of the bladder, and in sexual impotence not the result of organic disease, especially in combination with nux vomica and ergot.

The ordinary dosage is:
Extractum Cannabis Americanae, 0.01 gramme (1.5 grain).
Fluidextractum Cannabis Americanae, 0.05 cc. (1 minim).

The dosage of Cannabis Americana is the same as that of Cannabis Indica, as from our experiments we find that there is no therapeutic difference in the physiological action of the two drugs.

Cannabis Sativa, when grown in the United States (Cannabis Americana) under careful precautions, is found to be fully as active as the best imported Indian-grown Cannabis Sativa, as shown by the laboratory and clinical tests. The advantages of using carefully prepared solid and fluid extracts of the home-grown drug are apparent when it is considered that every step of the process, from planting of the drug to the final marketing of the finished product, is under the supervision of experts. The imported drug varies extremely in activity and much of it is practically inert or flagrantly adulterated.

The writer desires to acknowledge the able assistance given him in preparing the above notes by Mr. E. M. Holmes, F.L.S., and Mr. S. Jamieson, M.P.S. (Messrs. Parke, Davis and Co.) Readers acquiring further information on the subject are referred to the British Pharmaceutical Codex (1907) and Squire's "Companion to the British Pharmacopoeia," recently published.

A PHARMACEUTICAL STUDY

REFERENCES

Marshall, London *Lancet*, 1897, i. p. 235.
Dixon, *British Medical Journal*, 1899, ii p. 136.
Fraenkel, *Arch. f. exp. Path. u. Pharm.* xlix, p. 266.
Cushny, "Textbook of Pharmacology," 1906, p. 232.
Houghton and Hamilton, *Am. Jour. Pharm.*, January 1908.
Transactions Chem. Society, 1896, 69, 539.
Proceedings Chem. Soc. 1898, 14, 44, Feb. 17; *Ibid.* 1898, p. 184.
Squires, "Companion to British Pharmacopoeia," 1908.
Martindale's "Extra Pharmacopeia," 1908.
Hooper's "Medical Dictionary."
Chemist and Druggist.

E. WHINERAY, M.P.S., ETC.

SPECIAL SUPPLEMENT

JOHN ST. JOHN

THE RECORD OF THE MAGICAL RETIREMENT OF G. H. FRATER O∴M∴

PREFACE

NOBODY is better aware than myself that this account of my Retirement labours under most serious disadvantages.

The scene should have been laid in an inaccessible lamaserai in Tibet, perched on stupendous crags; and my familiarity with Central Asia would have enabled me to do it quite nicely.

One should really have had an attendant Sylph; and one's Guru, a man of incredible age and ferocity, should have frequently appeared at the dramatic moment.

A gigantic magician on a coal-black steed would have added to the effect: strange voices, uttering formidable things, should have issued from unfathomable caverns. A mountain shaped like a Svastika with a Pillar of Flame would have been rather taking; herds of impossible yaks, ghost-dogs, gryphons. ...

But my good, friends, this is not the way things happen. Paris is as wonderful as Lhassa, and there are just as many miracles in London as in Luang Prabang.

I did not even think it necessary to go into the Bois de Boulogne and meet those Three Adepts who cause bleeding at the nose, familiar to us from the writings of Macgregor Mathers.

THE EQUINOX

The Universe of Magic is in the mind of a man: the setting is but Illusion even to the thinker.

Humanity is progressing; formerly men dwelt habitually in the exterior world; nothing less than giants and Paynim and men-at-arms and distressed ladies, vampires and succubi, could amuse them. Their magicians brought demons from the smoke of blood, and made gold from baser metals.

In this they succeeded; the intelligent perceived that the gold and the lead were but shadows of thought. It became probable that the elements were but isomers of one element; matter was seen to be but a modification of mind, or (at least) that the two things matter and mind must be joined before either could be perceived. All knowledge comes through the senses, on the one hand; on the other, it is only through the senses that knowledge comes.

We then continue our conquest of matter; and we are getting pretty expert. It took much longer to perfect the telescope than the motor-car. And though, of course, there are limitations, we know enough to be able to predict them.

We know in what progression the Power to Speed coefficient of a steamboat rises—and so on.

But in our conquest of Nature, which we are making principally by the use of the rational intelligence of the mind, we have become aware of that world itself, so much so that educated men spend nine-tenths of their waking lives in that world, only descending to feed and dress and so on at the imperative summons of their physical constitution.

Now to us who thus live the world of mind seems almost as savage and unexplored as the world of Nature seemed to the Greeks.

JOHN ST. JOHN

There are countless worlds of wonder unpath'd and uncomprehended—and even unguessed, we doubt not.

Therefore we set out diligently to explore and map these

<blockquote>untrodden regions of the mind.</blockquote>

Surely our adventures may be as exciting as those of Cortes or Cook!

It is for this reason that I invite with confidence the attention of humanity to this record of my journey.

But another set of people will find another disappointment. I am hardly an heroic figure. I am not The Good Young Man That Died. I do not remain in holy meditation, balanced on my left eyelash, for forty years, restoring exhausted nature by a single grain of rice at intervals of several months.

You will perceive in these pages a man with all his imperfections thick upon him trying blindly, yet with all his force, to control the thoughts of his mind, so that he shall be able to say "I will think this thought and not that thought" at any moment, as easily as (having conquered Nature) we are all able to say "I will drink this wine, and not that wine."

For, as we have now learnt, our happiness does not at all depend upon our possessions or our power. We would all rather be dead than be a millionaire who lives in daily dread of murder or blackmail.

Our happiness depends upon our state of mind. It is the mastery of these things that the Magicians of to-day have set out to obtain for humanity; they will not turn back, or turn aside.

THE EQUINOX

It is with the object of giving the reins into the hands of others that I have written this record, not without pain.

Others, reading it, will see the sort of way one sets to work; they will imitate and improve upon it; they will attain to the Magistry; they will prepare the Red Tincture and the Elixir of Life—for they will discover what Life means.

PROLOGUE

IT hath appeared unto me fitting to make a careful and even an elaborate record of this Great Magical Retirement, for that in the first place I am now certain of obtaining some Result therefrom, as I was never previously certain.

Previous records of mine have therefore seemed vague and obscure, even unto the wisest of the scribes; and I am myself afraid that even here all my skill of speech and study may avail me little, so that the most important part of the record will be blank.

Now I cannot tell whether it is a part of my personal Kamma, or whether the Influence of the Equinox of Autumn should be the exciting cause; but it has usually been at this part of the year that my best Results have occurred. It may be that the physical health induced by the summer in me, who dislike damp and chill, may being forth as it were a flower the particular kind of Energy—Sammaváyamo—which gives alike the desire to perform more definitely and exclusively the Great Work, and the capacity to achieve success.

It is in any case remarkable that I was born in October (18—); suffered the terrible mystic trance which turned me toward the Path in October (18—); applied for admission to G∴ D∴ in October (18—); opened my temple at B——e in

October (18—); received the mysteries of L.I.L. in October (19—); and obtained the grade of $6° = 5°$; obtained the first true mystic results in October (19—); first landed in Egypt in October (19—); landed again in Egypt in October (19—); first parted from . . . in October (19—); wrote the B.-i-M. in October (19—), and obtained the grade of $7° = 4°$; received the great Initiation in October 19-; and, continuing, received . . . . in October 19—.

So then in the last days of September 19— do I begin to collect and direct my thoughts; gently, subtly, persistently turning them one and all to the question of retreat and communion with that which I have agreed to call the Holy Guardian Angel, whose Knowledge and Conversation I have willed, and in greater or less measure enjoyed, since Ten Years.

Terrible have been the ordeals of the Path; I have lost all that I possessed, and all that I love, even as at the Beginning I offered All for Nothing, unwitting as I was of the meaning of those words. I have suffered many and grievous things at the hands of the elements, and of the planets; hunger, thirst, fatigue, disease, anxiety, bereavement, all those woes and others have laid heavy hand upon me, and behold! as I look back upon these years, I declare that all hath been very well. For so great is the Reward which I (unworthy) have attained that the Ordeals seem but incidents hardly worthy to mention, save in so far as they are the Levers by which I moved the World. Even those dreadful periods of "dryness" and of despair seem but the necessary lying fallow of the Earth. All those "false paths" of Magic and Meditation and of Reason were not false paths, but steps upon the true Path; even a a tree must shoot downwards its roots into the Earth in order that it may flower, and bring forth fruit in its season.

So also now I know that even in my months of absorption in worldly pleasure and business, I am not really there, but stand behind, preparing the Event.

Imagine me, therefore, if you will, in Paris on the last day of September. How surprised was I—though, had I thought, I should have remembered that it was so—to find all my necessary magical apparatus to my hand! Months before, for quite other reasons, I had moved most of my portable property to Paris; now I go to Paris, not thinking of a Retirement, for I now know enough to trust my destiny to bring all things to pass without anxious forethought on my part—and suddenly, therefore, here do I find myself—and nothing is lacking.

I determined therefore to begin steadily and quietly, allowing the Magical Will to come slowly forth, daily stronger, in contrast to my old plan, desperation kindling a store of fuel dried by long neglect, despair inflaming a mad energy that would blaze with violence for a few hours and then go out—and nothing done. "Not hurling, according to the oracle, a transcendent foot towards Piety."

Quite slowly and simply therefore did I wash myself and robe myself as laid down in the Goetia, taking the Violet Robe of an Exempt Adept (being a single Garment), wearing the Ring of an Exempt Adept, and that Secret Ring which hath been entrusted to my keeping by the Masters. Also I took the Almond Wand of Abramelin and the Secret Tibetan Bell, made of Electrum Magicum with its striker of human bone. I took also the magical knife, and the holy Anointing Oil of Abramelin the Mage.

I began then quite casually by performing the Lesser Banishing Ritual of the Pentagram, finding to my great joy and some surprise that the Pentagrams instantly formulated themselves, visible to the material eye as it were bars of shining blackness deeper than the night.

I then consecrated myself to the Operation; cutting the Tonsure upon my head, a circle, as it were to admit the light of infinity: and cutting the cross of blood upon my breast, thus symbolising the equilibration of and the slaying of the body, while loosing the blood, the first projection in matter of the universal Fluid.

The whole formulating the Ankh—the Key of Life!

I gave moreover the signs of the grades from $0°=0°$ to $7°=4°$.

Then did I take upon myself the Great Obligation as follows:

    I. I, O.M. &c., a member of the Body of God, hereby bind myself on behalf of the whole Universe, even as we are now physically bound unto the cross of suffering:

   II. that I will lead a pure life, as a devoted servant of the Order:

  III. that I will understand all things:

  IV. that I will love all things

   V. that I will perform all things and endure all things

  VI. that I will continue in the Knowledge and Conversation of My Holy Guardian Angel:

 VII. that I will work without attachment:

    VIII. that I will work in truth:
      IX. that I will rely only upon myself:
       X. that I will interpret every phenomenon as a particular dealing of God with my soul.

And if I fail herein, may my pyramid be profaned, and the Eye be closed upon me!

All this did I swear and seal with a stroke upon the Bell.

Then I steadily sat down in my Asana (or sacred Posture), having my left heel beneath my body pressing into the anus, my right sole closely covering the phallus, the right leg vertical; my head, neck, and spine in one straight vertical line; my arms stretched out resting on their respective knees; my thumbs joined each to the fourth finger of the proper hand. All my muscles were tightly held; my breath came steady, slow and even through both nostrils; my eyes were turned back, in, up to the Third Eye; my tongue was rolled back in my mouth; and my thoughts, radiating from that Third Eye, I strove to shut in unto an ever narrowing sphere by concentrating my will upon the Knowledge and Conversation of the Holy Guardian Angel.

Then I struck Twelve times upon the Bell; with the new month the Operation was duly begun.

Oct. 1.   *The First Day*

    At Eight o'clock I rose from sleep and putting on my Robe, began a little to meditate. For several reasons—the journey and business of the day before, etc., etc., I did not feel fresh. But forcing myself a little I rose and went out to the Caf du Dôme where I took coffee and a biroche, after buying an exercise book in which to write this record.

This was about 8.45; and now (10.10) I have written thus far. [Including the Prologue, but not the Preface.—ED.]

10.45. I have driven over to the Hammam through the beautiful sunshine, meditating upon the discipline of the Operation.

It seems only necessary to cut off definitely dispersive things, aimless chatter and such; for the Operation itself will guide one, leading to disgust for too much food and so on. It there by upon my limbs any chain that requires a definite effort to break it, perhaps sleep is that chain. But we shall see—*solvitur ambulando*. If any asceticism be desirable later on, true wariness will soon detect any danger, and devise a means to meet it and overcome it.

12.0. Have finished bath and massage, during which I continued steadily but quite gently, "not by a strain laborious and hurtful but with stability void of movement," willing the Presence of Adonai.

12.5. I ordered a dozen oysters and a beefsteak, and now (12.10) find myself wishing for an apple chewed and swallowed by deglutition, as the Hatha Yogis do. The distaste for food has already begun.

12.12. Impressions already *failing to connect*.

I was getting into Asana and thinking "I record this fact," when I saw a jockey being weighed.

12.12. I thought of recording *my own* weight which I had not taken.
Good!

12.13. Pranayama [10 seconds to breath in, 20 seconds to
12.24. breathe out, 30 seconds to hold in the breath.] Fairly good; made me sweat again thoroughly. Stopped not from fatigue but from lunch.
[Odd memoranda during lunch.
Insist on pupils writing down their whole day; the play as well as the work. "By this means they will become ashamed, and prate no longer of 'beasts.' "]
I am now well away on the ascetic current, devising all sorts of privations and thoroughly enjoying the idea.

12.55. Having finished a most enjoyable lunch, will drink coffee and smoke, and try and get a little sleep. Thus to break up sleep into two shifts.

2.18. A nice sleep. Woke refreshed.

3.15. Am arrived home, having performed a little business and driven back.
Will sit down and do Asana, etc.

3.20. Have started.

3.28. 7 Pranayama cycles enough. Doubtless the big lunch is a nuisance.
I continue meditating simply.

3.36. Asana hurts badly, and I can no longer concentrate at all. Must take 5 minutes' rest and then persevere.

3.41. Began again. I shall take "Hua allalu alazi lailaha illa hua" for mantra [any sacred sentence, whose constant repetition produces many strange effects upon the mind.—ED.] if I want one, or: may Adonai reveal unto me a special mantra to invoke Him!

3.51. Broke down again, mantra and all.

3.52-
4.14. Went on meditating in "Hanged Man posture" [Legs crossed, arms below head, like the figure of the Hanged Man in the Tarot Cards.—ED.] to formulate sacrifice and pain self-inflicted; for I feel such a worm, able only to remain a few minutes at a time in a position long since "conquered." For this reason too I cut again the Cross of Blood; and now a third time will I do it. And I will take out the Magical Knife and sharpen it yet more, so that this body may fear me; for that I am Horus the terrible, the Avenger, the Lord of the Gate of the West.

4.15-
4.30. Read Ritual DCLXXI. [The nature of this Ritual is explained later.—ED.]

5.10 I have returned from my shopping. Strange how solemn and dignified so trivial a thing becomes, once one has begun to concentrate!

I bought two pears, half a pound of Garibaldi biscuits, and a packet of Gaufrettes. I had a citron pressé, too, at the Dôme.

At the risk of violating the precepts of Zoroaster 170 and 144 I propose to do a Tarot divination for this Operation.

5.10. I should explain first that I write this record for other eyes than mine, since I am now sufficiently sure of myself to attain something or other; but I cannot foretell exactly what form the attainment may take. Just so, if one goes to call upon a friend, he may be walking or riding or sleeping.

Thus, then, is Adonai hidden from me. I know where He lives; I know I shall be welcome if I call; but I do not know whether He will invite me to a banquet or ask me to go out with him for a long journey.

It may be that the Rota will give me some hint.

[We have omitted the details of this divination.—ED.]

I am never content with such divinations; trustworthy enough in material concerns, in the things of the Spirit one rarely obtains good results.

The first operation was rather meaningless; but one must allow (*a*) that it was a new way of dealing those cards for the opening of an operation; (*b*) that I had had two false starts.

The final operation is certainly most favourable; we shall see if it comes true. I can hardly believe it possible.

6.10. Will now go for a stroll, get some milk, and settle down for the evening.

10.50. I regret to have to announce that on going across to the Dôme with this laudable intention, Nina brought up that red-headed bundle of mischief, Maryt Waska. This being in a way a "bandobast" (and so inviolable), I took her to dinner, eating an omelette, and

10.50. some bread and Camembert, and a little milk. Afterwards a cup of coffee, and then two hours of the Vajroli Mudra badly performed.
All this I did with reluctance, as an act of self-denial or asceticism, lest my desire to concentrate on the mystic path should run away with me.
Therefore I think it may fairly be counted unto me for righteousness.
I now drink a final coffee and retire, to do I hope a more straightforward type of meditation.
So mote it be.
Naked, Maryt looks like Corregio's Antiope. Her eyes are a strange grey, and her hair a very wonderful reddish gold—a colour I have never seen before and cannot properly describe. She has Jewish blood in her, I fancy; this, and her method of illustrating the axiom "Post coitum animal triste" made me think of Baudelaire's "Une nuit que j'etais prés d'une affreuse Juive": and the last line

> Obscurcir la splendeur des tres froides prunelles.

and Barbey d'Aurevilly's "Rideau Cramoisi" suggested to me the following poem. [We omit this poem.—ED.]

11.30. Done! i' th' rough! i' th' rough! Now let me go back to my room, and Work!

(11.47.) Home—undressed—robed—attended to toilet—cut cross of Blood once more to affirm mastery of Body—sat down at 11.49 and ended the day with 10 Pranayamas, which caused me to perspire freely, but were not altogether easy or satisfactory.

JOHN ST. JOHN

The Second Day

The Stroke of Twelve found me duly in my Asana, practising Pranayama.
Let me continue this work; for it is written that unto the persevering mortal the Blessed Immortals are swift...
What then should happen to a persevering Immortal like myself?

12.7. Trying meditation and mantra.

12.18. I find thoughts impossible to concentrate; and my Asana, despite various cowardly attempts to "fudge" it, is frightfully painful.

12.20. In the Hanged Man posture, meditating and willing the Presence of Adonai by the Ritual "Thee I invoke, the Bornless One" and mental formulæ.

12.28. I'm hopelessly sleepy! Invocation as bad as bad could be—attention all over the place. Irrational hallucinations, such as a vision of either Eliphaz Levi or my father (I can't swear which!) at the most solemn moment!
But the irrational character of said visions is not bad. They come from nowhere; it is much worse when your own controlled brain breaks loose.

12.33. I will therefore compose myself to sleep: is it not written that He giveth unto His beloved even in sleep? "Others, even in sleep, He makes fruitful from His own strength."

7.29. Woke and forced myself to rise. I had a number of rather pleasing dreams, as I seem to remember. But their content is gone from me; and, in the absence of the prophet Daniel, I shall let the matter slide.

7.44. Pranayama. 13 cycles. Very tiring; I began to sweat. A mediocre performance.

8.0–8.20. Breakfast. Hatha Yogi—a pear and two gaufrettes.

8.53. Have been meditating in Hanged Man position. Thought dull and wandering; yet once "the conception of the Glowing Fire" seen as a planet (perhaps Mars). Just enough to destroy the concentration; then it went out, dammit!

10.40. Have attended to correspondence and other business and drunk a citron pressé.
The Voice of the Nadi began to resound.

10.50. Have done "Bornless One" in Asana. Good; yet I am filled with utter despair at the hopelessness of the Task. Especially do I get the Buddhist feeling, not only that Asana is intensely painful, but that all conceivable positions of the body are so.

11.0. Still sitting; quite sceptical; sticking to it just because I am a man, and have decided to go through with it.

11.13. Have done 10 P.Y. cycles. A bit better, and a slight hint of the Bhuchari Siddhi foreshadowed. Have been saying mantra; the question arises in my mind:

11.13. Am I mixing my drinks unduly? I think not; if one didn't change to another mystic process, one would have to read the newspaper.

11.20. This completes my half-hour of Asana. Legs very painful; yet again I find myself wishing for Kandy (not sugar candy, but the place where I did my first Hindu practices and got my first Results) and a life devoted entirely to meditation. But not for me! I'm no Pratyeka-Buddha; a Dhamma-Buddha every inch of me! [A Pratyeka-Buddha attains the Supreme Reward for himself alone; a Dhamma-Buddha renounces it and returns to hell (earth) to teach others the Way.—ED.]

I now take a few minutes "off" to make "considerations."

I firmly believe that the minutest dose of the Elixir would operate as a "detonator." I seem to be perfectly ready for illumination, if only because I am so perfectly dark. Yet my power to create magical images is still with me.

11.40- Hanged Man posture. Will invoke Adonai once more
12.0.   by pure thought. Got into a very curious state indeed; part of me being quite perfectly asleep, and part quite perfectly awake.

2.10. Have slept, and that soundly, though with many dreams. Awaking with the utmost horror and loathing of the Path of the Wise—it seemed somehow like a vast dragon-demon with bronze green wings iridescent that rose up startled and angry. And I saw that

2.10. the littlest courage is enough to rise and throw off sleep, like a small soldier in complete armour of silver advancing with sword and shield—at whose sight that dragon, not daring to abide the shock, flees utterly away.

2.15. Lunch, 3 Garibaldis and 3 Gaufrettes. Wrote two letters.

2.50. Going out walk with mantra.

8.3 This walk was in a way rather a success. I got the good mantra effects, *e.g.*, the brain taking it up of its own accord; also the distaste for everything but Adonai became stronger and stronger.
But when I returned from a visit to B——e on an errand of comradeship—$1\frac{1}{2}$ hours' talk to cut out of this mantra-yoga—I found all sorts of people at the Dôme, where I drank a citron pressé: they detained me in talk, and at 6.30 Maryt turned up and I had to chew a sandwich and drink coffee while she dined.
I feel a little headache; it will pass.
She is up here now with me, but I shall try to meditate. Charming as she is, I don't want to make love to her.

8.40. Mixed mantra and caresses rather a success. (At her request I gave M. a minimum dose of X.)

9.15. Asana and Meditation with mantra since 8.40. The blackness seems breaking. For a moment I got a vague glimpse of one's spine (or rather one's Sushumna) as a galaxy of stars, thus suggesting the stars as the ganglia of the Universe.

9.18 To continue.

10.18. Not very satisfactory. Asana got painful; like a

worm I gave up, and tried playing the fool; got amused by the New Monster, but did not perform the "Vajroli Mudra." [For this see the Shiva Sanhita, and other of the Holy Sanskrit Tantras.—ED.]

However, having got rid of her for the moment, one may continue.

10.24-
10.39.
P.Y. [Prana Yama.—ED.] 14 cycles. Some effort required; sweating appears to have stopped and Bhuchari hardly begun.

My head really aches a good deal.

I must add one or two remarks. In my walk I discovered that my mantra Hua allahu, etc., really belongs to the Visuddhi Cakkrâm; so I allowed the thought to concentrate itself there. [The Visuddhi-Cakkrâm: the "nerve centre," in Hindu mystic physiology, opposite the larynx.—ED.]

Also, since others are to read this, one must mention that almost from the beginning of this Working of Magick Art the changed aspect of the world whose culmination is the keeping of the oath "I will interpret every phenomenon as a particular dealing of God with my soul" was present with me. This aspect is difficult to describe; one is indifferent to everything and yet interested in it. The meaning of things is lost, pending the inception of their Spiritual Meaning; just as, on putting one's eye to the microscope, the drop of water on the slide is gone, and a world of life discovered, though the real import of that world is not apprehended, until one's knowledge becomes far greater than a single glance can make it.

10.55. Having written the above, I shall rest for a few moments to try and get rid of my headache.

A good simile (by the way) for the Yogi is to say that he watches his thought like a cat watching a mouse. The paw ready to strike the instant Mr. Mouse stirs.

I have chewed a Gaufrette and drunk a little water, in case the headache is from hunger. (P.S.—It was so; the food cured it at once.)

11.2. I now lie down as Hanged Man and say mantra in Visuddhi.

11.10. I must really note the curious confusion in my mind between the Visuddhi Cakkrâm and that part of the Boulevard Edgar Quinet which opens on to the cemetery. It seems an identity.

In trying to look *at* the Cakkrâm, I saw that.

Query: What is the connection, which appeared absolute and essential? I had been specially impressed by that gate two days ago, with its knot of mourners. Could the scene have been recorded in a brain-cell adjoining that which records the Visuddhi-idea? Or did I at that time unconsciously think of my throat for some other reason? Bother! These things are all dog-faced demons! To work!

11.17. Work: Meditation and Mantra.

11.35. No good. Went off into a reverie about a castle and men-at-arms. This had all the qualities of a true dream, yet I was not in any other sense asleep. I soon will be, though. It seems foolish to persist.

11.35. And indeed, though I tried to continue the mantra with its high aspiration to know Adonai, I must have slept almost at once.

The Third Day

6.55. Now the day being gloriously broken, I awoke with some weariness, not feeling clean and happy, not burning with love unto my Lord Adonai, though ashamed indeed for that thrice of four times in the night I had been awakened by this loyal body, urging me to rise and meditate—and my weak will bade it be at ease and take its rest—oh, wretched man! slave of the hour and of the worm!

7.0–7.16. Fifteen cycles of Prana Yama put me right mentally and physically: otherwise they had little apparent success.

7.30. Have breakfasted—a pear and two Garibaldis. (These by the way are the small size, half the big squares.)

7.50. Have smoked a pipe to show that I'm not in a hurry.

8.4 Hanged Man with mantra in Visuddhi. Thought I had been much longer. At one point the Spirit began to move—how the devil else can I express it? The consciousness seemed to flow, instead of pattering. Is *that* clear?

One should here note that there may perhaps be some essential difference in the operation of the Moslem and Hindu mantrams. The latter boom; the former ripple. I have never tried the former at all seriously until now.

THE EQUINOX

8.10- *Même jeu*—no good at all. Think I'll get up and have
8.32.   a Turker.

9.0.   Am up, having read my letters. Continuing mantra all the time in a more or less conscious way.

9.25.   Wrote my letters and started out.

10.38. Have reached the Cafe de la Paix, walking slowly with my mantra. I am beginning to forget it occasionally, mispronouncing some of the words. A good sign! Now and then I tried sending it up and down my spine, with good effect.

10.40. I will drink a cup of coffee and then proceed to the Hammam. This may ease my limbs, and afford an opportunity for a real go-for-the-gloves effort to concentrate.

It cannot be too clearly understood that nearly all the work hitherto has been preliminary; the intention is to get the Chittam (thought-stuff) flowing evenly in one direction. Also one practises detaching it from the Virttis (impressions). One looks at everything without seeing it.

O coffee! By the mighty Name of Power do I invoke thee, consecrating thee to the Service of the Magic of Light. Let the pulsations of my heart be strong and regular and slow! Let my brain be wakeful and active in its supreme task of self-control! That my desired end may be effected through Thy strength, Adonai, unto Whom be the Glory for ever! Amen without lie, and Amen, and Amen of Amen.

11.0.   I now proceed to the Hammam.

12.0. The Bath is over. I continued the mantra throughout, which much alleviated the torture of massage. But I could not get steady and easy in my Asana or even in the Hanged Man or Shavasana, the "corpse-position." I think the heat is exciting, and makes me restless. I continue in the cooling-room lying down.

12.10. I have ordered 12 oysters and coffee and bread and butter.
O oysters! be ye unto me strength that I formulate the 12 rays of the Crown of HVA! I conjure ye, and very potently command.
Even by Him who ruleth Life from the Throne of Tahuti unto the Abyss of Amennti, even by Ptah the swathed one, that unwrappeth the mortal from the immortal, even by Amoun the giver of Life, and by Khem the mighty, whose Phallus is like the Pillar in Karnak! Even by myself and my male power do I conjure ye. Amen.

12.20. I was getting sleepy when the oysters came. I now eat them in a Yogin and ceremonial manner.

12.45. I have eaten my oysters, chewing them every one; also some bread and butter in the same manner, giving praise to Priapus the Lord of the oyster, to Demeter the Lady of corn, and to Isis the Queen of the Cow. Further, I pray symbolically in this meal for Virtue, and Strength, and Gladness; as is appropriate to these symbols. But I find it very difficult to keep the mantra going, even in tune with the jaws; perhaps it is that this peculiar method of eating (25 minutes

- 12.45. for what could be done normally in 3) demands the whole attention.
- 1.30. Drifted into a nap. Well! we shall try what Brother Body really wants.
- 1.35. My attempt to go to sleep has made me supernaturally wakeful.
  I am—as often before—in the state described by Paul (not my masseur; the other Paul!) in his Epistle to the Romans, cap. vii. v. 19.
  I shall rise and go forth.
- 1.55. I have a good mind to try violent excitement of the Muladhara Cakkrâm; for the whole Sushumna seems dead. This at the risk of being labelled a Black Magician—by clergymen, Christian Scientists, and the "self-reliant" classes in general.
- 2.15. Arrived (partly by cab) at the Place. Certain curious phenomena which I have noticed at odd times—*e.g.*, on Thursday night—but did not think proper to record must be investigated. It seems quite certain that meditation-practices profoundly affect the sexual process: how and why I do not yet certainly know.
- 2.45. Rubbish! everything perfectly normal.
  Difficult, though, to keep mantram going.
- 3.0. Am sitting on the brink of the big fountain in the Luxembourg. This deadness of the whole system continues.
  To explain. Normally, if the thought be energetically directed to almost any point in the body, that point is

3.0. felt to pulse and even to ache. Especially this is the case if one vibrates a mantra or Magical name in a nerve-centre. At present I cannot do this at all. The Prana seems equilibrated in the whole organism: I am very peaceful—just as a corpse is.
It is terribly annoying, in a sense, because this condition is just the opposite of Dharana; yet one knows that it is a stage on the way to Samadhi. So I rise and give confidently the Sign of Apophis and Typhon, and will then regard the reflection of the sweet October Sun in the kissing waters of the fountain. (P.S.—I now remember that I forgot to rise and give the Sign.)

3.15. In vain do I regard the Sun, broken up by the lips of the water into countless glittering stars—abounding, revolving, whirling forth, crying aloud—for He whom my soul seeketh is not in these. Nor is He in the fountain, eternally as it jets and falls in brilliance of dew; for I desire the Dew Supernal. Nor is He in the still depths of the water; their lips do not meet His. Nor—O my soul!—is He anywhere to be found in thy secret caverns, unluminous, formless, and void, where I wander seeking Him—or seeking rest from that Search! O my soul!—lift thyself up; play the man, be strong; harden thyself against thy bitter Fate; for at the End thou shalt find Him; and ye shall enter in together into the Secret Palace of the King; even unto the Garden of Lilies; and ye shall be One for evermore. So mote it be!

3.15. Yet now—ah now!—I am but a dead man. Within me and without still stirs that life of sense that is not life, but is as the worms that feast upon my corpse. . . . Adonai! Adonai! my Lord Adonai! indeed, Thou hast forsaken me. Nay! thou liest, O weak soul! Abide in the meditation; unite all thy symbols into the form of a Lion, and be lord of thy jungle, travelling through the servile Universe even as Mau the Lion very lordly, the Sun in His strength that travelleth over the heaven of Nu in His bark in the mid-career of Day.

For all these thoughts are vain; there is but One thought, though that thought be not yet born—He only is God, and there is none other God than He!

3.30. Walking home with mantra; suddenly a spasm of weeping took me as I cried through the mantra—"My God, my God, why hast Thou forsaken me?"—and I have to stop and put it down!

A good thing; for it calms me.

3.45. At the Dome, master of myself. The Mantra goes just 30 times a minute, 1800 times an hour, 43,200 times a day. To say it a million times would take longer than Mrs. Glyn's heroine did to conceive. Yet I will get the result if I have to say it a hundred and eleven million times. But oh! fertilise my Akasic egg to-day!

This remark, one should notice, is truly characteristic of the man John St. John. I see how funny it is; but I'm quite serious withal. Ye dull dogs!

3.45. [The "Akasic Egg" is the sphere of the personality of man. A theosophic term.—ED.]

3.55. N.B.—Mantras might with advantage be palindromes.

3.56. I try to construct a magic square from the mantra. No good. But the mantra is going much better, quite mechanically and "without attachment" (*i.e.*, without conscious ulterior design. "Art for Art's sake" as it were).

4.10. I drink a "citron pressé."

4.25. Alas! here comes Maryt (with a sad tale of X. It appears that she fainted and spent some hours at the hospital. I should have insisted on her stying with me; the symptoms began immediately on her drinking some coffee. I have noticed with myself, that eating has started the action).

5.30. An hour of mingled nap and mantra.
I now feel alive again. It was very strange how calm and balanced I was: yet now I am again energised; may it be to the point of Enthusiasm!
People will most assuredly smile at this exalted mystic; his life seems made up of sleep and love-making. Indeed, to-day I have been shockingly under the power of Tamas, the dark sphere. But that is clearly a fatigue-effect from having worked so hard.
Oh Lord, how long?

5.50. The Mantra still ripples on. I am so far from the Path that I have a real good mind to get Maryt to let me perform the Black Mass on her at midnight. I would

5.50. just love to bring up Typhon, and curse Osiris and burn his bones and his blood!

At least, I now solemnly express a pious wish that the Crocodile of the West may eat up the Sun once and for all, that Set may defile the Holy Place, that the supreme Blasphemy may be spoken by Python in the ears of Isis.

I want trouble. I want to say Indra's mantram till his throne gets red-hot and burns his lotus-buttocks; I want to pinch little Harpocrates till he fairly yells . . . and I will too! Somehow!

6.15. I have now got into a sort of smug content, grinning all over like some sleepy Chinese god. No reason for it, Lord knows!

I can't make up my mind whether to starve or sandwich or gorge the beast St. John. He's not the least bit hungry, though he's had nothing to call a Meal since Thursday lunch. The Hatha-Yoga feeding game is certainly marvellous.

I should like to work marching and breathing with this mantra as I did of old with Aum Tat Sat Aum. Perhaps two steps to a mantra, and 4-8-16 steps to a breath-cycle? This would mean 28 seconds for a breath-cycle; quite enough for a marching man. We might try 4-8-8 to start; or even 8-8-8 (for the Chariot, wherein the Geburah of me rises to Binah—Strength winning the Wings of Understanding). [These symbols, allusions, and references will all be found in 777, just published by "The Equinox"—see advt.—ED.]

6.55. I shall now ceremonially defile the Beyt Allah with Pig, to express in some small measure my utter disgust and indignation with Allah for not doing His job properly. I say in vain "Labbaik!" [I am here.—ED.] He answers, "But I'm *not* here, old boy—another leg-pull!" He little knows His man, though, if He thinks He can insult me with impunity. Andre, un sandwich!
[Beyt Allah, the Mosque at Mecca, means "House of God"—ED.]

7.5. I shall stop mantra while I eat, so as to concentrate (*a*) on the chewing, (*b*) on defiling the House of God. Not so easy! the damned thing runs on like a prairie fire. Important then to stop it absolutely at will: even the Work itself may become an obsession.
11 hours with no real break—not bad.
The bad part of to-day seems the Asana, and the deadness. Or, perhaps worse, I fail to apprehend the true magical purport of my work: hence all sort of aimless formulae, leading—naturally enough—to no result.
It just strikes me—it may be this Isis Apophis Osiris IAO formula that I have preached so often. Certainly the first two days were Isis—natural, pleasant, easy events. Most certainly too to-day has been Apophis! Think of the wild cursing and black magic, etc. . . . we must hope for the Osiris section to-morrow or next day. Birth, death, resurrection! IAO!

7.35. The Sandwich duly chewed, and two Coffees drunk, I resume the mystic Mantra. Why? Because I dam well choose to.

7.50. 'Tis a rash thing to say, and I burn incense to the Infernal Gods that the Omen may be averted; but I seem to have conquered the real Dweller of the Threshold once and for all. For nowadays my blackest despair is tempered by the certainty of coming through it sooner or later, and that with flying colours.

9.30. The last ¾-hour I wasted talking to Dr. R——, that most interesting man. I don't mean talking; I mean listening. You are a bad, idle good-for-nothing fellow, O.M.! Why not stick to that mantra?

10.40. Have drunk two citrons pressés and gone to my room to work a mighty spell of magick Art.

11.0. Having got rid of Maryt (who, by the way, is Quite mad), and thereby (one might hope) of Apophis and Typhon, I perform the Great Ritual DCLXXI with good results magically; *i.e.*, I formulated things very easily and forcibly; even at one time I got a hint of the Glory of Adonai. But I made the absurd mistake of going through the Ritual as if I was rehearsing it, instead of staying at the Reception of the Candidate and insisting upon being *really* received.
I will therefore now (11.50) sit down again and invoke really hard on these same lines, while the Perfume and the Vision are yet formulated, though insensibly, about me. And thus shall end the Third day of my retirement.

The Fourth Day

12.15. So therefore begins the fourth day of this my great magical retirement; I bleed from the slashes of the

12.15. magick knife; I smart from the heat of the Holy Oil; I am bruised by the scourge of Osiris that hath so cruelly smitten me; the perfume yet fills the chamber of Art;—and I?

Oh Adonai my Lord, surely I did invoke Thee with fervour; yet Thou camest not utterly to the tryst. And yet I know that Thou wast there; and it may be that the morning may being rememberance of Thee which this consciousness does not now contain.

But I swear by Thine own glory that I will not be satisfied with this, that I will go on even unto madness and death if it be Thy will—but I will know Thee as Thou art.

It is strange how my cries died down; how I found myself quite involuntarily swinging back to the old mantra that I worked all yesterday.

However, I shall try a little longer in the Position of the Hanged Man, although sleep is again attacking me. I am weary, yet content, as if some great thing had indeed happened. But if I lost consciousness— a thing no man can be positive about from the nature of things —it must have happened so quietly that I never knew. Certainly I should not have thought that I had gone on for 25 minutes, as I did.

But I do indeed ask for a Knowledge and Conversation of the Holy Guardian Angel which is not left so much to be inferred from the good results in my life and work; I want the Perfume and the the Vision. . . .

Why am I so materially wallowing in grossness? It matters little; the fact remains that I do wallow.

12.15. I want that definite experience in the very same sense as Abramelin had it; and what's more, I mean to go on till I get it.

12.34. I begin, therefore, in Hanged Man posture, to invoke the Angel, within the Pyramid already duly prepared by DCLXXI.

12.57. Alas! in vain have I tried even the supreme ritual of Awaiting the Beloved, although once I thought—Ah! give unto Thy beloved in sleep!
How ashamed I should be, though! For an earthly lover one would be on tiptoe of excitement, trembling at every sound, eager, afraid ...
I will, however, rise and open (as for a symbol) the door and the window. Oh that the door of my heart were ever open! For He is always there, and always eager to come in.

1.0. I rise and open unto my Beloved.
... May it be granted unto me in the daylight of this day to construct from DCLXXI a perfect ritual of self-initiation, so as to avoid the constant difficulty of assuming various God-forms. Then let that ritual be a constant and perfect link between Us ... so that at all times I may be perfect in Thy Knowledge and Conversation, O mine Holy Guardian Angel! to whom I have aspired these ten years past.

1.5. And though as it may seem I now compose myself to sleep, I await Thee ... I await Thee!

7.35. I arise from sleep, mine eyes a little weary, my soul fresh, my heart restored.

8.0. Accordingly, I continue in gentle and easy meditation on my Lord Adonai, without fear or violence, quite directly and naturally.
One of the matters that came up last night with Dr. R——d was that of writing rubbish for magazines. He thought that one could do it in the intervals of serious work; but I do not think that one should take the risk. I have spent these many years training my mind to think cleanly and express beautifully. Am I to prostitute myself for a handful of bread?
I swear by Thyself, O Thou who art myself, that I will not write save to glorify Thee, that I will write only in beauty and melody, that I will give unto the world as Thou givest unto me, whether it be a consuming fire, or a cup of the wine of Iacchus, or a glittering dagger, or a disk brighter than the sun. I will starve in the street before I pander to the vileness of the men among whom I live—oh my Lord Adonai, be with me, give me the purest poesy, keep me to this vow! And if I turn aside, even for a moment, I pray Thee, warn me by some signal chastisement, that Thou art a jealous god, and that Thou wilt keep me veiled, cherished, guarded in Thine harem a pure and perfect spouse, like a slender fountain playing in Thy courts of marble and of malachite, of jasper, of topaz, and of lapis lazuli.
And by my magick power I summon all the inhabitants of the ten thousand worlds to witness this mine oath.

8.15. I will rise, and break my fast. I think it as well to go on with the mantra, as it started of its own accord.

9.0. Arrived at Pantheon, to breakfast on coffee and biroche and a peach.

I shall try and describe Ritual DCLXXI; since its nature is important to this great ceremony of initiation. Those who understand a little about the Path of the Wise may receive some hint of the method of operation of the L.V.X.

And I think that a description will help me to collect myself for the proper adaptation of this Ritual to the purpose of Self- initiation.

Oh, how soft is the air, and how serene the sky, to one who has passed through the black rule of Apophis! How infinitely musical are the voices of Nature, those that are heard and those that are not heard! What Understanding of the Universe, what Love is the prize of him that hath performed all things and endured all things!

The first operation of Ritual DCLXXI is the preparation of the Place.

There are two forces; that of Death and that of Natural Life.

Death begins the Operation by a knock, to which Life answers.

Then Death, banishing all forces external to the operation, declares the Speech in the Silence. Both officers go from their thrones and form the base of a triangle whose apex is the East. They invoke the Divine Word, and then Death slays with the knife, and embalms with the oil, his sister Life.

Life, thus prepared, invokes, at the summons of Death

9.0. the forces necessary to the Operation. The Word takes its station in the East and the officers salute it both by speech and silence in their signs; and they pronounce the secret Word of power that riseth from the Silence and returneth thereunto.

All this they affirm; and in affirming the triangular base of the Pyramid, find that they have mysteriously affirmed the Apex thereof whose name is Ecstasy. This also is sealed by that secret word; for that Word containeth All.

Into this prepared Pyramid of divine Light there cometh a certain darkling wight, who knoweth not either his own nature, or his origin or destiny, or even the name of that which he desireth. Before he can enter the Pyramid, therefore, four ordeals are required of him.

So, bound and blinded, he stumbles forward, and passes through the wrath of the Four Great Princes of the Evil of the World, whose Terror is about him on every side. Yet since he has followed the voice of the Officer who has prepared him, in this part of the Ritual no longer merely Nature, the great Mother, but Neschamah (his aspiration) and the representative of Adonai, he may pass through all. Yea, in spite of the menace of the Hiereus, whose function is now that of his fear and of his courage, he goes on and enters the Pyramid. But there he is seized and thrown down by both officers as one unworthy to enter. His aspiration purifies him with steel and fire; and there as he lies shattered by the force of the ritual, he hears—even as a

9.0.   corpse that hears the voice of Israfel—the Hegemon that chants a solemn hymn of praise to that glory which is at the Apex, and who invisibly rules and governs the whole Pyramid.

Now then that darkling wight is lifted by the officers and brought to the altar in the centre; and there the Hiereus accuses him of the two and twenty Basenesses, while the Hegemon lifting up his chained arms cries again and again against his enemy that he is under the Shadow of the Eternal Wings of the Holy One. Yet at the end, at the supreme accusation, the Hiereus smites him into death. The same answer avails him, and in its strength he is uplifted by his aspiration—and now he stands upright.

Now then he makes a journey in his new house, and perceives at stated times, each time preceded by a new ordeal and equilibration, the forces that surround him. Death he sees, and the Life of Nature whose name is Sorrow, and the Word that quickeneth these, and his own self—and when he hath recognised these four in their true nature he passes to the altar once more and as the apex of a descending triangle is admitted to the lordship of the Double Kingdom. Thus is he a member of the visible triad that is crossed with the invisible—behold the hexagram of Solomon the King! All this the Hiereus seals with a knock and at the Hegemon's new summons he—to his surprise—finds himself as the Hanged Man of the Tarot.

Each point of the figure thus formed they crown with light, until he glitters with the Flame of the Spirit.

9.0. Thus and not otherwise is he made a partaker of the Mysteries, and the Lightning Flash strikes him. The Lord hath descended from heaven with a shout and with the Voice of the Archangel, and the trump of God.
He is installed in the Throne of the Double Kingdom, and he wields the Wand of Double Power by the sings of the grade.
He is recognized an initiate, and the word of Secret Power, and the silent administration of the Sacrament of Sword and Flame, acknowledge him.
Then, the words being duly spoken and the deeds duly done, all is symbolically sealed by the Thirty Voices, and the Word that vibrateth from the Silence to the Speech, and from the Speech again unto the Silence.
Then the Pyramid is sealed up, even as it was opened; yet in the sealing thereof the three men partake in a certain mystical manner of the Eucharist of the Four Elements that are consumed for the Perfection of the Oil.
Konx Om Pax. [With these mystic words the Mysteries Eleusinian were sealed.—ED.]

10.0. Having written out this explanation, I will read it through and meditate solemnly thereupon. All this I wrote in the Might of the Secret Ring committed unto me by the Masters; so that all might be absolutely correct.
One thing strikes me as worthy of mention. Last night when I went into the restaurant to speak to

10.0. R——d, my distaste for food was so intense that the smell of it caused real nausea. To-day, I am perfectly balanced, neither hungry nor nauseated. This is indeed more important than it seems; it is a sure sign when one sees a person take up fads that he is under the black rule of Apophis. In the Kingdom of Osiris there is freedom and light. To-day I shall eat neither with the frank gluttony of Isis nor with the severe asceticism of Apophis. I shall eat as much and as little as I fancy; these violent means are no longer necessary. Like Count Fosco, I shall "go on my way sustained by my sublime confidence, self-balanced by my impenetrable calm."

10.50. I have spent half an hour wandering in the Musee du Luxembourg.

I now sit down to meditate on this new ritual. The following, so it appears, should be the outlines—damn it, I've a good mind to write it straight off—no! I'll be patient and tease the Spirit a little. I will be coquettish as a Spanish catamite.

1. Death summons Life and clears away all other forces.
2. The Invocation of the Word. Death consecrates Life, who in her whirling dance invokes that Word.
3. They salute the Word. The Signs and M——M must be a Chorus, if anything.
4. The Miraculous appearance of Iacchus, un-invoked.

10.50
1. The 3 Questions.
2. The 4 ordeals. Warning and comfort as an appeal to the Officers.
3. The Threshold.
   The Chorus of Purification.
   The Hymn "My heart, my mother!" as already written, years ago.
4. At the altar. The accusation and defence as antiphonies.
5. The journey. Bar and pass, and the 4 visions even as a mighty music.
6. The Hanged Man—the descent of Adonai.
7. The installation—signs, etc.

Sealing as for opening; but insert Sacrament.

1.15. During a lunch of 12 oysters, Cêpes Bordelaise, Tarte aux Cérises, Café Noir, dispatched without Yoga or ceremonial, I wrote the Ritual in verse, in the Egyptian Language. I don't think very well. Time must show: also experience. I'd recite Tennyson if I thought it would give Samadhi!
Now more mantra, though by the Lord I'm getting sick of it.

1.40. It occurs to me, now that I am seeing my way in the Operation a little more clearly, that one might consider the First Day as Osiris Slain ✠, the Second as that of the Mourning of Isis **L**, the third as that of the Triumph of Apophis **V**, and to-day that of Osiris Risen **X**; these four days being perfect in themselves as a $5° = 6°$ operation (or possibly with one or two more

1.40. to recapitulate L.V.X. Lux, the Light of the Cross). Thence one might proceed to some symbolic passage through the 6° = 5° grade—though of course that grade is really symbolic of this soul-journey, not *vice versâ*—and through 7° = 4°; so perhaps—if one could only dare to hope it!—to the 8° = 3° attainment. Certainly what little I have done so far pertains no higher than Minor adeptship though I have used higher formulæ in the course of my working.

1.55. My Prana is acting in a feverish manner; a mixture of fatigue and energy. This is not good: it probably comes from bolting that big lunch, and may mean that I must sleep to recover equilibrium. I will, however, use the Pentagram ritual on my Anahata Cakkrâm [the heart; a nerve-centre in Hindu mystical physiology.—ED.] and see if that steadies me. (P.S.—Yes: instantly). Notice, please, how in this condition of intense magical strain the most trifling things have a great influence. Normally, I can eat anything in any quantity without the slightest effect of any sort; witness my expeditions and debauches; nothing upsets me.
P.S.—But notice, please! Normally half a bottle of Burgundy excites me notably; while doing this magic it is like so much water. A "transvaluation of all values!"

3.55. Over a citron pressé I have revised the new Ritual. Also I have bought suitable materials for copying it fair; and this I did without solemnity or ceremonial.

3.55. but quite simply, just as anybody else might buy them. In short, I bought them in a truly Rosicrucian manner, according to the custom of the country.

I add a few considerations on the grade of Adeptus Major 6° = 5°.

(P.S.—Distinction is to be made between attainment of this grade in the natural and in the spiritual world. The former I long since possessed.)

1. It may perhaps mean severe asceticism. In case I should be going out on that path I will try and get a real good dinner to fortify myself.
2. The paths leading to Geburah are from Hod, that of the Hanged Man, and from Tiphereth, that of Justice, both equilibrated aspects of Severity, the one implying Self-Sacrifice, the other involuntary suffering. One is Free-will, the other Karma; and that in a wider sense than that of Suffering.
The Ritual DCLXXI will still be applicable: indeed, it may be considered sufficient; but of course it must be lived as well as performed.

(I must here complain of serious trouble with fountain pens, and the waste of priceless time fixing them up. They have been wrong throughout the whole operation, a thing that has not happened to me for near eight years. I hope I've got a good one at last—yes, thank God! this one writes decently.)

4.15. Somehow or other I have got off the track; have been fooling about with too many odd things, necessary as they may have been. I had better take a solid hour willing the Tryst with Adonai.

5.40. Have done all this, and a Work of Kindness. I will again revise the new ritual, dine, return and copy it fair for use.
Let Adonai the Lord oversee the Work, that it be perfect, a sure link with Him, a certain and infallible Conjuration, and Spell, and Working of true Magick Art, that I may invoke Him with success whenever seemeth good unto Him.
Unto Him; not unto Me! Is it not written that Except Adonai build the House, they labour in vain that build it?

6.15. Chez Lavenue. Not feeling like revision, will read through this record.
My dinner is to be Bisque d'Ecrevisses, Tournedos Rossini, a Coupe Jack, half a bottle of Meursault, and Coffee. All should now acquit adepts of the charge of not knowing how to do themselves well.

7.20. Dinner over, I return the Mantra-Yoga. One may note that I expected the wine to have an excessive effect on me; on the contrary, it has much less effect than usual.
This is rather important. I have purposely abstained from anything that might be called a drug, until now, for fear of confusing the effects.
With my knowledge of hashish-effects, I could very

7.20. likely have broken up the Apophis-kingdom of yesterday in a moment, and the truth of it would have been 5 per cent. drug and 95 per cent. magic; but nobody would have believed me. Remember that this record is for the British Public, "who may like me yet." God forbid! for I cannot echo Browning's hope. Their greasiness, hypocrisy, and meanness are such that their appreciation could only mean my vileness, not their redemption. Sorry if I seem pessimistic about them! A nasty one for me, by the way, if they suddenly started buying me! I should have, in mere consistency, to cut my throat!
Calm yourself, my friend! There is no danger.

7.40. At home again and robed. Am both tired and oppressed, even in my peace; for the day has been, and the evening is, close and hot, with a little fog, and, one may suspect, the air is overcharged with electricity. I will rest quietly with my mantra as Hanged Man, and perhaps sleep for a little.

8.10. No sleep—no rest for the wicked! 'Tis curious how totally independent is mantra-yoga of reverie. I can say my mantra vigorously while my thought wanders all over the world; yet I cannot write the simplest sentence without stopping it, unless with a very great effort, and then it is not satisfactory to either party!
Meditation—of the "rational" sort—on this leads me to suggest that active "radiant" thought may be incompatible with the mantra, itself being (?) active. One can

8.10. read and understand quite easily with the mantra going; one can remember things.

For example, I see my watch chain; I think. "Gold. Au, 196 atomic weight. $AuCl_3$, £3 10s. 0*d.* an ounce" and so on *ad infinitum;* but the act of writing down these things stops the mantra. This may be (partly) because I always say under my breath each word as I write it. [P.S.—But I do so, though less possibly, as I read.]

8.22. As I am really awake, I may as well do a little Pranayama.

8.40. How little I know of magic and the conditions of success! My 17 cycles of breath were not absolutely easy; yet I did them. After a big dinner!!! The sweating was quite suppressed, in spite of the heat of the night and the exercise; and the first symptoms of the Bhuchari-Siddhi—the "jumping about like a frog" —were well marked. I am encouraged to spend a few minutes (still in Asana) reading the Shiva Sanhita.

9.0. Asana very painful again. True, I was doing it very strictly.

I notice they give a second stage—trembling of the body—as preliminary to the jumping about like a frog —I had omitted this, as one is so obviously the germ of the other.

The Hindus seem to lack a sense of proportion. When the Yogi, by turning his tongue back for one half-minute, has conquered old age, disease and death; then instead of having good time he patiently (and rather pathetically, I think!) devotes his youthful

9.0. immortality to trying to "drink the air through the crow-bill" .... in the hope of curing a consumption of the lungs which he probably never had and which was in any case cured by his former effort!

9.40. Have been practising a number of these mudras and asanas.
Concerning the Visuddi Cakkram which is "of brilliant gold or smoke colour and has sixteen petals corresponding to the sixteen vowel sounds," one might make a good mantra of the English vowel sounds, or the Hebrew.
"Curiouser and curiouser!" The Yogis identify the Varana (Ganges) with the Ida-Nadi, the Asi (?) with the Pingala-Nadi, and Benares with the space between them. Like my identification of my throat with the Gate of the cimetière du Montparnasse.
Well, it requires very considerable discrimination and a good sound foundation of knowledge, if one means to get any sense at all out of these Hindu books.

10.20. A little Pranayama, I think.

10.22. Can't get steady and easy at all! Will try Hanged Man again.

10.42. Not much good. The mantra goes on, but without getting hold of the Chakkram.
'Tis difficult to explain; the best simile I can get is that of a motor running with the clutch out; or of a man cycling on a suspended machine.
There's no grip to it.

10.42. The fact of the matter is, I am quite unconcentrated. Evidently the Osiris Risen stage is over; and I think it is a case for violent measures.

If one were to slack off now and hope for the morning, like a shipwrecked Paul, one would probably wake up a mere man of the world.

The Question then arises: What shall I do to be saved?

The only answer—and one which is quite unconnected with the question—is that a Ritual of Adeptus Major should display the Birth of Horus and Slaying of Typhon. Here again Horus and Harpocrates—the twins of the twin signs of $0° = 0°$ ritual—are the slayers of Typhon. So all the rituals get mixed: the symbols recur, though in a different aspect. Anyway, one wants something a deal better than the path of Pe in $4° = 7°$ ritual.

I think the postulant should be actually scourged, tortured, branded by fire for his equilibrations at the various "Stations of the Cross" or points upon his mystic journey. He must assuredly drink blood for the sacrament—ah! now I see it all so well! The Initiator must kill him, Osiris; he must rise again as Horus and kill the Initiator, taking his place in the ceremony thence to the end. A bit awkward technically, but 'twill yield to science. They did it of old by a certain lake in Italy!

Well, all this is dog-faced demon, ever seducing me from the Sacred Mysteries. I can't go out and kill anybody at this time o'night! We might make a start,

10.42. though, with a little scourging, torturing, and branding by fire. . . .
Anything for a quiet life!

11.0. But scourging oneself is not easy with a robe on; and though one could take it off, there is this point to be considered: that one can never (except by a regrettable accident) hurt oneself more than one wants to. In other words, it is impossible thus to inflict pain, and so flagellants have been rightly condemned as mere voluptuaries. The only way to do so would be to inflict some torture whose severity one could not gauge at the time: *e.g.*, one might dip oneself in petroleum and set light to it, as the young lady mystic did—I suppose in Brittany!—the other day. It's not the act that hurts, but the consequences; so, although one knows only roughly what will happen, one can force oneself to the act.
This, then, is a possible form of self-martyrdom. Similarly, mutilations; though it is perhaps just to observe that all these people are mad when they do these things, and their standard of pleasure and pain consequently so different from the sane man's as to be incomprehensible.
Look at my Uncle Tom! who goes about the world bragging of his chastity. The maniac is probably happy—a peacock who is all tail! And squawk. Look at the Vegetarians and Wallaceites and all that crew of lunatics. They are paid in the coin of self-conceit. I shall waste no pity on them!

11.3. Rather pity myself, who cannot even make sensible "considerations" for a Ritual of Adeptus Major.

The only thing to do in short is to go steadily on, with a little extra courage and energy—no harm in that!—on the same old lines. The Winding of the Way must necessarily lead me just where it may happen to go. Why deliberately go off to Geburah? Why not aspire direct by the Path of the Moon-Ray unto the Ineffable Crown? Modesty is misplaced here!

Very good. Then how aspire? Who is it that standeth in the Moon-Ray? The Holy Guardian Angel. Aye! O my Lord Adonai, Thou art the Beginning and the End of the Path. For as Thou אתה thou art also 406 = תו Tau the material world, the Omega. And as He הוא Thou art 12, the rays of the Ineffable Crown. (A disaster has occurred; viz., a sudden and violent attack of that which demands a tabloid of Pepsin, Bismuth, and Charcoal—and gets it. On my return, 11.34, I continue.)

And as אני Ani "I" thou art also אין the Negative, that is beyond these on either side!

But this illness is a nuisance. I must have got a little chill somehow. Its imminence would account for my lack of concentration. And I could doubtless go on gloriously, but that another disaster has occurred! Enter Maryt, sitting and clothed and in her right mind—or comparatively so!

11.38. I suppose, then, I must quit the game for a minute or two.

11.56. Got rid of her, thank God. I may say in self-defence that I would never have let her in but for the accident of my being outside the room and the door left open, so that she was inside on my return.
Let me get into Asana.

The Fifth Day

12.26. So beginneth the Fifth Day of this great Magical Retirement. With two and twenty breath-cycles did I begin. This practice was a little easier; but not much better. It ought to become quite simple and natural before one devotes the half-minute of Kambhakam (breath held-in), when one is rigid to a strong projection of Will toward Adonai, as has been my custom. I hope to-day will be more hard definite magical Work, less discourse, less beatific state of mind—which is the very devil! the real Calypso, none the less temptress because her name happens to be Penelope. Ah Lord Adonai, my Lord! Grant unto me the Perfume and the Vision; let me attain the desirable harbour; for my little ship is tossed by divers tempests, even by Euroclydon, in the Place where Four Winds meet.

12.35. Therefore I shall go to rest, letting my mind rest ever in the Will toward Adonai. Let my sleep be toward Him, or annihilation; let my waking be to the music of His name; let the day be full to the uttermost of Him only.

2.18. My good friend the body woke me at this hour by means of disturbed dreams about a quite imaginary

2.18. relative of whom nobody for years had ever seen anything but his head, which he would poke out of a waterproof sheet. He was supposed to be an invalid. I am glad to say that I woke properly and got quite automatically on to the mantra.

My Prana, however, seems feverish and unbalanced. So I eat a biscuit or two and drink some water and will put it right with the Pentagram Ritual.

Done, but oh! how hard. Sleep fights me as Apollyon fought Christian! but I will up and take him by the throat.

(See; 'tis 2.30. Twelve minutes to do that little in!) And look at the handwriting!

3.6. How excellent is Prana Yama, a comfort to the soul! I did thirty-two cycles, easy and pleasant; could have gone on indefinitely. The muscles went rigid, practically of their own accord; so light did I feel that I almost thought myself to be "that wise one" who "can balance himself on his thumb." Sleep is conquered right away from the word "jump." Indeed, if

> Satan trembles when he sees
> The weakest saint upon his knees;

then surely:

> Satan flees, exclaiming "Damn!"
> When any saint starts Pranayam!

So happy, indeed, was I in the practice that I devoted myself by the Waiting formula to Adonai; and that I got to "neighbourhood-concentration" is shewn by the fact that I several times forgot altogether about Adonai, and found myself saying the silly old Mantram.

3.6. I despair of asking my readers to distinguish between the common phenomenon of wandering thought and this phenomenon which is at the very portal of true and perfect concentration; yet it is most important that the distinction should be seized. The further difficulty will occur—I hope!—of distinguishing between the vacancy of the idiot, and that destruction of thought which we call Shivadarshana, or Nirvikalpa-samadhi. [We must again refer the reader to the Hindu classics. —ED.]

The only diagnostic I can think of is this; that there is (I can't be sure about it) no rational connection between the thought one left behind one and the new thought. In a simple wandering during the practice of concentration one can very nearly always (especially with a little experience) trace the chain. With neighbourhood-concentration this is not so. Perhaps there is a chain, but so great already is the power of preventing the impressions from rising into consciousness that one has no knowledge of the links, each one having been automatically slaughtered on the threshold of the consciousness.

Of course, the honest and wary practitioner will have no difficulty in recognising the right kind of wandering; with this explanation there is no excuse for him if he does.

I have another theory, though. Perhaps this is not a wandering at all, but a complete annihilation of all thought. Affirming Adonai, I lop off the heads of all others; and Adonai's own head falls. But in the

3.6. momentary pause which this causes, some old habitual thought (to-night my mantra) rises up. A case of the Closure followed by the Moving of the Previous Question.
Oh Lord! when wilt Thou carry a Motion to Adjourn, nay, to Prorogue, nay! to Dissolve this Parliament?

3.32. I am not sleepy; yet will I again compose myself, devoting myself to Adonai.

7.7. Again woke and continued mantra.

8.10. I ought to have made more of it at 7.7; I went off again to sleep; the result is that I am rather difficult to wake again.
However, let me be vigilant now.

8.45. I have dressed and from 8.35-8.45 performed the Ritual of the Bornless One.
Though I performed it none too well (failing, *e.g.*, to make use of the Geometric Progression on the Mahalingam formula in the Ieou section [We cannot understand this passage. It presumably refers to the "Preliminary Invocation" in the "Goetia" of King Solomon, published S.P.R.T., Boleskine Foyers, N.B., 1904.—ED], and not troubling even to formulate carefully the Elemental Hosts, or to marshal them about the circle) I yet, by the favour of IAO, obtained a really good effect, losing all sense of personality and being exalted in the Pillar. Peace and ecstasy enfolded me. It is well.

8.50. But as I was ill last night, and as the morning has broken chill and damp, I will go to the Café du Dôme

8.50. and break my fast humbly with Coffee and Sandwich. May it strengthen me in my search for the Quintessece, the Stone of the Wise, the Summum Bonum, True Wisdom and Perfect Happiness!

9.0. I hope (by the way) that I have made it quite clear that all this time even a momentary cessation of active thought has been accompanied by the rising-up of the mantra. The rhythm, in short, perpetually dominates the brain; and becomes active on every opportunity. The liquid Moslem mantra is much easier to get on to than is the usual Hindu type with its *m* and *n* sounds predominating: but it does not shake the brain up so forcibly. Perhaps 'tis none the worse for that. I think the unconscious training of the brain to an even rhythm better than startling it into the same by a series of shocks.

I should like, to to remark that the suggestions in the "Herb Dangerous" [We hope to publish this essay in No. 2 of "The Equinox"—ED.] for a ritual seem the wrong way round. It seems to me that the Eastern methods are very arid, and chiefly valuable as a training of the Will, while the Ceremonies of the Magic of Light tune up the soul to that harmony when it is but one step to the Crown.

The real plan is, then, to train the Will into as formidable an engine as possible, and then, at the moment in the Ritual when the real work should be done, to fling forth flying that concentrated Will "whirling forth with re-echoing Roar, so that it may comprehend with

9.0. invincible Will ideas omniform, which flying forth from that one Fountain issued: whose Foundation is One, One and Alone."

As therefore Discipline of whatever kind is only one way of going into a wood at midnight on Easter Eve and cutting the magic wand with a single blow of the magic knife, etc. etc. etc., we can regard the Western system as the essential one. Yet of course Pranayama, for one thing, has its own definite magical effect, apart from teaching the practitioner that he must last out those three seconds—those deadly long last three seconds—even if he burst in the process.

All this I am writing during breakfast.

My devotees may note, by the way, how the desire to sleep is breaking up.

Night   I. $7\frac{1}{2}$ hours, unbroken from 12.30.
  ,,   II.   7 hours nearly, with dreams.
  ,,   III.   8 hours nearly; but woke three or four times, and if I had not been a worm would have scattered it like chaff!
  ,,   IV.   6 1/2 hours; and I wake fresh.
  ,,   V. $1\frac{3}{4} + 4\frac{1}{2} + 1$ hour; and real good work done in the intervals.

[P.S. ,,   VI.   Probably 4 hours.
  ,,   VII. $2 + 2 + \frac{1}{2}$ hours.
  ,,   VIII.   6 hours much broken.
  ,,   IX. $1\frac{1}{2} + 2 + 2$ hours.
  ,,   X. $4 + 1\frac{1}{4}$ hours.
  ,,   XI. $1\frac{3}{4} + 4\frac{1}{2}$ hours.
  ,,   XII.   Back to the normal—7 hours perfect sleep.]

11.30. Have been walks with the mantra arranging for and modelling a "saddle" whereby to get Asana really steady and easy; also for some photographs illustrating some of the more absurd positions, for the instruction of my devotees.

I must now copy out the new Ritual.

This, you will readily perceive, is all wrong. Theoretically, everything should be ready by the beginning of the Operation; and one should simply do it and be done with it.

But this is a very shallow view. One never knows what may be required; *i.e.*, a beginner like myself doesn't. Further, one cannot write an effective Ritual till one is already in a fairly exalted state . . . and so on.

We must just do the best we can, now as always.

2.0 I have been concentrating solely on the Revision and copying of the Ritual. Therefore I now live just as I always live in order to get a definite piece of work done: concentrating as it were *off* the Work. As Levi also adjures us by the Holy Names.

Coming back from lunch (a dozen Marennes Vertes and an Andouillette aux Pommes) I met Zelina Visconti, more lovely-ugly than ever in her wild way. She says that she is favourably disposed towards me, on the recommendation of her concierge ! ! ! "The tongue of good report hath already been heard in his favour. Advance, free and of good report!"

4.45. And only two pages done! but the decorations "marvelious"!

5.15. Another half-hour gone! in mere titivating the Opus! and now I'm too tired to as much as start Prana Yama. I will go to the Dôme and see what a citron pressé and a sandwich does for me, at the same time taking over the MS. of Liber DCCCCLXIII., which has been given me to correct, and doing it.
Please the pigs, the Visconti will cheer me up in the evening; and I shall get a good day in to-morrow.

6.35. Still at Liber DCCCCLXIII. [To be published shortly by "The Equinox."—ED.] I should like to write mantrams for each chapter.

7.20. Still at Liber DCCCCLXIII. I need hardly say that I am perfectly aware that in one sense all this working and ritual making and copying and illuminating is but a crowd of dog-faced demons, since the One Thought of Unity with Adonai is absent.
But I do it on purpose, making each thing I do into that Magic Will.
So if you ask me "Are you correcting Liber DCCCCLXIII.?" I reply, "No! I am Adonai!"

7.50. Arrival of the Visconti.

8.50. Departure of the Visconti. Really a necessary rest: for my head had begun to ache, and her kiss, half given and half taken, much refreshed me.

9.50. Have done Liber DCCCCLXIII. 'Tis hardly thinkable that one could have read it (merely) in the

9.50. time. Say three and a half hours! Well, if it doesn't count as Tapas, and Jap, and Yama, and Niyama, and all the rest of it, all I can say is that I think They don't play fair. I will now go and get something to eat, and (God willing) on my return settle down to real work, for I need daylight to copy my Ritual.

11.30. A sandwich and two coffees at the Versailles and a citron pressé at the Dome, some little chatter with M——e, B——e, H——s, and others. In fact, I'm a lazy unconcentrated hound. I started Mantra again, though; of course it goes quite easily.

11.50. Undressed, and the mantra going, and the Will toward Adonai less unapparent.

To-day I began ill, full of spiritual pride—look at the records of my early hours! One might have thought me a great master of magic loftily condescending to explain a few elementary truths suited to the capacity of his disciples.

The fact is that I am a toad, ugly and venomous, and if I do wear a precious jewel in my hand, that jewel is Adonai, and—well, come to think of it, I am Adonai. But St. John is not Adonai; and St. John had better do a little humiliation to-morrow. Nothing being more humiliating than Prana Yama, I will begin with that.

The Sixth Day

12.5. Thus then—oh ye great gods of Heaven!—begins the Sixth Day of the Great Magical Retirement of that

12.5. Holy Illuminated Man of God our Greatly Honoured Frater, O.M., Adeptus Exemptus 7° = 4° Brother-Elect of the Most Secret and Sublime Order A∴ A∴

He does with great difficulty (and no interior performance) just four breath-cycles.

Somebody once remarked that it had taken a hundred million years to produce me; I may add that I hope it will be another hundred million before God makes such another cur.

12.15. Have performed the Equilibrating Ritual of the Scourge, the Dagger, and the Chain; with the Holy Anointing Oil that bringeth the informing Fire into their Lustral Water.

12.35. I am so sleepy that I cannot concentrate at all. (I was trying the "Bornless One.") The magic goes well; good images and powerful, but I slack right off into sleep. It's the hour for heroic measures or else to say: A good night's rest, and start fresh in the morning! I suppose, as usual, I shall say the first and do the second.

12.45. Have risen, washed, performed the ritual "Thee I invoke, the Bornless One" physically.

The result fair. One gets better magical sight and feeling when one is performing a ritual in one's Astral Body, so called. For one is on the same plane as the things one's dealing with.

If, however, serious work is wanted, one must be all there. To get "materialized" "spirits"—pardon the absurd language!—one should (nay, must!) work inside

12.45. one's body. So, too, I think, for the highest spiritual work; for that Work extends from Malkuth to Kether.

Here is the great value of the rationalistic Eastern systems. [P.S. Of course scientifically worked with pencil, note-book, and stop-watch. The Yogi is usually in practice just as vague a dreamer as the mystic.] They keep one always balanced by common sense. One might go off on lines of pleasing illusion for years, until one was lost on the "Astral Plane."

All this, observe, is very meaningless, very vague at the best. What is the Astral Plane? Is there such a thing? How do its phantoms differ from those of absinthe, reverie, and love, and so on?

We may admit their unsubstantiality without denying their power; the phantoms of absinthe and love are potent enough to drive a man to death or marriage; while reverie may end in anti-vivisectionism or nut-food-madness.

On the whole, I prefer to explain the many terrible catastrophes I have seen caused by magic misunderstood by supposing that in magic one is working with some very subtle and essential function of the brain, whose disease may mean for one man paralysis, for another mania, for a third melancholia, for a fourth death. It is not *à priori* absurd to suggest that there may be some one particular thought that would cause death. In the man with heart disease, for instance, the thought "I will run quickly upstairs" might cause death quite as directly as "I will shoot myself." Yet of

12.45. course this thought acts through the will and the apparatus of nerves and muscles. But might not a sudden fear cause the heart to stop? I think cases are on record.

But all this is unknown ground, or, as Frank Harris would say, Unpath'd Waters. We are getting dangerously near "mental arsenic" and "all—god—good—bones—truth—lights—liver—mind—blessing—heart—one and not of a series—ante and pass the buck."

The common sense of the practical man of the world is good enough for me!

1.10. Will G. R. S. Mead or somebody wise like that tell me why it is that if I get out of my body and face (say) East, I can turn (in the "astral body") as far as West-Sou'-West or thereabouts, but no further except with very great difficulty and after long practice? In making the circle, just as I got to West, I would swing right back to West-Nor'-West: turn easily enough, in short, to any point but due West, within perhaps 5°, but never pass that point. I have taught myself to do it, but always with an effort.

Is this a common experience?

I connect it with my faculty of knowing direction, which all mountaineers and travellers who have been with me admit to be quite exceptional.

If I leave my tent or hut by a door facing, say, South-West, throughout that whole day, over all kinds of ground, through any imaginable jungle, in all kinds

1.10. of weather, fog, blizzard, blight, by night or day, I know within 5° (usually within 2°) the direction in which I faced when I left that tent or hut. And if I happen to have observed its compass bearing, of course I can deduce North by mere judgment of angle, at which I am very accurate.

Further, I keep a mental record, quite unconsciously, of the time occupied on a march; so that I can always tell the time within five minutes or so without consulting my watch.

Further, I have another automatic recorder which maps out distance plus direction. Suppose I were to start from Scott's and walk (or drive; it's all the same to me) to Haggerston Town Hall (wherever Haggerston may be; but say it's N.E.), thence to Maida Vale. From Maida Vale I could take a true line for Piccadilly again and not go five minutes walk out of my way, bar blind alleys, etc., and I should know when I got close to Scott's again before I recognised any of the surroundings.

It always seems to me that I get an intuition of the direction and length of line A (Scott's to Haggerston bee-line; in spite of any winding, it would make little odds if I went via Poplar), another intuition of line B (Haggerston to Maida Vale), and obtained my line C (back to Scott's) by "Subliminal trigonometry." In this example I am assuming that I had never been in London before. I have done precisely similar work in dozens of strange cities, even a twisted warren like Tangier or Cairo. I am worse in Paris than

1.10. anywhere else; I think because the main thoroughfares radiate from stars, and so the angles puzzle one. The power, too, suits ill with civilized life; it fades as I live in towns, revives as I get back to God's good earth. A seven-foot tent and the starlight—who wants more?

1.35. Well, I've woke myself writing this. The point that really struck me was this: what would happen if by severe training I forced my "astral body"—damn it! isn't there a term for it free from L. . . . –prostitution? (One speaks of "les deux prostitutions"; so it's all right.) My Scin-Laeca, then—what would happen if I forced my Scin-Laeca to become a Whirling Dervish? I couldn't get giddy, because my Semicircular canals would be at rest.
I must really try the experiment.
[Scin-Laeca. See Lord Lytton's "Strange Story."—ED.]

1.58. I will now devote myself to sleep, willing Adonai. Lord Adonai, give me deep rest like death, so that in very few hours I may be awake and active, full of lion-strength of purpose toward Thee!

7.35. My heroic conduct was nearly worth a "Nuit Blanche." For, being so thoroughly awake, I had all my Prana irritated, a feeling like the onset of a malarial attack, twelve hours before the temperature rises. I dare say it was after 3 o'clock when I slept; I woke too, several times, and ought to have risen and done Prana Yama but I did not. O worm! the sleepiest bird can easily catch *thee*! . . . I am not nicely awake, though it is to

- 7.35. my credit that I woke saying my mantra with vigour. 'Tis a bitter chill and damp the morn; yet must I rise and toil at my fair Ritual.
- 7.55. Settling down to copy.
- 10.12. Have completed my two prescribed pages of illumination.
  Will go and break my fast and do my business.
- 10.30. After writing letters went out and had coffee and two brioches.
- 11.50. At Louvre looking up some odd points in the lore of Khemi [Egypt.—ED.] for my Ritual.
- 12.20. I cannot understand it; but I feel faint for lack of food; I must get back to strict Hatha-Yoga feeding.
- 1.00. Half-dozen oysters and an entrecôte aux pommes.
- 2.05. Back to work. I am in a very low physical condition; quite equilibrated, but exhausted. I can hardly walk upright!
  Lord Adonai, how far I wander from the gardens of thy beauty, where play the fountains of the Elixir!
- 2.55. Wrote two pages; the previous were not really dry; so I must wait a little before illuminating.
  I will rest—if I can! In the Hanged Man posture.
- 4.30. I soon went to sleep and stayed there.
  It is useless to persist. . . . Yet I persist.
- 5.40. I was so shockingly cold that I went to the Dôme and had milk, coffee, and sandwich, eaten in Yogin manner.

5.40. But it has done no good as far as energy is concerned. I'm just as bad or worse than I was on the day which I have called the day of Apophis (third day). The only thing to my credit is the way I've kept the mantra going.

5.57. One thing at least is good; if anything does come of this great magical retirement—which I am beginning to doubt—it will not be mixed up with any other enthusiasm, poetic, venereal, or bacchanalian. It will be purely mystic. But as it has not happened yet—and just at present it seems incredible that it should happen—I think we may change the subject.

. . . . What a fool I am, by the way! I say that "He is God, and that there is no other God than He" 1800 times an hour; but I don't *think* it even once a day.

6.30. All my energy has suddenly come back.
Was it that Hatha-Yoga sandwich?
I go on copying the Ritual.

7.10. Copying finished. I will go and dine, and learn it by heart, humbly and thoughtfully. The illumination of it can be finished, with a little luck, in two more days.

I am disinclined to use the Ritual until it is beautifully coloured. As Zoroaster saith: "God is never so much turned away from man, and never so much sendeth him new paths, as when he maketh ascent to divine speculations or works, in a confused or disordered manner, and (as the oracle adds) with unhallowed lips, or unwashed feet. For of those who are thus

7.10. negligent the progress in imperfect, the impulses are vain, and the paths are dark."

7.40. Chez Lavenue. Bisque d'Ecrevisses, demi-perdreau à la Gelée, Cêpes Bordelaise, Coupe Jack. Demi Clos du Roi. I am sure I made a serious mistake in the beginning of this Operation of Magick Art. I ought to have performed a true Equilibration by an hour's Prana Yama in Asana (even if I had to do it without Kambhakham) at midnight, dawn, noon, and sunset, and I should have allowed nothing in heaven above, or in earth beneath, or in the waters under the earth, to have interfered with its due performance.
Instead I thought myself such a fine fellow that to get into Asana for a few minutes every midnight and the rest go-as-you-please would be enough. I am well punished.

8.30. This food, eaten in a Yogin and ceremonial manner, is doing me good. I shall end, God willing, with coffee, cognac, and cigar. It is a fatal error to knock the body to pieces and leave the consciousness intact, as has been the case with me all day. It is true that some people find that if they hurt the body, they make the mind unstable. True; they predispose it to hallucination.
One should use strictly corporeal methods to tame the body; strictly mental methods to control the mind.
This latter restriction is not so vitally important. Any weapon is legitimate against a public enemy like the mind. No truce nor quarter!

8.30. On the contrary, to use the spiritual forces to secure health, as certain persons attempt to do to-day, is the vilest black magic. This is one of the numerous reasons for supposing that Jesus Christ was a Brother of the Left-Hand Path.

Now my body has been treating me well, waking nicely at convenient hours, sleeping at suitable times, keeping itself to itself . . . an admirable body. Then why shouldn't I take it out and give it the best dinner Lavenue can serve? . . . Provided that it doesn't stop saying that mantra!

It would be so easy to trick myself into the belief that I had attained! It would be so easy to starve myself until there was "visions about"! It would be so easy to write a sun-splendid tale of Adonai my Lord and my lover, so as to convince the world and myself that I had found Him! With my poetic genius, could I not outwrite St. John (my namesake) and Mrs. Dr. Anna Bonus Kingsford? Yea, I could deceive myself if I did not train and fortify my scepticism at every point. That is the great usefulness of this record; one will be able to see afterwards whether there is any trace of poetic or other influence. But this is my sheet-anchor: I cannot wrote a lie, either in poetry or about magic. These are serious things that constitute my personality; and I could more easily blow out my brains that write a poem which I did not feel. The apparent exception is in case of irony.

[P.S. I wonder whether it would be possible to draw up a mathematical table, showing curves of food (and

8.30. digestion), drink, other physical impulses, weather, and so on, and comparing them with the curve of mystic enthusiasm and attainment.
Through it is perhaps true that perfect health and *bien-être* are the bases of any true trance or rapture, it seems unlikely that mere exuberance of the former can excite the latter.
In other words there is probably some first matter of the work which is not anything we know of as bodily. On my return to London, I must certainly put the matter before more experienced mathematicians, and if possible, get a graphic analysis of the kind indicated.]

9.20. How difficult and expensive it is to get drunk, when one is doing magic! Nothing exhilarates or otherwise affects one. Oh, the pathos and tragedy of those lines:

> Come where the booze is cheaper !
> Come where the pots hold more !

How I wish I had written them!

10.08. Having drunk a citron pressé and watched the poker game at the Dôme for a little, I now return home. I thought to myself, "Let me chuck the whole thing overboard and be sensible, and get a good night's rest"—and perceived that it would be impossible. I am so far into this Operation that

> pausing to cast one last glance back
> O'er the safe road—'twas gone!

10.08. I must come out of it either an Adept or a maniac. Thank the Lord for that! It saves trouble.

10.20. Undressed and robed. Will do an Aspiration in the Hanged Man position, hoping to feel rested and fit by midnight.
The Incense has arrived from London; and I feel its magical effects most favourable.
O creature of Incense! I conjure thee by Him that sitteth upon the Holy Throne and liveth and reigneth for ever as the Balance of Righteousness and Truth, that thou comfort and exalt my soul with Thy sweet perfume, that I may be utterly devoted to this Work of the Invocation of my Lord Adonai, that I may fully attain thereto, beholding Him face to face—as it is written "Before there was Equilibrium, Countenance beheld not Countenance"—yea, being utterly absorbed in His ineffable Glory—yea, being That of which there is no Image either in speech or thought.

10.55. What a weary world we live in! No sooner am I betrayed into making a few flattering remarks about my body that I find everything wrong with it, and two grains of Cascara Sagrada necessary to its welfare!
. . . . I wish I knew where I was! I don't at all recognise what Path I am on; it doesn't seem like a Path at all. As far as I can see, I am drifting rudderless and sailless on a sea of no shore—the False Sea of the Qliphoth. For in my stupidity I began to try a certain ritual of the Evil Magic, so called. . . . Not

10.55. evil in truth, because only that is evil (in one sense) which does not lead to Adonai. (In another sense, all is evil which is not Adonai.) And of course I had the insane idea that this ritual would serve to stimulate my devotion. For the information of the Z.A.M., I may explain that this ritual pertained to Saturn in Libra; and, though right enough in its own plane, is a dog-faced demon in this operation. Is it, though? I am so blind that I can no longer decide the simplest problems. Else, I see so well, and am so balanced, that I see both sides of every question.
In chess-blindness one used to abjure the game. I never tried to stick it through; I wish I had. Anyhow, I have to stick this through!
O Lord of the Eye, let thine Eye be ever open upon me! For He that watcheth Israel doth not slumber nor sleep!
Lord Shiva, open Thou the Eye upon me, and consume me altogether in its brilliance!
Destroy this Universe! Eat up thine hermit in thy terrible jaws! Dance Thou upon this prostrate saint of Thine!
. . . I suffer from thirst . . . it is a thirst of the body . . . yet the thirst of the soul is deeper, and impossible to quench.
Lord Adonai! Let the Powers of Geburah plunge me again and again into the Fires of Pain, so that my steel may be tempered to that Sword of Magic that invoketh Thy Knowledge and Thy Conversation.
Hoor! Elohim Gibor! Kamael! Seraphim! Graphiel!

10.55. Bartzabel! Madim! I conjure ye in the Number Five.

By the Flaming Star of my Will! By the Senses of my Body! By the Five Elements of my Being! Rise! Move! Appear! Come ye forth unto me and torture me with your fierce pangs ... for why? because I am the Servant of the Same your God, the True Worshipper of the Highest.

Ol sonuf vaoresaji, gono Iadapiel, elonusaha cælazod.

I rule above ye, said the Lord of Lords, exalted in power.
[From Dr. Dee's MSS.—ED.]

11.17. Will now try the Hanged Man again.

11.30. Very vigorous and good, my willing of Adonai. . . . I should like to explain the difficulty. It would be easy enough to form a magical Image of Adonai: and He would doubtless inform it. But it would only be an Image. This may be the meaning of the commandment "Thou shalt not make any graven image," etc., just as "Thou shalt not have any other Gods but me" implies single-minded devotion (Ekâgrata) to Adonai. So any mental or magical Image must necessarily fall short of the Truth. Consequently one has to will that which is formless; and this is very difficult. To concentrate the mind upon a definite thing is hard enough; yet at least there is something to grasp, and some means of checking one's result. But in this case, the moment one's will takes a magical shape—and the will simply revels in creating shapes—at the moment one knows that one has gone off the track.

11.30. This is of course (nearly enough) another way of expressing the Hindu Meditation whose method is to kill all thoughts as they arise in the mind. The difference is that I am aiming at a target, while they are preventing arrows from striking one. In my aspiration to know Adonai, I resemble their Yogis who concentrate on their "personal Lord"; but at the same time it must be remembered that I am not going to be content with what would content them. In other words, I am going to *define* "the Knowledge and Conversation of my Holy Guardian Angel" as equal to Neroda-Samapatti, the trance of Nibbana.
I hope I shall be able to live up to this!

11.55. Have been practising Asana, etc. I forgot one thing in the last entry: I had been reproaching Adonai that for six days I had evoked Him in vain. . . . I got the reply, "The Seventh Day shall be the Sabbath of the Lord thy God."
So mote it be!

The Seventh Day.

12.17. I began this great day with Eight breath-cycles; was stopped by the indigestion trouble in its other form. (P.S.—Evidently the introduction of the Cascara into my sensitive aura made its action instantaneous.) My breathing passages were none too clear, either; I have evidently taken a chill.
Now, O, my Lord Adonai, thou Self-Glittering One, wilt Thou not manifest unto Thy chosen one? For see

12.17. me! I am as a little white dove trembling upon thine altar, its throat stretched out to the knife. I am as a young child bought in the slave market . . . and night is fallen! I await Thee, O my Lord, with a great longing, stronger than Life; yet am I as patient as Death.
There was a certain Darwesh whose turban a thief stole. But when they said to him, "See! he hath taken the road to Damascus!" that holy man answered, as he went quietly to the cemetery, "I will await him here!"
So, therefore, there is one place, O thou thief of my heart's love, Adonai, to which thou must come at last; and that place is the tomb in which lie buried all my thoughts and emotions, all that which is "I, and Me, and Mine." There will I lay myself and await thee, even as our Father Christian Rosenkreutz that laid himself in the Pastos in the Vault of the Mountain of the Caverns, Abiegnus, on whose portal did he cause to be written the words, "Post Lux Crucis Annos Patebo." So Thou wilt enter in (as did Frater N. N. and his companions) and open the Pastos; and with thy Winged Globe thou wilt touch the Rosy Cross upon my breast, and I shall wake into life—the true life that is Union with Thee.
So therefore—perinde ac cadaver—I await Thee.

12.43. I wrote, by the way, on some previous day (IV. 12.5? A.M.) that I used the Supreme formula of Awaiting. . . . Ridiculous mouse! is it not written in the Book of the

12.43. Heart that is girt about with the Serpent that "To await Thee is the End, not the Beginning"?
It is as silly as rising at midnight, and saying, "I will go out and sleep in the sun."
But I am an Irishman, and if you offer me a donkey-ride at a shilling the first hour and sixpence the second, you must not be surprised at the shrewd silliness of my replying that I will take the second hour first.
But that is always the way; the love of besting our dearest friends in a bargain is native to us: and so, even in religion, when we are dealing with our own souls, we try to cheat. I go out to cut an almond rod at midnight, and, finding it inconvenient, I "magically affirm" that ash is almond and that seven o'clock is twelve. It seems a pity to have become a magician, capable of forcing Nature to accommodate herself to your statements, for no better use to be made of the power than this!
Miracles are only legitimate when there is no other issue possible. It is waste of power (the most expensive kind of power) to "make the spirits bring us all kinds of food" when we live next door to the Savoy; that Yogi was a fool who spent forty years learning to walk across the Ganges when all his friends did it daily for two pice; and that man does ill when he invokes Tahuti to cure a cold in the head while Mr. Lowe's shop is so handy in Stafford Street.
But miracles may be performed in an extremity; and are.
This brings us round in a circle; the miracle of the

12.43. Knowledge and Conversation of the Holy Guardian Angel is only to be performed when the magus has rowed himself completely out; in the language of the Tarot, when the Magus has become the Fool.
But for my faith in the Ritual DCLXXI. I should be at the end of my spells.
Well? We shall see in the upshot.

1.25. I really almost begin to believe IT will happen.
For I lay down quite free of worry or anxiety (hugging myself, as it were), perfectly sure of Him in the simple non-assertive way that a child is sure of its mother, in a state of pleased expectancy, my thoughts quite suppressed in an intent listening, as it were for the noise of the wind of His chariot, as it were for the rustle of His wings.
For lo! through the heaven of Nu He rideth in His chariot—soon, soon He will be here!
Into this state of listening come certain curious things—formless flittings, I know not what. Also, what I used to call "telephone-cross" voices—voices of strange people saying quite absurd commonplace things—"Here, let's feel it!" "What about lunch?" "So I said to him: Did you . . ." and so on; just as if one were overhearing a conversation in a railway carriage. I beheld also Kephra, the Beetle God, the Glory of Midnight. But let me compose myself again to sleep, as did the child Samuel.
If He should choose to come, He can easily awaken me.

3.35. I have been asleep a good deal—one long dream in which P——t, Lord M——y of B——n and my wife are all staying with me in my mother's house. My room the old room, with one page torn out—for I conceived it as part of a book, somehow! Oh such a lot of this dream! Most of it clearly due to obvious sources—I don't see where Lord M——y comes in. Very likely he is dead. I have had that happen now and again. [P.S.—this was not the case.]

The dream changed, too, to a liner; where Japanese stole my pipe in a series of adventures of an annoying type—every one acted as badly as he knew how, and as unexpectedly.

Waking just now, and instantly concentrating on Adonai, I found my body seized with a little quivering, very curious and pleasant, like

> trembling leaves in a continuous air.

I think I have heard this state of Interior Trembling described in some mystic books. I think the Shakers and Quakers had violent shudderings. Abdullah Haji of Shiraz writes:—

> Just as the body shudders when the Soul
> Gives up to Allah in its quick career
> Itself....

It is the tiniest, most intimate trembling, not unlike that of Kambhakham or "Vindu-siddhi" [see the Shiva Sanhita.—ED.] properly performed; but of a female quality. I feel as if I were being shaken; in

3.35. the other cases I recognize my own ardour as the cause. It is very gentle and sweet.
So now I may turn back to wait for Him.

3.50. The Voice of the Nadi has changed to a music faint yet very full and very sweet, with a bell-like tone more insistent than the other notes at intervals.

5.45. Again awake, and patient-eager. The dreams flow through me ceaselessly.
This time a house where I, like a new Bluebeard, have got to conceal my wives from each other. But my foolish omission to knife them brings it about that I have thirty-nine secret chambers, and only one open one in each case.
Oh, yards of it! And all sorts of people come in to supper—which there isn't any, and we have to do all sorts of shifts—and all the wives think themselves neglected—as they are bound to do, if one is insane enough to have forty—and I loathed them all so! it was terrible having to fly round and comfort and explain; the difficulty increases (I should judge) as about the fifth power of the number of wives...
I'm glad I'm awake!
Yea, and how glad when I am indeed awake from this glamour life, awake to the love my Lord Adonai!
It is bitter chill at dawn. A consecrating cold it seems to me—yet I will not confront it and rejoice in it—I am already content, having ceased to strive.

7.15. Again awake, deliciously rested and refreshed.

9.45. Again awake, ditto.

11.35. I will now break my fast with a sandwich and coffee, eaten Yogin-wise.

I seem like one convalescent after a fever; very calm, very clean, rather weak, too weak, indeed, to be actually happy: but content.

I spent the morning posing for Michael Brenner, a sculptor who will one day be heard of. Very young yet, but I think the best man of his generation—of those whose work I have seen. By the way, I am suffering from a swollen finger, since yesterday morning or possibly earlier. I have given it little attention, but it is painful.

I want to explain why I have so carefully recorded the somewhat banal details of all I have eaten and drunk.

1. All food is a species of intoxicant; hence a fruitful source of error. Should I obtain any good result, I might say "You were starved" or "You were drunk." It is very easy to get visions of sorts by either process, and to delude oneself into the idea that one has attained, mistaking the Qliphoth for Kether.

2. In keeping the vow "I will interpret every phenomenon as a particular dealing of God with my soul" the mere animal actions are the most resistant. One cannot see the nature of the phenomenon; it seems so unimportant; one is inclined to despise it. Hence I enter it in the record as a corrective.

3. If others are to read this, I should like them to see that elaborate codes of morality have nothing to do with my system. No question of sin and grace ever enters it.

If a chemist wants to prepare copper sulphate from its oxide, he does not hesitate on the ground that sulphuric acid, thrown in the eyes, hurts people. So I use the moral drug which will produce the desired result, whether that drug be what people commonly call poison or no. In short, I act like a sensible man; and I think I deserve every credit for introducing this completely new idea into religion.

12.25. That function of my brain which says "You ought to be willing Adonai" sometimes acts. But I am willing Him! It is so active because all this week it has been working hard, and doesn't realise that its work is done. Just as a retired grocer wakes up and thinks "I must go and open the shop."

In Hindu phrase, the thought-stuff, painfully forced all these days into one channel, has acquired the habit [*i.e.*, of flowing naturally in it.—ED.] I am Ekâgrata—one-pointed.

Just as if one arranges a siphon, one has to suck and suck for a while, and then when the balance in the two arms of the tube is attained, the fluid goes on softly and silently of its own act. Gravitation which was against us is now for us.

So now the whole destiny of the Universe is by me overcome; I am impelled, with ever-gathering and irresistible force, toward Adonai.

12.25. Vi Veri Vniversvm Vivvs Vici!

12.57. Back home to illuminate my beautiful Ritual.

3.30. Two pages done and set aside to dry. I think I will go for a little walk and enjoy the beautiful sun.
Also to the chemist's to have my finger attended to.

4.05. The chemist refused to do anything; and so I did it myself. It is the romantic malady of ingrowing nail; a little abscess had formed. Devilish painful after the clean-up. Will go the walk aforesaid.

4.17. I ought to note how on this day there is a complete absence of all one's magical apparatus. The mantra has slowed down to (at a guess) a quarter of its old pace. The rest in unison. This is because the feeling of great power, etc. etc., is the mere evidence of conflict—the thunder of the guns. Now all is at peace; the power of the river, no more a torrent.
The Concourse of the Forces has become the Harmony of the Forces; the word Tetragrammation is spoken and ended; the holy letter Shin is descended into it. For the roaring God of Sinai we have the sleeping Babe of Bethlehem. A fulfilment, not a destroying, of the Law.

4.45. Am at home again. I will lie down in the Position of the Hanged Man, and await the coming of my Lord.

6.00. Arisen again to go out to diner. I was half-asleep some of the time.

6.15. Dinner—Hors d'Œuvre—Tripes à la Mode de Caen—Filet de Porc—Glace—$\frac{1}{2}$ Graves. Oh, how the world

6.15. hath inflexible intellectual rulers! I eat it in a semi-Yogin manner.

6.20. I am wondering whether I have not made a mistake in allowing myself to sleep.
It would be just like me, if there were only one possible mistake to make, to make it! I was perfect, had I only watched. But I let my faith run away with me. . . . I wonder.

6.45. Dinner over, I go on as I am in calm faith and love. Why should I expect a catastrophic effect? Why should not the circumstances of Union with God be compatible with the normal consciousness? Interpenetrating and illuminating it, if you like; but not destroying it. Well, I don't know why it shouldn't be; but I bet it isn't! All the spiritual experience I have had argues against such a theory.
On the contrary, it will leave the reason quite intact, supreme Lord of its own plane. Mixing up the planes is the sad fate of many a mystic. How many do I know in my own experience who tell me that, obedient to the Heavenly Vision, they will shoot no more rabbits! Thus they found a system on trifles, and their Lord and God is some trumpery little elemental masquerading as the Almighty.
I remember my Uncle Tom telling me that he was sure God would be displeased to see me in a blue coat on Sunday. And to-day he is surprised and grieved that I do not worship his god—or even my own tailor, as would be surely more reasonable!

7.32. How is it that I expect the reward at once? Surely I am presuming on my magical power, which is an active thing, and therefore my passivity is not perfect. Of course, when IT happens, it happens out of time and space—now or ten years hence it is all the same. All the same to IT; not all the same to me, O.M. So O.M. (the dog!) persists irrationally in wanting IT, here and now. Surely, indeed, it is a lack of faith, a pandering to the time-illusion . . . and so forth. Yes, no doubt it is all magically wrong, even magically absurd; yet, though I see the snare, I deliberately walk into it. I suppose I shall be punished somehow . . . Good! there's the excuse I wanted. Fear is failure: I must dare to do wrong. Good!

7.50. It has just occurred to me that this Waiting and Watching is the supreme Magical strain. Every slight sound or other impression shocks one tremendously. It is easy enough to shut out sounds and such when one is concentrating in active magic: I did all my early evocations in Chancery Lane. But now one is deliberately opening all the avenues of sense to admit Adonai! One has destroyed one's own Magic Circle. The whole of that great Building is thrown down. . . . Therefore I am in a worse hole that I ever was before—and I've only just realized it. A footfall on the pavement is most acute agony—because it is not Adonai. My hearing, normally rather dull, is intensely sharpened; and I am thirty yards from the electric trams of the Boulevard Montparnasse at the busiest hour of the evening. . . .

7.50. And the Visconti may turn up! . . .
Eli, Eli, lama sabacthani!

8.45. I went out to the Dôme to drink my final citron pressé and to avoid the Visconti. Am returned, and in bed. I shall try and sleep now, waking in time for midnight and the quiet hours.

8.53. I have endured the supreme temptation and assault of the Enemy.
In this wise. First, I found that I did not want sleep—I couldn't stop "Waiting." Next, I said "Since last night that Black Ritual (see entry 10.55) did at least serve to turn all my thoughts to the One Thought, I will try it again . . ."
Then I said: "No; to do so is not pure 'waiting.;' "
And then—as by a flash of lightning—the Abyss of the Pit opened, and my whole position was turned. I saw my life from the dawn of consciousness till now as a gigantic "pose"; my very love of truth assumed for the benefit of my biographer! All these strange things suffered and enjoyed for no better purpose than to seem a great man. One cannot express the horror of this thought; it is The thought that murders the soul—and there is no answer to it. So universal is it that it is impossible to prove the contrary. So one must play the man, and master it and kill it utterly burying it in that putrid hell from which it sprang Luckily I have dealt with it before. Once when I lived at Paddington J——s and F——r were with me talking, and, when they went, thoughtfully left this devil-thought behind—the agony is with me yet

8.53. That, though, was only a young mild devil, though of the same bad brood. It said: "Is there any Path or Attainment? Have you been fooled all along?"

But to-night's thought struck at my own integrity, at the inmost truth of the soul and of Adonai.

As I said, there is no answer to it; and as these seven days have left me fairly master of the fortress, I caught him young, and assigned him promptly to the oubliette.

I put down this—not as a "pose"—but because the business is so gigantic. It encourages me immensely; for if my Dweller on the Threshold be that most formidable devil, how vast must be the Pylon that shelters him, and how glorious must be the Temple just beyond!

9.30. It seems that there was one more mistake to make; for I've made it!

I started to attempt to awaken the Kundalini—the magical serpent that sleeps at the base of the spine; coiled in three coils and a half around the Sushumna; and instead of pumping the Prana up and down the Sushumna until Siva was united with Sakti in the Sahasrara-Cakkram, I tried—God knows why; I'm stupider than an ass or H . . . C . . . .—to work the whole operation in Muladhara—with the obvious result.

There are only two more idiocies to perform—one, to take a big dose of Hashish and record the ravings as if they were Samadhi; and two, to go to church. I may as well give up.

9.30. Yet here answers me the everlasting Yea and Amen: Thou canst not give up, for I will bring thee through. Yet here I lie, stripped of all magic force, doubting my own peace and faith, farther from Adonai than ever before—and yet—and yet—

Do I not know that every error is a necessary step in the Path? The longest way round is the shortest way home. But it is disgusting! There's a grim humour in it, too. The real Devil of the Operation must be sitting with sardonic grin upon his face, enjoying my perplexity—

For that Dweller-of-the-Threshold-thought was not as dead as I supposed; as I write he comes again and again, urging me to quit the Path, to abandon the unequal contest. Luckily, friend Dweller, you prove too much! Your anxiety shows me that I am not as far from attainment as my own feelings would have me think. At least, though, I am thrown into the active again; I shall rise and chant the Enochian Calls and invoke the Bornless One, and clear a few of the devils away, and get an army of mighty angels around me—in short, make another kind of fool of myself, I wonder?

Anyway, I'll do it. Not a bad idea to ask Thoth to send me Taphtatharath with a little information as to the route—I do not know where I am at all. This is a strange country, and I am very lonely.

This shall be my ritual.
   1. Banishing Pentagram Ritual.
   2. Invoking ditto. [These will appear in No. 2 "Liber O." --- ED.]

3. "The Bornless One." [See the "Goetia."—ED.]
4. The Calls I—VI with the rituals of the five Grades. [From Dr. Dee's and the G∴ D∴ MSS.—ED.]
5. Invocation of Thoth.
6. (No: I will *not* use the New Ritual, nor will I discuss th matter.) An impromptu invocation of Adonai.
7. Closing formulae.

To work, then!

11.15. The ceremony went well enough; the forces invoked came readily and visibly; Thoth in particular as friendly as ever—I fancy He takes this record as a compliment to Him—He's welcome to it, poor God!
The L.V.X. came, too but not enough to pierce the awful shroud of darkness that by my folly I have woven for myself.
So at the end I found myself on the floor, so like Rodin's Cruche Cassée Danaide Girl as never was . . . As I ought to have been in the beginning! Well, one thing I got (again!), that is, that when all is said and done, I am that I am, and all these thoughts of mine, angels and devils both, are only fleeting moods of me. The one true self of me is Adonai. Simple! Yet I cannot remain in that simplicity.
I got this "revelation" through the Egyptian plane, a partial illumination of the reason. It has cleared up the mind; but alas! the mind is still there. This is the strength and weakness both of the Egyptian plane,

11.15. that it is so lucid and spiritual and yet so practical. When I say weakness, I mean that it appeals to my weakness; I am easily content with the smaller results, so that they seduce me from going on to the really big ones. I am quite happy as a result of my little ceremony—whereas I ought to be taking new and terrible oaths! Yet why should Tahuti be so kind to me, and Asar Unnefer so unkind?

The answer comes direct from Tahuti himself: Because you have learned to write perfectly, but have not yet taught yourself to suffer.

True enough, the last part!

Asar Un-nefer, thou perfected One, teach me Thy mysteries! Let my members be torn by Set and devoured by Sebek and Typhon! Let my blood be poured out upon Nile, and my flesh be given to Besz to devour! Let my Phallus be concealed in the maw of Mati, and my Crown be divided among my brethren! Let the jaws of Apep grind me into poison! Let the sea of poison swallow me wholly up!

Let Asi my mother rend her robes in anguish, and Nepti weep for me unavailing.

Then shall Asi being forth Hoor, and Heru-pa-kraat shall leap glad from her womb. The Lord of Vengeance shall awaken; Sekhet shall roar, and Pasht cry aloud. Then shall my members be gathered together, and my bonds shall be unloosed; and my khu shall be mighty in Khem for ever and ever!

11.37. I return to he place of the Evil Triad, of Ommo Satan that is before the altar. There to expiate my folly in

11.37. attaching myself to all this great concourse of ideas that I have here recorded, instead of remaining fixed in the single stronghold of Unity with Myself.

11.54. And so this great day draws to its end.
These are indeed the Qliphoth, the Qliphoth of Kether, the Thaumiel, twin giant heads that hate and tear each other.
For the horror and darkness have been unbelievable; yet again, the light and brilliance have been almost insupportable.
I was never so far, and never so near . . . But the hour approaches. Let me collect myself, and begin the new day in affirmation of my Unity with my Lord Adonai!

The Eighth Day

12.3. Thus the Eighth day, the Second Week, begins. I am in Asana. For some reason or other, Pranayama is quite easy. Concentrating on Adonai, I was in Kambhakham for a whole minute without distress.
It *is* true, by the way. I was—and am—in some danger of looking on this Record as a Book; *i.e.*, of emphasising things for their literary effect, and diminishing the importance of others which lend themselves less obviously.
But the answer to this, friend Satan! is that the Canon of Art is Truth, and the Canon of Magic is Truth; my true record will make a good book, and my true book will make a good record.

12.3. *Ekam evam advaitam* ! friend Satan! One and not two. *Hua allahu alazi lailaha illa Hua!*

But what shall by my "considerations" for this week? I am so absolutely become as a pantomorphous Iynx that all things look alike to me; there are just as many pros and cons to Pranayama as to Ceremonial, etc. etc., —and the pros and cons are so numerous and far reaching that I simply dare not start discussing even one. I can see an endless avenue in every case. In short, like the hashish-drunkard in full blast, I am overwhelmed by the multitude of my own magical Images. I have become the great Magician—Mayan, the Maker of Illusion—the Lord of the Brethren of the Left-hand Path.

I don't "wear my iniquity as an aureole, deathless in Spiritual Evil," as Mr. Waite thinks; but it's nearly as bad as that. There seems only one reply to this great question of the Hunchback (I like to symbolize the spirit of Questioning by "?"—a little crooked thing that asks questions) and that is to keep on affirming Adonai, and refusing to be obsessed by any images of discipline or magic.

Of course! but this is just the difficulty—as it was in the Beginning, is now, and every shall be, world without end! My beautiful answer to the question, How will you become a millionaire? is: I will possess a million pounds. The "answer" is not an answer; it is a begging of the question.

What a fool I am! and people think me clever. *Ergo* perhaps!

12.3. Anyhow I will now (12.37) go quietly to sleep—as I am always saying, and never do when I say it!—in the hope that daylight may bring counsel.

7.40. Woke fresh and comfortable. Sleep filled with dreams and broken into short lengths. I ought to observe that this is a very striking result of forging this magic chain; for in my normal life I am one of the soundest sleepers imaginable. Nine solid hours without turning once is my irreducible minimum.

9.10. Having done an hour's illumination of the New Ritual, will go and break my fast with coffee and a brioche, and thence proceed to Michael Brenner's studio.

12.15. I have spent the morning in modelling Siddhasana—a more difficult task than appeared. Rather like THE task!
But I went on with the mantra, and made some Reflections upon Kamma.
I will now have a Yogin coffee and sandwich, and return to my illumination of the Ritual.
In the desert of my soul, where no herb grows, there is yet one little spring. I am still one-pointed, at least in the lower sense that I have no desire or ambition but this of accomplishing the Great Work.
Barren is this soul of mine, in these $3\frac{1}{2}$ years of drought (the $3\frac{1}{2}$ coils of the Kundalini are implied by this) and this Ekâgrata is the little cloud like a hand (Yod, the Lingam of great Shiva). And, though I catch up my robe and run before the chariot of the King into Jezreel, it may be

12.15. that before I reach those gates the whole sky may be one black flame of thundercloud, and the violet swords of the lightning may split asunder its heavy womb, and the rain, laughing like a young child, may dance upon the desert!

12.58. The Light beginneth to dawn upon the Path, so that I see a little better where I stand. This whole journey seems under some other formula than IAO—perhaps a Pentagram formula with which I am not clearly acquainted. If I knew the Word of the Grade, I could foretell things: but I don't.
I think I will read through the whole Record to date and see if I can find an Ariadne-clue.

1.15. Back, and settled to Ritual-painting.

2.30. Finished: bar frontispiece and colophon, which I can design and execute to-morrow.

3.0. Took half an hour off, making a silly sketch of a sunset. Will now read through the Record, and Reflect upon it.

4.15. "Before I was blind; now I see!" Yesterday I was right up to the Threshold, right enough; but got turned back by the Dweller. I did not see the Dweller till afterwards (8.53 entry) for he was too subtle. I will look carefully back to try and spot him; for if I "knew his Name" I could pass by—*i.e.*, next time I climb up to the Threshold of the Pylon.
I think the entries 1.25 and 3.35 A.M. explain it "Hugging myself, as it were." How fatally

4.15. accurate! I wrote it and never saw the hellish snare! I ought to have risen up and prepared myself ceremonially as a bride, and waited in the proper magical manner. Also I was too pleased with the Heralds of my Lord's coming—the vision of Khephra, etc. It was perhaps this subtle self-satisfaction that lost me ... so I fell to the shocking abyss of last night!

The Dweller of the Threshold is never visible until after one has fallen; he is a Veiled God and smites like the Evil Knight in Malory, riding and slaying—and no man seeth him.

But when you are tumbled headlong into Hell, where he lives, then he unveils his Face, and blasts you with its horror!

Very good, John St. John, now you know! You are plain John St. John and you have to climb right up again through the paths to the Threshold; and remember this time to mortify that self-satisfaction! Go at it more reverently and humbly—oh, you dog, how I loathe you for your Vileness! To have risen so high, and—now—to be thus fallen!

4.40. The question arises: how to mortify this self-satisfaction?

Asceticism notoriously fosters egoism; how good am I to go without dinner! How noble! What renunciation!

On the other hand, the good wine in one says: "A fine fellow I have made my coffin of!"

The answer is simple, the old answer: *Think not of*

4.40. *St. John and his foolishness; think of Adonai!* Exactly: the one difficulty!

My best way out will be to concentrate on the New Ritual, learn it perfectly by heart, work it at the right moment. . . .

I will go, with this idea, to have a Citron pressé; thence to my Secret Restaurant, and dine, always learning the Ritual.

I will leave off the mantra, though it is nearly as much part of me as my head by now; and instead repeat over and over again the words of the Ritual so that I can do it in the end with perfect fluency and comprehension. And this time may Adonai build the House!

6.10. Instead I met Dr. R——, who kindly offered to teach me how to obtain astral visions! (P.S.—The tone of this entry wrongs me. I sat patiently and reverently, like a *chela* with his *guru*, hoping to hear the Word I needed.) Thence I went my long and lonely walk to my Secret Restaurant, learning the Ritual as I went.

7.15. Arrived at the Secret Restaurant. Ordered 6 oysters, Rable de Lièvre poivrade purée de marrons, and Glace "Casserole" with a small bottle of Perrier Water.

I know the New Ritual down to the end of the Confession.

It was hard to stop the mantra—the moment my thought wandered, up it popped!

8.3. I shall add Café Cognac Cigare to this debauch.

I continue learning the Ritual.

8.40. I will return and humble myself before the Lord

8.40. Adonai. It is near the night of the Full Moon; in my life the Full Moon hath ever been of great augury. But tonight I am too poor in spirit to hope.

Lo! I was travelling on the paths of Lamed and of Mem, of Justice and the Hanged Man, and I fell into both the pitfalls thereof. Instead of the Great Balance firmly held, I found only Libra, the house of Venus and of the exaltation of Saturn; and these evil planets, smiling and frowning, overcame me. And so for the sublime Path of Man; instead of that symbol of the Adept, his foot set firmly upon heaven, his whole figure showing forth the Reconciler with the Invisible, I found but the stagnant and bitter water of selfishness, the Dead Sea of the Soul. For all is Illusion. Who saith "I" denieth Adonai, save only if he mean Adonai. And Daleth the Door of the Pylon, is that Tree whereon the Adept of Man hangeth, and Daleth is Love Supernal, that if it be inserted in the word ANI, "I," giveth ADNI, Adonai.

Subtle art thou and deadly, O Dweller of the Threshold (P.S.—This name is a bad one. *Dweller beside the Pylon* is a better term; for he is not in the straight path, which is simple and easy and open. He is never "overcome"; to meet him is the proof of having strayed. The Key fits the Door perfectly; but he who is drunken on the bad wine of Sense and Thought fumbles thereat. And of course there is a great deal of door, and very little key- hole), who dost use my very love of Adonai to destroy me!

Yet how shall I approach Him, if not with reverent

8.40. joy, with a delicious awe? I must wash His feet with my tears; I must die at His gateway; I must . . . I know not what . . .
Adonai, be thou tender unto me Thy slave, and keep my footsteps in the Way of Truth! . . . I will return and humble myself before the Lord Adonai.

10.18. Home again; have done odd necessary things, and am ready to work. I feel slack; and I feel that I have been slack, though probably the Record shows a fair amount of work done. But I am terribly bruised by the Great Fall; these big things leave the body and mind no worse, apparently; but they hurt the Self, and later that is reflected into the lower parts of the man as insanity or death.
I must attain, or . . . an end of John St. John.
An end of him, one way or the other, then!
Good-bye, John!

10.30. Ten minutes wasted in sheer mooning! I'm getting worse every minute.

10.40. Fooled away ten minutes more!

10.57. Humiliation enough! For though I made the cross with Blood and Flame, I cannot even remain concentrated in humiliation, which yet I feel so acutely What a wormy worm I am! I tried the new strict Siddhasana, only to find that I had hurt myself so this morning with it that I cannot bear it at all, even with the pillow to support the instep.
I will just try and do a little Pranayama, to see if I can

10.57. stay doing any one simple thing for ten minutes at a stretch!

11.30. Twenty-five Breath-Cycles . . . But it nearly killed me. I was saying over the Ritual, and did so want to get to the Formulation of the Hexagram at least, if not to the Reception. As it was, I broke down during the Passage of the Pylons, luckily not till I had reached that of Tahuti.
But it is a good rule; when in doubt play Pranayama. For one can no longer worry about the Path: the Question is reduced to the simple problem: Am, I, or am I not, going to burst?
I got all the sweating and trembling of the body that heart could desire; but no "jumping about like a frog" or levitation. A pity!

11.45. I shall read for a little in the Yoga-Shastra as a rest. Then for the end of the day and the Beginning of the Ninth Day. Zoroaster (or Pythagoras?) informs us that the number Nine is sacred, and attains the summit of Philosophy. I'm sure I hope so!

11.56. I get into Asana . . . and so endeth the Eighth Lesson.

The Ninth Day

12.2. Thus I began this great day, being in my Asana firm and easy, and holding in my breath for a full minute while I threw my will with all my might towards Adonai.

12.19. Have settled myself for the night. Will continue a little, learning the Ritual.

12.37. Having learnt a few passages of a suitable nature to go to sleep upon, I will do so.

. . . Now I hope that I shall; surely the Reaction of Nature against the Magical Will must be wearing down at last!

2.12. I wake. It takes me a little while to shake off the dominion of sleep, very intense and bitter.

3.4 Thus John St. John—for it is not convenient further to speak as "I"—performed 45 Breath-cycles; for 20 minutes he had to struggle against the Root of the Powers of Sleep, and the obstruction of his left nostril.

During his Kambhakham he willed Adonai with all his might.

Let him sleep, invoking Adonai!

5.40. Well hath he slept, and well awakened.

The last entry should extend to 3.30 or thereabouts; probably later; for, invoking Adonai, he again got the beginnings of the Light, and the "telephone-cross" voices very strongly. But this time he was fortunately able to concentrate on Adonai with some fervour, and these things ceased to trouble. But the Perfume and the Vision came not, nor any full manifestation of the L.V.X., the Secret Light, the light that shineth in darkness.

John St. John is again very sleepy. He will try and concentrate on Adonai without doing Pranayama—much harder of course. It is a supreme effort to keep both eyes open together.

5.40. He must do his best. He does not wish to wake too thoroughly, either, lest afterward he oversleep himself, and miss his appointment with Michael Brenner to continue moulding Siddhasana.

7.45. Again I awake.... [O swine! thou hast felt in thyself "Good! Good! the night is broken up nicely; all goes very well"—and thou hast written "I!" O swine, John St. John! When wilt thou learn that the least stirring of thy smug content is the great Fall from the Path?] It will be best to get up and do some kind of work; for the beast would sleep.

8.25. John St. John has arisen, after doing 20 breath-cycles, reciting internally the ritual, 70 per cent. of which he now knows by heart.

8.35. To the Dôme—a café-croissant. Some proofs to correct during the meal.

10.25. Having walked over to the studio reciting the Ritual (9.25-9.55 approximately), John St. John got into his pose, and began going for the gloves. The Interior Trembling began, and the room filled with the Subtle Light. He was within an ace of Concentration; the Violet Lotus of Ajna appeared, flashing like some marvellous comet; the Dawn began to break, as he slew with the Lightning-Flash every thought that arose in him, especially this Vision of Ajna; but fear —dread fear!—gripped his heart. Annihilation stood before him, annihilation of John St. John that he had

10.25. so long striven to obtain: yet he dared not. He had the loaded pistol to his head; he could not pull the trigger. This must have gone on for some time; his agony of failure was awful; for he knew that he was failing; but though he cried a thousand times unto Adonai with the Voice of Death, he could not—he could not. Again and again he stood at the gate, and could not enter. And the Violet Flames of Ajna triumphed over him.

Then Brenner said: "Let us take a little rest!"—oh irony!—and he came down from his throne, staggering with fatigue. . . .

If you can conceive all his anger and despair! His pen, writing this, forms a letter badly, and through clenched teeth he utters a fierce curse.

Oh Lord Adonai, look with favour upon him!

11.30 After five minutes rest (to the body, that is), John St. John was too exhausted on resuming his pose, which, by the way, happens to be the Sign of the Grade $7° = 4°$, to strive consciously.

But his nature itself, forced through these days into the one channel of Will towards Adonai, went on struggling on its own account. Later, the conscious man took heart and strove, though not so fiercely as before. He passed through the Lightnings of Ajna whose two petals now spread out like wings above his head, and the awful Corona of the Interior Sun with its flashing fires appeared, and declared itself to be his Self. This he rejected; and the Formless Ocean of

11.30   White Brilliance absorbed him, overcame him; for he could not pass therethrough. This went on repeating itself, the man transformed (as it were) into a mighty Battering Ram hurling itself again and again against the Walls of the City of God to breach them.—And as yet he has failed. Failed. Failed. Physical and mental exhaustion are fairly complete.
Adonai, look with favour upon Thy slave!

12.20. He has walked, reciting the Ritual, to Dr. R—— and H—— for lunch. They have forgotten the appointment, so he continues and reaches Lavenue's at 12.4 after reading his letters and doing one or two necessary things. He orders Epinards, Tarte aux Fraises, Glace au Café, and ½ Evian. The distaste for food is great; and for meat amounts to loathing. The weather is exceedingly hot; it may be arranged thus by Adonai to enable John St. John to meditate in comfort. For he is vowed solemnly "to interpret every phenomenon as a particular dealing of God with his soul."

12.50. During lunch he will go on correcting his proofs.

1.35.   Lunch over, and the proofs read through.

1.45.   He will make a few decorations further in his Ritual, and perhaps design the Fontispiece and Colophon. He is very weary, and may sleep.

2.25.   He has done the illumination, as far as may be. He will now lie down as Hanged Man, and invoke Adonai.

4.45. He was too tired to reach nearer than the neighbourhood of that tremendous Threshold; wherefore he fell from meditation into sleep, and there his Lord gave him sweet rest thereof.
He will arise, and take a drink—a citron pressé—at the Dôme; for the day is yet exceeding hot, and he has had little.

4.53. One ought to remark that all this sleep is full extravagant dreams; rarely irrational and never (of course) unpleasant, or one would be up and working with a circle every night. But O.M. thinks that they show an excited and unbalanced condition of John St. John's brain, though he is almost too cowed to express an opinion at all, even were the question, Is grass green?
Every small snatch of sleep, without exception, in the last three or four days, has these images.
The ideal condition seems likely to be perfect oblivion —or (in the Adept) is the Tamo-Guna, the Power of elemental Darkness, broken once and for ever, so that His sleep is vivid and rational as another man's waking; His waking another man's Samadhi; His Samadhi—to which He ever strives—— ? ? ? ? ?
At least this later view is suggested by the Rosicrucian formula of Reception:

> May thy mind be open unto the Higher!
> May thy heart be the Centre of Light!
> May thy body be the Temple of the Rosy Cross!

and by the Hindu statement that in the attained Yogin

4.53. the Kundalini sleeps in the Svadistthana, no more in the Muladhara Cakkrâm.
See also the Rosicrucian lecture on the Microcosmos, where this view is certainly upheld, the Qliphoth of an Adept being balanced and trained to fill his Malkuth, vacated by the purified Nephesch which has gone up to live in Tiphereth.
Or so O.M. read it.
The other idea of the Light descending and filling each principle with its glory is, it seems to him, less fertile, and less in accord with any idea of Evolution.
(What would Judas McCabbage think?)
And one can so readily understand how tremendous a task is that of the postulant, since he has to glorify and initiate all his principles and train them to their new and superior tasks. This surely explains better the terrible dangers of the path....
Some years back, on the Red River in China, John St. John saw at every corner of that swift and dangerous stream a heap of wreckage.
... He, himself in danger, thought of his magical career. Alcoholism, insanity, disease, faddism, death, knavery, prison—every earthly hell, reflection of some spiritual blunder, had seized his companions. By dozens had that band been swept away, dashed to pieces on one rock or another. He, alone almost upon that angry stream, still held on, his life each moment the plaything of giant forces, so enormous as to be (once they were loose) quite out of proportion to all human wit or courage or address—and he held on his course, humbly,

4.53. not hopelessly, not fearfully, but with an abiding certainty that he would endure unto the end.
And now?
In this great Magical Retirement he has struck many rocks, sprung many leaks; the waters of the False Sea foam over the bow, ride and carry the quarter—is he perchance already wrecked, his hopeless plight concealed from him as yet by his own darkness? For, dazzled as he is by the blinding brilliance of this morning's Spiritual Sun, which yet he beheld but darkly, to him now even the light of earth seems dark. Reason the rudder was long since unshipped; the power of his personality has broken down, yet under the tiny storm-sail of his Will to Adonai, the crazy bark holds way, steered by the oar of Discipline—Yea, he holds his course. Adonai! Adonai! is not the harbour yet in sight?

6.7. He has returned home and burnt (as every night since its arrival) the holy incense of Abramelin the Mage.
The atmosphere is full of vitality, sweetened and strengthened; the soul naturally and simply turns to the holy task with vigour and confidence; the black demons of doubt and despair flee away; one respires already a foretaste of the Perfume, and obtains almost a premonition of the Vision.
So, let the work go on.

6.23. 7 Breath-cycles, rather difficult. Clothes are a nuisance and make all the difference.

6.31. John St. John is more broken up by this morning'

6.31. failure than he was ready to admit. But the fact stands; he cannot concentrate his mind for three seconds together. How utterly hopeless it makes one feel! One thinks one is at least always good for a fair average performance—and one is undeceived.

This, by the way, is the supreme use of a record like this. It makes it impossible to cheat oneself.

Well, he has got to get up more steam somehow, though the boiler bursts. Perhaps early dinner, with Ritual, may induce that Enthusiastic Energy of which the Gnostics write.

This morning the whole Sankhara-dhatu (the tendency of the being John St. John) was operating aright. Now by no effort of will can he flog his tired cattle along the trail.

So poor a thing is he that he will even seek an Oracle from the book of Zoroaster.

Done. Zoroaster respectfully wishes to point out that "The most mystic of discourses informs us—his wholeness is in the Supra-Mundane Order; for there a Solar World and Boundless light subsist, as the Oracles of the Chaldeans affirm."

Not very helpful, is it?

As if divination could ever help on such exalted planes! As if the trumpery elementals that operate these things possessed the Secrets of the Destiny of an Adept, or could help him in his agony!

For this reason, divination should be discarded from the start: it is only a "mere toy, the basis of mercenary fraud" as Zoroaster more practically assures us.

6.31. Yet one can get the right stuff out of the Tarot (or other inconvenient method) by spiritualising away all the meaning, until the intuition pierces that blank wall of ignorance.
Let O.M. meditate upon this Oracle on his way to feed John St. John's body—and thus feed his own!

6.52. Out, out, to feed!

6.57. Trimming his beard in preparation for going out, he reflects that the deplorable tone (as one's Dean would say) of the last entry is not the cry of the famished beast, but that of the over-driven slave.
"Adonai, ply Thou thy scourge! Adonai, load Thou the chain!"

7.25. What the devil is the matter with the time? The hours flit just like butterflies—the moon, dead full, shines down the Boulevard. My moon—full moon of my desire! (Ha, ha, thou beast! are "I and Me and Mine" not dead yet?)
Yea, Lord Adonai! but the full moon means much to John St. John; he fears (*fears*, O Lord of the Western Pylon!) lest, of once that full moon pass, he may not win through. . . .
"The harvest is over, the summer is ended, and we are not saved!"
Yet hath not Abramelin lashed the folly of limiting the spiritual paths by the motions of the planets? And Zoroaster, in that same oracle just quoted?

7.35. Hors d'Œuvres, Bouillabaisse, contrefilet rôti, Glace. Graves.

7.35. The truth is that the Chittam is excited and racing, the control being impaired; and the Ego is springing up again.

7.50. This racing of the Chittam is simply shocking. John St. John must stop it somehow. Hours and hours seem to have passed since the last entry.

7.57. ! ! ! He is in such a deuce of a hurry that (in a lucid moment) he finds himself trying to eat bread, radish, beef and potato at a mouthful.
Worse, the beast is pleased and excited at the novelty of the sensation, and takes delight in recording it.
Beast! Beast!

8.3. ! ! ! ! After myriads of æons. He has drunk only about one third of his half-bottle of light white wine; yet he's like a hashish- drunkard, only more so. The loss of the time-sense which occurs with hashish he got during his experiments with that drug in 1906, but in an unimportant way. (Damn him! he is so glad. He calls this a Result. A result! Damn him!) O.M. who writes this is so angry with him that he wants to scrawl the page over with the most fearful curses! and John St. John has nearly thrown a bottle at the waiter for not bringing the next course. He will not be allowed to finish his wine! He orders cold water.

8.12. Things a little better. But he tries 100 small muscular movements, pressing on the table with his fingers in tune, and finds the tendency to hurry almost irresistible. This record is here written at lightning speed. . . . Attempt to write slowly is painful.

8.20. The thought too, is wandering all over the world. Since the last entry, very likely, the beast has not thought even once of Adonai.

8.35. The Reading of the Ritual has done much service, though things are still far from calm. Yet the mighty flood of the Chittam is again rolling its tremendous tide toward the sea—the Sea of annihilation. Amen.

9.0. Returning home, with his eyes fixed on the supreme glory of the Moon, in his heart and brain invoking Adonai, he hath now entered into his little chamber, and will prepare all things for the due performance of the New Ritual which he hath got by heart.

9.35. Nearly ready. In a state of very intense magical strain—anything might happen.

9.48. Washed, robed, temple in order. Will wait until 10 o'clock and begin upon the stroke. O.M. $7° = 4°$ will begin; and then solemnly renounce all his robes, weapons, dignities, etc., renouncing his grades even by giving the Signs of them backwards and downwards toward the outer. He will keep only one thing, the Secret Ring that hath been committed unto him by the Masters; for from that he cannot part, even if he would. That is his Password into the Ritual itself; and on his finger it shall be put at the moment when all else is gone.

11.5. Ceremony works admirably. Magical Images strong. At Reception behold! the Sigil of the Supreme Order itself in a blaze of glory not to be spoken of. And the half seen symbol of my Lord Adonai therewith as a mighty angel glittering with infinite light.

11.5. According to the the Ritual, O.M. withdrew himself from the Vision; the Vision of the Universe, a whirling abyss of coruscating suns in all the colours, yet informed and dominated by that supernal brilliance. Yet O. M. refused the Vision; and a conflict began and was waged through many ages—so it seemed. And now all the enemies of O. M. banded themselves against him. The petty affairs of the day; even the irritations of his body, the emotions of him, the plans of him, worry about the Record and the Ritual and—O! everything!—then, too, the thoughts which are closer yet to the great Enemy, the sense of separateness; that sense itself at last—so O. M. withdrew from the conflict for a moment so that the duty of this Record done might leave him free for the fight.
It may have been a snare—may the Lord Adonai keep him in the Path.
Adonai! Adonai!
(P.S.—Add that the "ultra-violet" or "astral" light in the room was such that it seemed bright as daylight. He hath never seen the like, even in the ceremony which he performed in the Great Pyramid of Gizeh.)

11.14-
11.34. O. M. then passed from vision unto vision of unexampled splendour. The infinite abyss of space, a rayless orb of liquid and colourless brilliance fading beyond the edges into a flame of white and gold. . . . The Rosy Cross flashing with lustre ineffable. . . . and more, much more which ten scribes could hardly catalogue in a century.

11.14   The Vision of the Holy Guardian Angel itself; yet was He seen as from afar, not intimately. . . .
Therefore is O. M. not content with all this wonder; but will now orderly close the temple, that at the Beginning of the Tenth Day—and Ten are the Holy Sephiroth, the Emanations of the Crown; Blessed be He! . . . He may make new considerations of this Operation whereby he may discover through what error he is thus betrayed again and again into failure.
Failure. Failure.

11.49. The Temple is closed.
Now then, O Lord Adonai! Let the Tenth Day be favourable unto O. M. For in the struggle he is as nothing worth. Nor valiant, nor fortunate, nor skilful —except Thou fight by his side, cover his breast with Thy shield, second his blows with Thy spear and with Thy sword.
Aye! let the Ninth Day close in silence and in darkness, and let O.M. be found watching and waiting and willing Thy Presence.
Adonai! Adonai! O Lord Adonai! Let Thy Light illumine the Path of that darkling wight John St. John, that being who, separate from Thee, is separate from all

Light, Life, Love.

Adonai! Adonai! let it be written of O. M. that "The Lord Adonai is about him like a thunderbolt and like a Pylon and like a Serpent and like a Phallus—and in the midst thereof like the Woman that jetteth the Milk

11.49. of the Stars from Her paps; yea, the Milk of the Stars from Her paps."

The Tenth Day

12.17. Now that the perfume of the incense is clearly away, one may most potently perceive the Invoked Perfume of the Ceremony Itself. And this mystical perfume of Adonai is like pure Musk, but infinitely subtilised—far stronger, and at the same time far more delicate. (P.S.—Doubt has arisen about this perfume, as to whether there was not a commonplace cause. On the balance of the evidence, carefully considered, one would pronounce for the mystic theory.)
One should add a curious omen. On sitting down for the great struggle (11.14) John St. John found a nail upon the floor, at his feet. Now a nail is Vau in Hebrew, and the Tarot Trump corresponding to Vau is the Hierophant or Initiator—whereby is O. M. greatly comforted.
So poor a thing hath he become!
Even as a little child groping feebly for the breast of its mother, so gropeth Thy little child after Thee, O Thou Self-Glittering One!

12.55. He hath read through Days VIII. and IX.
... He is too tired to understand what he reads. He will, despite of all, do a little Pranayama, and then sleep, ever willing Adonai.
For Pranayama with its intense physical strain is a great medicine for the mind. Even as the long trail of the desert and the life with the winds and the stars,

12.55. the daily march and its strife with heat, thirst, fatigue, cure all the ills of the soul, so does Pranayama clear away the phantoms that Mayan, dread maker of Illusion, hath cumbered it withal.

1.13. 10 Breath-Cycles; calm, perfect, without the least effort; enough to go to sleep upon.
He will read through the Ritual once, and then sleep. (The Pranayama precipitated a short attack of diarrhœa, started by the chill of the Ceremony.)

6.23. He slept from 1.45 (approximately) till now. The morn is cold and damp; rain has fallen.
John St. John is horribly tired; the "control" is worn to a thread. He takes five minutes to make up his mind to go through with it, five more to wash and write this up. And he has a million excuses for not doing Pranayama.

6.51. 15 Breath-cycles, steady and easy enough.
The brain is cool and lucid; but no energy is in it. At least no Sammaváyamo. And at present the Superscription on John St. John's Cross is

FAILURE.

Marvellous and manifold as are his results, he hath renounced them and esteemeth them as dross. . . . This is right, John St. John! yet how is it that there is place for the great hunchbacked devil to whisper in thine ear the doubt: Is there in truth any mystic path at all? Is it all disappointment and illusion?
And the "Poor Thing" John St. John moves off

6.51. shivering and sad, like a sot who has tried to get credit at a tavern and is turned away—and that on Christmas Eve!

There is no money in his purse, no steam in his boilers—that's what's the matter with John St. John.

It is clear enough, what happened yesterday. He failed at the four Pylons in turn; in the morning Fear stopped him at that of Horus and so on; while in the evening he either failed at the Pylon of Thoth, *i.e.*, was obsessed by the necessity (alleged) of recording his results, or failed to overcome the duality of Thoth. Otherwise, even if he comprehended the base, he certainly failed at the apex of the Pyramid.

In any case, he cannot blame the Ceremony, which is most potent; one or two small details may need correction, but no more.

Here then he is down at the bottom of the hill again, a Rosicrucian Sisyphus with the Stone of the Philosophers! An Ixion bound to the Wheel of Destiny and of the Samsara, unable to reach the centre, where is Rest.

He must add to the entry 1.13 that the "telephone-cross" voices came as he composed himself to sleep, in the Will to Adonai. This time he detached a body of cavalry to chase them to oblivion. Perhaps an unwise division of his forces; yet he was so justly indignant at the eternal illusions that he may be excused.

Excused! To whom? Thou must succeed or fail! O Batsman, with thy frail fortress of Three-in-One, the Umpire cries "Out"; and thou explainest to thy friends

6.51. in the pavilion. But thy friends have heard that story before, and thy explanation will not appear in the score. *Mr. J. St. John, b. Maya*, o, they will read in the local newspaper. There is no getting away from that!
Failure! Failure! Failure!
Now then let me (7.35) take the position of the Hanged Man and invoke Adonai.

9.0. Probably sleep returned shortly. Not a good night, through dreamless, so far as memory serves.
The rain comes wearily down, not chasing the dryness, but soddening the streets.
The rain of autumn, not the rain of spring!
So is it in this soul, Lord Adonai. The thought of Thee is heavy and uneasy, flabby and loose, like an old fat woman stupid-drunk in her slum; which was as a young maiden in a field of lilies, arrow-straight, sun-strong, moon-pure, a form all litheness and eagerness, dancing, dancing for her own excess of life.
Adonai! Adonai!

9.17. Rose, dressed, etc., reflecting on the Path. Blinder than ever! The brain is in revolt; it has been compressed too long. Yet it is impossible to rest. It is too late. The Irresistible God, whose name is Destiny, has been invoked, and He hath answered.
The matter is in His hands; He must end it, either with that mighty spiritual Experience which I have sought, or else with black madness, or with death. By the Body of God, swear thou that death would come—welcome, welcome, welcome!

9.17. And to Thee, and from Thee, O thou great god Destiny, there is no appeal. Thou turnest not one hair's breadth from Thy path appointed.

That which "John St. John" *means* (else is it a blank name) is that which he must be—and what is that? The issue is with Thee—cannot one wait with fortitude, whether it be for the King's Banqueting-House or for the Headsman and the Block?

9.45. Breakfast—croissant, sandwich, 2 coffees. Concentrating *off* the Work as well as possible.

10.10. Arrived at Brenner's studio. The rest has produced one luminous idea: why not end it all with destruction? Say a great ritual of Geburah, curses, curses, curses! John St. John ought not to have forgotten how to curse. In his early days at Wastdale Head people would travel miles to hear him!

Curse all the Gods and all the demons—all those things in short which go to make up John St. John. For *that*—as he now knows—is the Name of the great Enemy, the Dweller upon the Threshold. It was that mighty spirit whose formless horror beat him back, for it was he!

So now to return to concentration and the Will toward Adonai.

10.20. One thing is well; the vow of "interpreting every phenomenon as a particular dealing of God with my soul" is keeping itself. Whatever impression reaches the consciousness is turned by it into a symbol or a simile of the Work.

11.18. The pose over; recited Ritual, now known by heart; then willed Adonai; hopelessly unconcentrated.

... To interpret this Record aright, it must, however, be understood that the "Standard of Living" goes up at an incredible rate. The same achievement would, say five days ago, have been entered as "High degree of concentration; unhoped-for success."
The phenomena which to-day one dismisses with annoyed contempt are the same which John St. John worked four years continuously to attain, and when attained seemed almost to outstrip the possible of glory. The flood of the Chittam is again being heaped up by the dam of Discipline. There is less headache, and more sense of being on the Path—that is the only way one finds of expressing it.

11.45. Worse and worse; though pose even better held. In despair returned to a simple practice, the holding of the mind to a single imagined object; in this case the Triangle surmounted by the Cross. It seems quite easy to do nowadays; why shouldn't it lead to the Result? It used to be supposed to do so.

Might be worth trying anyway; things can hardly be worse than they are.

Or, one might go over to the Hammam, and have a long bath and sleep—but who can tell whether it would refresh, or merely destroy the whole edifice built up so laboriously in these ten days?

12.15. At Panthéon. $\frac{1}{2}$ dozen Marennes, Rognons Brochette Lait chaud.

JOHN ST. JOHN

12.15. John St. John is aching all over, cannot get comfortable anyhow; is hungry, and has no appetite; thirsty, and loathes the thought of drinking!

He must do something—something pretty drastic, or he will find himself in serious trouble of body and mind, the shadows of his soul, that is sick unto death. For "where are now their gods?" Where is the Lord, the Lord Adonai?

12.35. The beast feels decidedly better; but whether he is more concentrated one may doubt. Honestly, he is now so blind that he cannot tell!

Perhaps a "café, cognac, et cigare" may tune him up to the point of either going back to work, or across Paris to the Hammam. He will make the experiment, reading through his proofs the while.

One good thing; the Chittam is moving slowly. The waiters all hurry him—what a contrast to last night!

1.15. Proofs read through again. John St. John feels far from well.

2.15. A stroll down the Boul' Mich' and a visit to M——'s studio improve matters a good deal.

3.30. The cure continued. No worry about the Work, but an effort to put it altogether out of the mind. A café crème, forty minutes at the Academie Marcelle—a gruelling bout without gloves—and J. St. J. is at the Luxembourg to look at the pretty pictures.

3.40. The proof of the pudding, observes the most mystic of discourses (surely!), is in the Eating.

3.40. One might justly object to any Results of this Ten days' strain. But if abundant health and new capacity to do great work be the after-effect, who then will dare to cast a stone?
Not that it matters a turnip-top to the Adept himself. But others may be deterred from entering the Path by the foolish talk of the ignorant, and thus may flowers be lost that should go to make the fadeless wreath of Adonai. Ah, Lord, pluck *me* up utterly by the root, and set that which Thou pluckest as a flower upon thy brow!

4.10. Walked back to the Dôme to drink a citron pressé through the lovely gardens, sad with their fallen leaves. Reflecting on what Dr. Henry Maudsley once wrote to him about mysticism "Like other bad habits (he might have said 'Like all living beings') it grows by what it feeds on." Most important, then, to use the constant critical check on all one's work. The devotion to Adonai might itself fall under suspicion, where it not for the definition of Adonai.
Adonai is that thought which informs and strengthens and purifies, supreme sanity in supreme genius. Anything that is not that is not Adonai.
Hence the refusal of all other Results, however glorious; for they are all relative, partial, impure Anicca, Dukkha, Anatta: Change, sorrow, Unsubstantiality; these are their characteristics, however much they may appear to be Atman, Sat, Chit, Ananda, Soul Being, Knowledge, Bliss.
But the main consideration was one of expediency

JOHN ST. JOHN

4.10. Has not John St. John possibly been stuffing himself both with Methods and Results?

Certainly this morning was more like the engorgement of the stomach with too much food than like the headache after a bout of drunkenness.

A less grave fault, by far; it is easy and absurd to get a kind of hysterical ecstasy over religion, love, or wine. A German will take off his hat and dance and jodel to the sunrise—and nothing comes of it! Darwin studies Nature with more reverence and enthusiasm, but without antics—and out comes the Law of Evolution. So it is written "By their fruits ye shall know them."

But about this question of spiritual overfeeding --- what did Darwin do when he got to the stage (as he did, be sure! many a time) when he wished every pigeon in the world at the devil?

Now this wish has never really arisen in John St. John; however bad he feels, he always feels that Attainment is the only possible way out of it. This is the good Karma of his ten years' constant striving.

Well, in the upshot, he will get back to Work at once, and hope that his few hours in the world may prove a true strategic movement to the rear, and not a euphemism for rout!

5.4. There are further serious considerations to be made concerning Adonai. This title for the Unknown Thought was adopted by O. M. in November, 19—, in Upper Burma, on the occasion of his passing through the ordeal and receiving the grade which should be really attributed to Daath (on account of its nature, the

5.4. Mastery of the Reason), though it is commonly called 7° = 4°.

It appeared to him at that period that so much talk and time were wasted on discussing the nature of the Attainment—a discussion foredoomed to failure, in the absence of all Knowledge, and in view of the Self-Contradictory Nature of the Reasoning Faculty, as applied to Metaphysics—that it would be wiser to drop the whole question, and concentrate on a simple Magical Progress.

The Next Step for humanity in general was then "the Knowledge and Conversation of the Holy Guardian Angel."

One thing at a time.

But here he finds himself discussing and disputing with himself the nature of that Knowledge.

Better far act as hitherto, and aspire simply and directly, as one person to another, careless of the critical objections (quite insuperable, of course) to this or any other conception.

For as this experience transcends reason, it is fruitless to argue about it.

Adonai, I invoke Thee!

Simpler, then, to go back to the Egoistic diction, only remembering always that by "I" is meant John St. John or O. M., or Adonai according to the context.

5.30. Having read some of THE Books to induct myself again into the Work.

Therefore will I kindle the holy Incense, and turn myself again to the One Thought.

6.27. All this time in Hanged Man position, and thinking of everything else.
As bad as it was on the very first day!

7.10. More waste time aimlessly watching a poker game. Walked down to Café de Versailles. Dinner. Hors d'Œuvre, Escargots, Cassoulet de Castelnaudry, Glace, $\frac{1}{2}$ Evian. Am quite washed-out. I have not even the courage of despair. There is not enough left in me to despair.
I don't care.

7.35. One gleam of light illumines the dark path—I can't enjoy my dinner. The snails, as I prong them forth, are such ugly, slimy, greasy black horrors—oh! so like my soul! . . . Ugh!
I write a letter to F———r and sign myself with a broken pentagram.
It makes me think of a "busted flush." . . .
But through all the sunlight peeps: *e.g.*, These six snails were my six inferior souls; the seventh, the real soul, cannot be eaten by the devourer.
How's that for high?

8.3. Possibly a rousing mantra would fix things up; say the Old Favorite:

Aum Tat Sat Aum

and give the Hindus a chance.
We can but try.
So I begin at once.

9.10. This is past all bearing. Another hour wasted chatting to Nina and H———. The mantra hardly remem-

9.10. bered at all. I have gone to bed, and shall take things in hand seriously, if it kills me.

9.53. Since 9.17 have done Pranayama, though allowing myself some irregularities in the way of occasional omission of a Kambhakham.
'Tis very hard to stick to it. I find myself, at the end of above sentence, automatically crawling into bed. No, John!

10.14 Have been trying to extract some sense from that extraordinary treatise on mysticism, "Konx Om Pax." Another failure, but an excusable one.
I will now beseech Adonai as best I may to give me back my lost powers.
For I am no more even a magician! So lost am I in the illusions that I have made in the Search for Adonai, that I am become the vilest of them all!

10.27. A strange and unpleasant experience. My thought suddenly transmuted itself into a muscular cry, so that my legs gave a violent jerk. This I expect is at bottom the explanation of the Bhuchari-Siddhi. A very bad form of uncontrolled thought. I was on the edge of sleep; it woke me.
The fact is, all is over! I am done! I have tried for the Great Initiation and I have failed: I am swept away into strange hells.
Lord Adonai! let the fires be informing; let them "balance, assain assoil."
I suppose this rash attempt will end in Locomotor Ataxia or G. P. I.

10.27. Let it! I'm going on.

11.47. The first power to return is the power to suffer. The shame of it! The torture of it!
My slept in patches as a man sleeps that is deadly ill. I am only afraid of failing to wake for the End of the day.
God! what a day!
... I dare not trust my will to keep me awake; so I rise, wash, and will walk about till time to get into my Asana. Thirst! Oh how I thirst!
I had not thought that there could be such suffering.

The Eleventh Day

12.19. It seems a poor thing to be proud of, merely to be awake. Yet I was flushed with triumph as a boy that wins his first race.
The powers of Asana and Pranayama return. I did 21 Breath-cycles without fatigue.
Energy returns, and Keenness to pursue the Path—all fruits of that one little victory over sleep.
How delicate are these powers, so simple as they seem! Let me be very humble, now and for every more! Surely at least that lesson has been burnt into me.
And how gladly I would give all these powers for the One Power!

2.33. Another smart attack of diarrhœa. I take 4 gr. Plumb c. Opio and alter my determination to stay out of bed all night, as chill is doubtless the chief cause.
... It is really extraordinary how the smallest success

12.33. awakes a monstrous horde of egoistic devils, vain, strutting peacocks, preening and screaming!
This is simply damnable. Egoism is the spur of all energy, in a way; and in this particular case it is the one thing that is not Adonai (whatever else may be) and so the antithesis of the Work.
 Bricks without straw, indeed! That's nothing to it. This job is like being asked to judge a Band contest and being told that one may do anything but listen. Only worse! One could form some idea of how they were playing through other senses; in this case *every* faculty is the enemy of the Work. At first sight the problem seems insoluble. It may be so, for me. At least, I have not solved it. Yet I have come very near it, many a time, of old; have solved it indeed, though in a less important sense than now I seek. I am not to be content with little or with much; but only with the Ultimate Attainment.
Apparently the method is just this; to store up—no matter how—great treasures of energy and purity until they begin to do the work themselves (in the way that the Hindus call Sukshma).
Just so the engineer—five feet six in his boots—and his men build the dam. The snows melt on the mountains the river rises, and the land is irrigated, in a way that is quite independent of the physical strength of that Five foot Six of engineer. The engineer might even be swept away and drowned by the forces he had himself organized. So also the Kingdom of Heaven.

JOHN ST. JOHN

12.33. And now (12.57) John St. John will turn himself to sleep, invoking Adonai.

1.17. Can neither sleep nor concentrate.
Instead grotesque "astral" images of a quite base gargoylish type.
I suppose I shall have to pentagram them off like a damned neophyte.
Je m'emmerde!

3.8. Praise the Lord, I wake! If that can be called waking which is a mere desperate struggle to keep the eyes open.

3.18. Pranayama all wrong—very difficult. Rose, washed, drank a few drops of water. (N.B.—To-night have drunk several times, a mouthful at a time; other nights, and days, no. All entries into body recorded duly.)

3.30. Have done 10 Breath-Cycles; am quite awake.

It will therefore now be lawful again to sleep.

8.12. Awoke at 7.40, read a letter which arrived, and tried quite vainly to concentrate.

8.52. Have risen, written a letter. Will break my fast—café croissant—and go a walk with the New Mantra, using my recently invented method of doing Pranayama on the march. The weather is again perfect.

9.14. Breakfast—eaten Yogin-wise—at an end. The walk begins.

1.15. The walk over. Kept mantra going well enough.

11.15. Made also considerations concerning the Nature of the Path.

The upshot is that it does not matter. Acquire full power of Concentration; the rest is only leather and prunella.

Don't worry; work!

I shall now make a pantacle to aid the said faculty of concentration.

The Voice of the Nadi (by the way) is resounding well, and the Chittam is a little better under control.

1.5. Have worked well on the Pantacle, thinking of Adonai. Of course we are now reduced to a "low anthropomorphic conception"—but what odds? Once the Right Thought comes it will transcend any and all conceptions. The objection is as silly as the objection to illustrating Geometry by Diagrams, on the ground that printed lines are thick—and so on.

This is the imbecility of the "Protestant" objection to images. What fools these mortals be!

The Greeks, too, after exhausting all their sublimest thoughts of Zeus and Hades and Poseidon, found that they could not find a fitting image of the All, the supreme—so they just carved a goat-man, saying: Let this represent Pan!

Also in the holiest place of the most secret temple there is an empty shrine.

But whoso goes there in the first instance thinks; There is no God.

He who goes there at the End, when he has adored all the other deities, knoweth that No God.

1.5. So also I go through all the Ritual, and try all the Means; at the End it may be I shall find No rituals and No means, but an act or a silence so simple that it cannot be told or understood.
Lord Adonai, bring me to the End!

1.25. After writing above, and adding a few touches to the Pantacle, am ready to go to lunch.

1.45. Arrived at Panthéon, with mantra.
Rumpsteak aux pommes soufflées, poire, $\frac{1}{2}$ Evian, and the three Cs.
Was meditating on asceticism. John Tweed once told me that Swami Vivekananda, towards the end of his life, wrote a most pathetic letter deploring that his sanctity forbad his "going on the bust."
What a farce is such sanctity! How much wiser for the man to behave as a man, the God as a God!
This is my real bed-rock objection to the Eastern systems. They decry all manly virtue as dangerous and wicked; and they look upon Nature as evil. True enough, everything is evil relatively to Adonai; for all stain is impurity. A bee's swarm is evil—inside one's clothes. "Dirt is matter in the wrong place." It is dirt to connect sex with statuary, morals with art.
Only Adonai, who is in a sense the True Meaning of everything, cannot defile any idea. This is a hard saying, though true, for nothing of course is dirtier than to try and use Adonai as a fig-leaf for one's shame.
To seduce women under pretence of religion is un-

1.45. utterable foulness; though both adultery and religion are themselves clean.

To mix jam and mustard is a messy mistake.

2.5. It also struck me that this Operation is (among other things) an attempt to prove the proposition: Reward is the direct and immediate consequence of Work.

Of all the holy illuminated Men of God of my acquaintance, I am the only one that holds this opinion.

But I think that this Record, when I have time to go through it, and stand at some distance, to get the perspective, will be proved a conclusive proof of my thesis.

I think that every failure will be certainly traceable to my own dam foolishness; every little success to courage, skill, wit, tenacity.

If I had but a little more of these!

2.22. I further take this opportunity of asserting my Atheism. I believe that all these phenomena are as explicable as the formation of hoar-frost or of glacier tables. I believe "Attainment" to be a simple supreme sane state of the human brain. I do not believe in miracles; I do not think that God could cause a monkey, clergyman, or rationalist to attain.

I am taking all this trouble of the Record principally in hope that it will show exactly what mental and physical conditions precede, accompany, and follow "attainment" so that others may reproduce, through those conditions, that Result.

2.22. I believe in the Law of Cause and Effect—and I loathe the cant alike of the Superstitionist and the Rationalist.

The Confession of St. Judas McCabbage

I believe in Charles Darwin Almighty, maker of Evolution; and in Ernst Haeckel, his only son our Lord Who for us men and for our salvation came down from Germany: who was conceived of Weissmann, born of Büchner, suffered under du Bois-Raymond, was printed, bound, and shelved: who was raised again into English (of sorts), ascended into the Pantheon of the Literary Guide and sitteth on the right hand of Edward Clodd: whence he shall come to judge the thick in the head.

I believe in Charles Watts; the Rationalist Press Association; the annual dinner at the Trocadero Restaurant; the regularity of subscriptions, the resurrection in a sixpenny edition, and the Book-stall everlasting.
AMEN.

3.0. Arrived at Brenner's studio, and went on with the "moulage" of my Asana.

4.20. Left the Studio; walk with mantra.

4.55. Mantra-march. Pranayama; quick-time. Very bracing and fatiguing, both.
At Dôme to drink a citron press.
Reflections have been in my mind upon the grossness of the Theistic conception, as shewn even in such pictures as Raphael's and Fra Angelico's.

4.55. How infinitely subtler and nobler is the contemplation of

>> The Utmost God
> Hid i' th' middle o' matter,

the inscrutable mystery of the nature of common things. With what awe does the wise man approach a speck of dust!
And it is this Mystery that I approach!
For Thou, Adonai, art the immanent and essential Soul of Things; not separate from them, or from me; but That which is behind the shadow-show, the Cause of all, the Quintessence of all, the Transcender of all.
And Thee I seek insistently; though Thou hide Thyself in the Heaven, there will I seek Thee out; though Thou wrap Thyself in the Flames of the Abyss, even there will I pursue Thee; Though Thou make Thee a secret place in the Heart of the Rose or at the Arms of the Cross that spanneth all-embracing Space though Thou be in the inmost part of matter, or behind the Veil of mind; Thee will I follow; Thee will I overtake; Thee will I gather into my being.
So thus as I chase Thee from fastness to fastness of my brain, as Thou throwest out against me Veil after Magic Veil of glory, or of fear, or of despair, or of desire; it matters nothing; at the End I shall attain to Thee—oh my Lord Adonai!
And even as the Capture is delight, is not the Chase also delight? For we are lovers from the Beginning though it pleasure Thee to play the Syrinx to my Pan

4.55. Is it not the springtide, and are these not the Arcadian groves?

5.31. At home; settling to strictest meditation upon Adonai my Lord; willing His presence, the Perfume and the Vision, even as it is written in the Book of the Sacred Magick of Abramelin the Mage.

8.6. Soon this became a sleep, though the will was eager and concentrated.
The sleep, too, was deep and refreshing. I will go to dinner.

8.22. Arrived, with mantra, at the Caf de Versailles.

9.10. ½ doz. Marennes, Rable de Liévre, citron pressé.
I am now able to concentrate OFF the Path for a little. Whether this means that I am simply slipping back into the world, or that I am more balanced on, and master of, the Path, I cannot say.

10.4. Have walked home, drunk a citron pressé at the Dôme, and prepare for the night.
As I crossed the boulevard, I looked to the bright moon, high and stately in the east, for a message. And there came to me this passage from the Book of Abramelin:
"And thou wilt begin to inflame thyself in praying" ...
It is the sentence which goes on to declare the Result. (P.S.—With this rose that curious feeling of confidence, sure premonition of success, that one gets in most physical tasks, but especially when one is going to get

10.4. down a long putt or a tricky one. Whether it means more than that perception and execution have got into unison (for once) and know it, I cannot say.)

It is well that thus should close this eleventh day of my Retirement, and the thirty-third year of my life. Thirty and three years was this temple in building. . . .

It has always been my custom on this night to look back over the year, and to ask: What have I done?

The answer is invariably "Nothing."

Yet of what men count deeds I have done no small share. I have travelled a bit, written a bit . . . I seem to have been hard at it all the time—and to have got nothing finished or successful.

One Tragedy—one little comedy—two essays—a dozen poems or so—two or three short stories—odds and ends of one sort and another: it's a miserable record, though the Tragedy is good enough to last a life. It marks an epoch in literature, though nobody else will guess it for fifty years yet.

The travel, too, has been rubbish. It's been a petty peddling year.

The one absolute indication is: on no account live otherwise than alone.

But it is 10.35; these considerations, though in a way pertaining to the Work, are not the Work itself.

Let me *begin to inflame myself in praying!*

The Twelfth Day

12.17. When therefore I had made ready the chamber, so that all was dark, save for the Lamp upon the Altar,

12.17. began as recorded above, to inflame myself in praying, calling upon my Lord; and I burned in the Lamp that Pantacle which I had made of Him, renouncing the Images, destroying the Images, that Himself might arise in me.

And the Chamber was filled with that wondrous glow of ultra- violet light self-luminous, without a source, that hath no counterpart in Nature unless it be in that Dawn of the North. . . .

And there were reveled unto me certain Words of Power . . .

And I invoked my Lord and recited the Book Ararita at the Altar . . .

This holy inspired book (delivered unto me in the winter of last year) was now at last understanded of me; for it is, though I knew it not, a complete scheme of this Operation.

For this cause I will add this book Ararita at the end of the Manuscript. [This has not been permitted. The Book Ararita will be issued by the A∴ A∴ in due course.—ED.] I also demanded of mine Angel the Writing upon the Lamen of Silver; a Writing of the veritable Elixir and supernal Dew. And it was granted unto me.

Then subtly, easily, simply, imperceptibly gliding, I passed away into nothing. And I was wrapped in the black brilliance of my Lord, that interpenetrated me in every part, fusing its light with my darkness, and leaving there no darkness, but pure light.

Also I beheld my Lord in a figure and I felt the interior

12.17. trembling kindle itself into a Kiss—and I perceived the true Sacraments—and I beheld in one moment all the mystic visions in one; and the Holy Graal appeared unto me, and many other inexpressible things were know of me.

Also I was given to enjoy the subtle Presence of my Lord interiorly during the whole of this twelfth day. Then I besought the Lord that He would take me into His presence eternally even now.

But He withdrew Himself, for that I must do that which I was sent hither to do; namely, to rule the earth.

Therefore with sweetness ineffable He parted from me; yet leaving a comfort not to be told, a Peace ... the Peace. And the Light and the Perfume do certainly yet remain with me in the little Chamber, and I know that my Redeemer liveth, and that He shall stand at the latter day upon the earth.

For I am He that liveth, and was dead; and behold! I am alive for evermore, and have the Keys of Hell and of Death. I am Amoun the Sun in His rising; I have passed from darkness into Light. I am Asar Un-nefer the Perfected One. I am the Lord of Life, triumphant over death. . . .

There is no part of me that is not of the Gods. . . .

> The dead man Ankh-af-na-khonsu
>   Saith with his voice of truth and calm:
> Oh Thou that has a single arm!
>   O Thou that glitterest in the moon!
> I weave Thee in the spinning charm;
>   I lure thee with the billowy tune.

JOHN ST. JOHN

The dead man Ankh-af-na-khonsu
   Hath parted from the darkling crowds,
Hath joined the dwellers of the light,
   Opening Duant, the star-abodes;
      Their keys receiving.
The dead man Ankh-af-na-khonsu
   Hath made his passage into night,
His pleasure on the earth to do
      Among the living.

      Amen
   Amen without lie
Amen, and Amen of Amen.

12.40. I shall lie down to sleep in my robes, still wearing the Ring of the Masters, and bearing my wand in my hand.

For to me now sleep is the same as waking, and life the same as death.

In Thy L.V.X. are not light and darkness but twin children that chase each other in their play?

7.55. Awoke from long sweet dreamless sleep, like a young eagle that soars to greet the dawn.

9.20. After breakfast, have strolled, on my way to the studio, through the garden of the Luxembourg to my favourite fountain. It is useless to attempt to write of the dew and the flowers in the clear October sunlight.

Yet the light which I behold is still more than sunlight. My eyes too are quite weak from the Vision; I cannot bear the brilliance of things.

The clock of the Senate strikes; and my ears are ravished with its mysterious melody. It is the Infinite interior movement of things, secured by the co-exten-

9.20. sion of their sum with the all, that transcends the deadly opposites; change which implies decay, stability which spells monotony.

I understand all the Psalms of Benediction; there is spontaneous praise, a fountain in my heart. The authors of the Psalms must have known something of this Illumination when they wrote them.

9.30. It seems, too, that this Operation is transformed. I suppose it must read as a patchwork of most inharmonious colour, a thing without continuity or cohesion. To me, now, it appears from the very start a simple direct progress in one straight line. I can hardly remember that there were checks.

Of course my rational memory picking out details finds otherwise. But I seem to have two memories almost as if belonging to two strata of being. In Qabalastic language, my native consciousness is now Neschamah. not Ruach or Nephesch.

... I really cannot write more. This writing is a descent into Ruach, and I want to abide where I am.

11.17. At 10.0 arrived at Brenner's studio, and took the pose. At once, automatically, the interior trembling began again, and again the subtle brilliance flowed through me.

The consciousness again died and was reborn as the divine, always without shock or stress.

How easy is magic, once the way is found!

How still is the soul! The turbid spate of emotion has ceased; the heavy particles of thought have sunk t

11.17. the bottom; how limpid, how lucid is its glimmer. Only from above, from the overshadowing Tree of Life, whose leaves glisten and quiver in the shining wind of the Spirit, drops ever and anon, self- luminous, the Dew of Immortality.

Many and wonderful also were the Visions and powers offered unto me in this hour; but I refused them all; for being in my Lord and He in me, there is no need of these toys.

12.0. The pose over. On this second sitting, practically no thoughts arose at all to cloud the Sun; but a curious feeling that there was something more to come.

Possibly the Proof, that I had demanded, the Writing on the Lamen...

12.40. Chez Lavenue. Certain practical considerations suggest themselves.

One would have been much better off with a proper Magical Cabinet, a disciple to look after things, proper magical food ceremonially prepared, a private garden to walk in ... and so on.

But at least it is useful and important to know that things can be done at a pinch in a great city and a small room.

1.14. The lunch is good; the kidneys were well cooked; the tarte aux fraises was excellent; the Burgundy came straight from the Vat of Bacchus. The Coffee and Cognac are beyond all praise; the cigar is the best Cabaña I ever smoked.

THE EQUINOX

1.14. I read through this volume of the Record; and I dissolve my being into quintessential laughter.
The entries are some of them so funny! ... Previously, this had escaped me.

1.32. And now the Rapture of it takes me!

1.25. The exquisite beauty of the women in the Restaurant ... what John St. John would have called old hags!

1.27. My soul is singing ... my soul is singing!

1.30. It matters nothing what I do ... everything goes infinitely, incredibly right!
"The Lord Adonai is about me as a Thunderbolt and as a Pylon and as a Serpent and as a Phallus." ...

3.17. Have had a long talk of Art with B——. "The master considers himself always a student." So, therefore, whatever one may have attained, in this as in Art, there is always so much more possible that one can never be satisfied.
Much less, then, satiated.

11.15. Having gone back into the life of the world—yet a world transfigured!—I did all my little work, my little amusements, all the things that one does, very quietly and beatifically.
About 10.30 the rapture began to carry me away; yet withstood it and went on with my game of Billiards, for politeness' sake.
And even there in the Café du Dôme was the glory within me, and I therein; so that every time that I failed at a stroke and stood up and drank in tha

11.15. ambrosial air, I was night falling for that intense sweetness that dissolved away the soul. Even as a lover that swoons with excess of pleasure at the first kiss of the belovéd, even so was I, oh my Lord Adonai!
Wherefore I am come hither to my chamber to enflame myself in praying at the Altar that I have set up.
And I am ready, robed, armed, anointed . . . .

11.35. Ardesco ! . . . .

The Thirteenth Day.

It is Eight o'clock in the morning.
Being entered into the Silence, let me abide in the Silence!

AMEN

The Equinox by Aleister Crowley - Hardcover and Paperback

$100 or $250 for 10 volumes!

www.lulu.com/equinox_crowley

Made in the USA
Columbia, SC
24 January 2025